What Your Colleagues Ar

"In this wonderfully honest book, Justin Stygles shows how our traditional ways of teaching reading—our use of scores, labels, interventions, judgments—are shame-inducing for many students, who retreat to avoidance behavior ("reading is boring!") or learn to fake it. Stygles is open about how, for a time, he went along with these practices but broke free to pay attention, build relationships, ask questions, become a model, and provide the support students need. It's a stirring journey."

—Thomas Newkirk
Professor emeritus, University of New Hampshire
Author, *Embarrassment: And the Emotional Underlife of Learning*

"'*I Hate Reading': Overcoming Shame in the Reading Classroom*, based on Justin Stygles's years of teaching, narrates the author's journey into helping students understand themselves as readers, including the why behind their choices of books, avoidance through fake reading, and how they perceive themselves as readers, thinkers, and learners. Rich in diverse ways to get to know students, how to use writing about reading to reveal each student's feelings and reactions to books, and techniques and questions that can help students construct positive reading identities, Justin continually models the importance of being honest yet nonjudgmental while interacting with students. It's the powerful stories about individual students and sample conferences between Justin and a student that breathe energy, passion, and deep meaning into his teaching suggestions, inviting you to return to them to reread and re-experience the honesty and pain expressed by students and how Justin responds. An essential guide for teachers in all grades, the book is compelling because it's written with love and honesty and based on Justin's teaching and learning journey as well as grounded in research. You'll return to parts again and again as you strive to create a safe environment for students and give them all the time they need to shift from hating and avoiding reading to choosing to become a reader!"

—Laura Robb
Author, *Guided Practice for Reading Growth* and *Read, Talk, Write: 35 Lessons That Teach Students to Analyze Fiction and Nonfiction*

"Justin Stygles *sees* his students. He acknowledges the layers students bring into a classroom, from trauma, poverty, and negative self-perceptions to the perfectionist who performs for others. He is conscious of how shame permeates the lives of his students and how they have become disconnected from reading. Through building an interpersonal bridge with students, he is able to construct a space where students do not fail but rather discover who they are through reading. Stygles' pedagogy gives merit to the power of relationships; students not only develop a stronger sense of self but also emerge as authentic readers. *'I Hate Reading': Overcoming Shame in the Reading Classroom* delves into why many students loathe reading and gives tangible, student-centered methods that generate intrinsic motivation in our students to treasure reading. To demonstrate his approach to students and reading, Stygles incorporates ample student examples with each strategy outlined. This book changes the way we have traditionally tried to engage students and asks educators everywhere to pause and think about the individual, the student, the reader."

—Laura Mewa
Assistant Principal

"*'I Hate Reading'* looks closely not just at what reluctant readers do but also how they feel. When we uncover and acknowledge shame, we create the context for students to experience other feelings as readers, such as joy and pride. Thank goodness Stygles brings his years of experience as a teacher and a scholar to help us all ask a different set of questions about the student readers we support. Full of research, relatable vignettes, and concrete tools to try, this book will change the way you view the student readers who keep you up at night."

—Gravity Goldberg
Author, *Teach Like Yourself* and
Mindsets and Moves

"Justin Stygles's book offers new insight into finding connections and reaching our students where they are. We all know teaching is about building relationships, but Stygles looks at the intersection of years of established reading pedagogy and everything we know about building relationships and then takes a step backward to focus on the barriers to both, which are rooted in shame. He then offers practical solutions for breaking down those barriers. My students are in high school, yet the dysfunctional behaviors Stygles attributes to shame are still apparent at that level—perhaps more so. The research in this book offers hope that it is not too late to discover and eliminate those barriers and to instill a love of reading in my most reluctant learners. This book is a thorough examination of the ways in which shame holds our students back, an honest look at the role we may play in perpetuating the shame cycle, and a guide to inform our actions going forward as we continue in our efforts to build resilient readers."

—Stephanie Fearn
Literacy coach, secondary English teacher,
and adjunct professor

"As much as we'd like all students to associate reading with joy, often students come to our classrooms with negative perceptions of themselves as readers. In his powerful self-reflection, Justin is brave enough to unpack his instructional practices that have had unintended negative consequences on his students. I'll admit it: At some points, it was hard for me to read Justin's words as he stirred up my own shameful memories of when I had failed my own students. But ultimately, this book pushed me to understand how to better connect to students for whom reading does not equate with joy. Full of candid conversations and classroom resources, this book helps us transform reading shame into reading pleasure."

—Molly Ness
Author, *Every Minute Matters*, and
Think Big With Think Alouds, Grades K-5

"Justin Stygles has done what no other author has done: He's discussed students' reading identity in relationship to the delicate subject of shame. Justin gives teachers a means to help students grow their ability and passion to read while guiding their emotional growth and development as learners. This book provides a path for teachers to take to heal students' emotional selves and also develop their passion as readers. The tips for assessment and instruction focus also work well in classrooms where students may be learning to work together in groups and where students are becoming part of a reading community."

—Nancy Akhavan
Author, *The Big Book of Literacy Tasks, Grades K–8*

"This book is a labor of love. Justin Stygles unequivocally gets to the heart of what our students need. This is a must-read by all educators who want to grow and refine their practice as literacy teachers. What matters the most is that all our students are successful, accepted, and embraced in all classrooms, regardless of reading levels."

—Kara DiBartolo
Director of Curriculum, Instruction, and Innovation
The Sherman Public Schools, Sherman, CT

"Justin's book cuts through the competing agendas within schools to remind us that our job as educators is to improve the lives of our students."

—Talya Edlund
Assistant Principal, 2016 Maine Teacher of the Year

"Justin's passion for engaging his learners and his clear descriptions of how to attain solid literacy development are encouraging and refreshing. It warms my heart as an experienced school administrator that he has worked diligently to get his message out to other educators and parents on proven practices to improve literacy. My hope is for Justin to continue teaching and share further professional development on how to develop student confidence and security in their reading and writing."

—Ken Spinney II
Special Education Director

"I Hate Reading"

"I Hate Reading"

Overcoming Shame in the Reading Classroom

Justin M. Stygles

resources.corwin.com/ihatereading

CORWIN Literacy

FOR INFORMATION:

Corwin
A SAGE Company
2455 Teller Road
Thousand Oaks, California 91320
(800) 233-9936
www.corwin.com

SAGE Publications Ltd.
1 Oliver's Yard
55 City Road
London EC1Y 1SP
United Kingdom

SAGE Publications India Pvt. Ltd.
B 1/I 1 Mohan Cooperative Industrial Area
Mathura Road, New Delhi 110 044
India

SAGE Publications Asia-Pacific Pte. Ltd.
18 Cross Street #10-10/11/12
China Square Central
Singapore 048423

President: Mike Soules
Vice President and
Editorial Director: Monica Eckman
Director and Publisher,
Corwin Classroom: Lisa Luedeke
Senior Content Development
Manager: Julie Nemer
Editorial Assistant: Nancy Chung
Project Editor: Amy Schroller
Copy Editor: Deanna Noga
Typesetter: C&M Digitals (P) Ltd.
Proofreader: Lawrence W. Baker
Indexer: Integra
Cover Designer: Rose Storey
Marketing Manager: Margaret O'Connor

Printed in Canada

Library of Congress Cataloging-in-Publication Data

Names: Stygles, Justin M., author.

Title: I hate reading : overcoming shame in the reading classroom / Justin M. Stygles.

Description: Thousand Oaks, California : Corwin Literacy, [2023] | Series: Corwin literacy | Includes bibliographical references and index.

Identifiers: LCCN 2022028323 | ISBN 9781071844823 (paperback) | ISBN 9781071894422 (epub) | ISBN 9781071894439 (epub) | ISBN 9781071894446 (pdf)

Subjects: LCSH: Reading (Elementary) | Reading comprehension—Study and teaching (Elementary) | Teacher-student relationships. | Learning, Psychology of.

Classification: LCC LB1573 .S898 2023 | DDC 372.4—dc23/eng/20220803
LC record available at https://lccn.loc.gov/2022028323

This book is printed on acid-free paper.

22 23 24 25 26 10 9 8 7 6 5 4 3 2 1

CONTENTS

LIST OF ONLINE RESOURCES

From Chapter 3

Figure 3.2: My Reading Life—Memories Matrix

Reading Prompts Questions

Questions to Support Student Writing

Figure 3.8: Reader Self-Perception Scale

Figure 3.9: Reading Process Self-Evaluation

From Chapter 4

Figure 4.8: The Reading Visa

From Chapter 5

Figure 5.1: Tracking Literary Elements Matrix

Figure 5.2: *George Crum and the Saratoga Chip* Literary Elements Matrix

Figure 5.9: Empathetic Annotation Template

From Chapter 7

Sample Prompts

Figure 7.3: Managing My Reading Life: The VOWELS Checklist (Beginner Version)

Figure 7.4: VOWEL Checklist (Advanced Version)

Figure 7.5: Favorites Bookshelf Assignment Overview

Student Example—Top Ten Bookshelf

Visit the "*I Hate Reading*" companion website at **resources.corwin.com/ihatereading** for these downloadable resources.

PREFACE

Hi. My name is Deven Johnson. I know you don't like me. You're always upset with me because I "never do anything," especially reading.

Remember last Thursday? You were mad at me because I didn't write a response during test prep. You snapped at me this time. That was new. I told you I wasn't interested in what I read, so I didn't answer the question.

You said, "That's unacceptable! You're better than that."

I am, though? Really?

Then you looked at me with that disappointed look you always give me. You know the one where you know you can't "fix" anything about me, even though you want to?

Remember last week? You said I reminded you of you when you were my age?

You said that you didn't have a dad much growing up.

You said that you went to school looking scrappy, with cigarette-scented clothes?

You talked about how you overcame it, and I could, too, if integrity mattered to me. (What's integrity anyway?)

You said something funny like, "If you hold yourself to a high standard, despite what is happening in your life, you will rise above."

It sounded stupid, and I don't know what you meant.

Here's what I do know. Every other teacher tried being nice to me, but I know they only did it because they felt bad for me.

Remember last month? You caught me reading the same picture book again? I said I left my book at home. Again. Actually, I don't know where it is. You'll say I lost it. You've also never been to my house. Worse, I hate it when you catch me. It's like you're "targeting" me.

Even though every other teacher was nice, why can't you ignore me like they did? Don't you have a favorite you can go smile with and leave me alone?

So what if I left my book at home? Don't people expect that of me? I always do it, then they say, "It's ok, just try to remember it tomorrow." I try. I just don't remember. (You're probably going to think I don't care.) And also, why is it my fault that I can't think of anything I'm interested in reading?

Why do you even ask me if I have time to read? Everyone tells me where I need to be and what I need to be doing. After that, I find myself all alone. My parents are on their phones; my brother is playing his games. And if I start reading, I'm going to be told I'm supposed to be doing what they said. I don't even know what it is!! I'm so tired. I hate myself because I can do nothing right, and I (feel like I) get in trouble for it all the time!

Imagine you live in a world where the only thing you do is go home and play video games and watch movies. I don't go anywhere! You always talk about going to Portland. I've never been there!

You know what else? I know you hate that you actually kneel next to me and try to "understand the way I think." I'm dumb. Everyone gets it but me. And there you are again. You never go away. I hate that you're not brushing me off. You said something like, "Accountability is compassion . . ." and then something like, "If you expect something of me, it's your responsibility to be right alongside me," something stupid like that. Something teachers are supposed to say.

That's why you're so annoying. You try to be nice to me. You expect me to "become someone," as you say. I'm just glad you don't say something like "GRIT" or use a "growth mindset," whatever that means, like some of my last teachers. Am I supposed to be inspired by you saying words to me? Do you think I'm actually in control of my life? Why do you think I'm smart? No one else does! That's what none of you get. No one cares about me! Sure, they say they do, when I have to read aloud as they show me how bad I am as a reader.

And I'm not done! Next, you say that you "get me." Even though I want to disagree, I wonder, "Why do I half think you know my secret?"

***

Think of the possibility of not knowing what to do or who you are because all those who you rely on dictate your existence? Moreover, those same loved ones abandon you, only to repeatedly tell you all you do is wrong. Imagine a world where any sense of creativity or autonomy is extinguished because you're not what you're expected to be. What if your biggest hope was to be able to do the very thing you were most certain you couldn't do? A hope so big, so overwhelming, that your best strategy was avoidance. Why not live what you've always known—failure?

What am I talking about? I'm talking about what we love so much. Reading.

ACKNOWLEDGMENTS

Thanking people is hard. Saying thank you is one thing. Truly conveying that sentiment is another. Sometimes you simply cannot express the appreciation felt so deep down inside.

First off, I owe this book to Penny Kittle. She pulled out a cell phone in the middle of my conference session one sunny September afternoon in Portland to call Lisa Luedeke, who would become the most patient and supportive project manager. Over 9 years, and so many ups and downs, Lisa remained faithful to this project and helped me in so many capacities. Lisa, you are a true friend, not just for the book, but also for your humanity. Without you, this book would not survive, nor would my aspiration to contribute.

Thank you to Joanna Davis Swing for your preliminary editorial work during days I couldn't make sense of anything. Thank you, Paula Stacy, for digging the ideas out from underneath the rubble of poor writing. You did more than I can say. Thank you to Sara Johnson, who, when I had given up all hope of this project, stepped in to wrap things up. Thank you for keeping my voice alive and staying true to my perceptions of the world.

Thank you to Julie Ann Peterson, LCSW. Without you and a broken finger, this project would have never taken place. You helped me realize the shame in my life. You opened the door to writing this idea by insisting I start reading, attempting to find a single shred of hope that my thinking might be worth hearing. You helped me find the message I needed to share through the recognition of shame in my existence and the impact I had on others, not to mention a dedicated path to recovery.

Thank you, Jody Cyr, LCSW. You laughed and cried with me. You knew how much this book meant to me and saw me through it. You never gave up on me. You recognized what I still had inside and what light I could shine.

I want to share special thanks to Desiree Dunn. You stood by me in the darkest hours, when no other soul did. You looked beyond my challenges, knowing that the true me was still inside.

I also send my sincere gratitude to Meghan Schofield. From your first days as a teacher, you were curious about my research and how you could better reach readers. Thank you.

And to the most unsuspecting of all teachers, Anna Golendukhina. You taught me what it was to be dedicated to students. You always made sure to make me feel a part of the group and something bigger than myself. Not to mention all the times you called me out for my *tiempo*.

I also want to express my thanks to Kara DiBartolo, Molly Ness, Cheryl Mizerny, and Michelle Best. No matter what, you were always willing to put together proposals on this topic with me for NCTE.

I cannot forget Sam Murray and Alyssa Perkins at Bingas Stadium, who, after way too many diesel buffalo tenders, always made time to talk and inquire about the book.

Thank you, Rhiana, for teaching me so much as teacher and father. I'm sorry you've faced so much. Hopefully you can learn from my mistakes and become the courageous blessing you are.

I hope you understand.

Publisher's Acknowledgments

Corwin gratefully acknowledges the contributions of the following reviewers:

Christina Nosek
Teacher and Author
Mountain View, CA

Lynn Angus Ramos
Curriculum & Instruction Coordinator
Decatur, GA

ABOUT THE AUTHOR

Justin M. Stygles has served readers as an intermediate and middle-grades teacher for 19 years. For many years he taught Grades 4–6 in rural and coastal Maine schools. His other experiences include working in summer literacy programs in rural, suburban, and private schools. He currently teaches fourth grade in Portland, Maine. Justin is from a military background and graduated with an associate's degree in harness racing before becoming an educator. He's served on committees with the International Literacy Association and National Council of Teachers of English. Previous publications include articles in *Literacy Today, Voices from the Middle,* and *Hoof Beats. "I Hate Reading"* is his first professional book.

To Rhiana

It's not your fault.

INTRODUCTION

What would you do if you could answer the question, "Why do kids stop reading by the end of elementary school?" Gallagher (2010) brought this to our attention in his seminal text, *Readicide*. What if we could find the answer:

- Not by looking at cognitive abilities, but affect—the child's physical response, emotions, and perceptions—rather than by traditional means, like reading comprehension scores?
- With compassion—through a long-term investment with readers and by using relationships, or the interpersonal bridge, to rectify self-perception and build competence and mastery so students become truly independent, lifelong readers because reading matters to them?
- By questioning our practices—what if the answers to why kids stop reading don't come in test scores but merely by looking into their eyes and listening to their story?

I found myself asking these questions about 7 years ago after life forced me into a deep self-reflection. When I began studying books like *Shame: The Power of Caring*, by renowned shame researcher Kaufman (1993), I saw more than myself on the pages, I saw my maturing readers. My students, subjected to traditional reading pedagogy, manifested the shame-based behaviors I was reading in those pages. I continued to read, drawing links between shame research and education literature about reading instruction. The connections were alarming. Following years of self-reflection and instructional adaptations, I developed my own theories, many of which are presented in this text.

This book is an attempt to reconsider and reexamine reading joy, reading achievement, and affective processes. It is intended to help educators understand and implement the practices I discovered that mentor students through a process of becoming engaged in their reading development. In this book, educators can consider the isolation or abandonment readers may feel as a result of many current practices in the teaching of reading. What I am talking about here is shame—the internalized sense of inadequacy, faultiness, contempt, rejection, and the loss of personal integrity—those readers may feel. By the end of this book, educators will know how to lift students out of the dejection they may associate with learning to read.

> This book is an attempt to reconsider and reexamine reading joy, reading achievement, and affective processes.

In a world consumed by data-driven practices and the quest for external affirmation promoted by social media, students are more vulnerable than ever to "rejecting" themselves in favor of developing an appearance they believe is more favorable to others. Yet from the research and our knowledge of child development, we know the driving forces that support maturing children are competency, agency, and self-efficacy. In other words, students need and deserve a strong sense of self that allows them to develop resilience or embrace the "gift" of who they are from within. This includes reading instruction that promotes a healthy sense of self. We have an opportunity, today, to reverse a trend in literacy education where the child is the receiver of teaching and is "told" who they are. We can embrace this goal of self-efficacy and actualization and truly help our students become lifelong readers with a strong sense of who they are as readers.

> We know the driving forces that support maturing children are competency, agency, and self-efficacy. In other words, students need and deserve a strong sense of self.

How Can You Approach This Book?

Up front, I will say that some of the content in this book will challenge you. What is presented here comes from actual classroom experiences. These stories are from a variety of settings including classrooms, intervention settings, and summer programs. These environments are rural, suburban, and urban communities in which I lived and worked. Every single teaching environment I've worked in was 50% free- and reduced-school lunch or higher. Most of my students live within the profound impacts of poverty, be it financial, emotional, or generational (Payne, 1998). The stories I share are tales of the errors I made and the shifts I needed to make to encourage students to assume reading into their lives. I am hoping by sharing my vulnerability, it will help you outgrow your current self as an educator.

However, some of the terms used might cause you to recoil a bit. I don't like to use labels. However, at times you will see terms such as *struggling reader* or *dumb*. These are the definitions readers apply to themselves, not the labels I place on them. I cannot change the internalizations or self-perceptions that students bring with them into the classroom. I can only help show them a more promising future where they have the tools and the power to change their own narrative. Sometimes that means I have to forsake agendas like data-driven aspirations to "roll up my sleeves" and put the reader before myself.

As you read each chapter, I hope you will find yourself on a journey. First, we start with what *shame* means. From there we learn about the reader's narrative through assessments. Next, we look at ways to bring students into reading, how to manage their reading lives, and how to help them develop a reading process. Finally, we look at data-based interventions and how to invite students to define their reading legacy through writing about reading.

If at any point you find yourself challenged or overwhelmed, please take time for yourself. It took me nearly a decade of self-reflection and baby steps just to reach this point. I encourage you to pause and reflect when you need to. Just remember, this book is based on what I've experienced in nearly 20 years of teaching. I'm sharing my perspective to support your classroom, to help you to continue evolving as an educator at a time when students and readers need us most.

At the end of each chapter is a section titled Reflect and Act. The purpose of this section is to give you an opportunity to process what you have read. As we know, shifting our practice takes reflection and time. The great news about teaching is that every day we can start fresh. Within the framework of this conversation, I encourage you to think about what can be done tomorrow, or next week, or even what you will do differently in the coming school year.

1

DISRUPTING PEDAGOGY

Prioritizing Students in the Shadows of Shame

iStock.com/PeopleImages

"Every child has a legitimate need to be noticed, understood, and taken seriously."

—*Alice Miller*

It's 2:55. The students have finally gotten themselves packed up and out the door. You look at the clock and sigh. You have 5 minutes to get things together and get to the faculty meeting. It's been a long day. The morning schoolwide assembly went on longer than planned as the school debated the final agenda item: What to name the school's new fish, a colorful Beta. It was the second assembly this week to interrupt your language arts block, leaving half an hour to squeeze in some independent reading and meet with a group of students who cannot seem to find that "love for books."

Now in your fifth year of teaching, you are finally feeling comfortable grouping students and engaging them productively. But this group has proved especially challenging. Richard seemed to make every group hard. Like today, knowing your time was limited, you kept the focus narrow—practicing the strategy of prediction, something you have been working on for a week. It all fell apart when you asked Richard for his prediction about what might happen next to a character who recently broke his leg, and he muttered, "He would get a cast."

Everyone laughed. You would have laughed, too, maybe if this was a different student, but this was characteristic of Richard and his attitude that year: disengaged, discouraged, distant, and even outright defiant at times. He rarely remembered to bring his independent reading book, and when he did, he mostly pretended to read. You tried all the traditional accountability techniques—keeping him in at recess, sitting with him while he read, calling home. Once he was given extra credit. Nothing worked. Last year he barely achieved a "meets standards score" on the state test. This year you doubted he could do that.

Your mind spins as you walk to the library for the meeting. How can I reteach prediction so that Richard will, in spite of himself, see its value? How can I get him, and all the students really, to take it seriously? If they could only seriously engage the strategies! If they could find a pathway to true comprehension, they might find a path to stronger engagement. But how? You sift back through *Strategies That Work* (Harvey & Goudvais, 2000, 2007) and Ellery's (2008) *Creating Strategic Readers* to find an answer. As you scan the library for a place to sit, ideally in the back, your mind wanders. You consider changing the reading material, maybe finding something less challenging.

As your mind wanders, the principal announces the topic at hand. You look up and see the following words projected in huge type on the screen at the front of the room.

"Every child has a legitimate need to be noticed, understood, and taken seriously."

—Alice Miller, author of *The Drama of the Gifted Child*

Then the principal turns to the room and says with a smile intended to encourage the staff, "This quote represents our focus." Instead, your heart sinks. "I'm already trying!" you think to yourself.

Acknowledging Reality: What's Happening?

Undoubtedly, we as educators are working hard to manage a complex set of agendas and needs every single day. There are state and district mandates, pacing guides, and new curriculums to learn. Students are coming to our classes with trauma histories and negative self-perceptions, not to mention poverty, food insecurity, and/or a sense of feeling unloved. We have students who need room to cry, sleep, or just want a relationship in which to feel valued. Then there is instruction—who needs scaffolding, reteaching, extended time, and interventions?

The list is endless, and it is always on your mind; perhaps, enough so that the tears begin to fall just after students leave. I know. It happens to me regularly.

When I started reading about shame, initially for my purposes, I began to *see* my readers in the details and definitions provided by researchers. I was quite confident about my abilities to raise reading scores and improve reading achievement, almost too proud. And it came at a cost. It was the shame research that led me to redefine my approach and what *success* meant, and to whom, in the classroom.

I remember vividly the first time I asked a student in a reading conference to share her thoughts about herself and reading. I turned to her student and said, *"What do you think about yourself as a reader, and what is it like when you read?"* She looked back at me with a perplexed face almost as if saying, *"You mean I'm supposed to be taking something from this?"*

I'd recently completed an M.A. program in literacy, thinking I had established a new, enlightening pedagogy as a literacy specialist and teacher. Now, I had this young lady, Angelina, age 11, sitting in front of me. She'd moved into my fifth-grade class about mid-year. Like many students, Angelina's benchmark assessment and reading achievement scores didn't identify a need for intervention. But something lurked beneath the surface that made me uneasy about her reading and her academic future. When I listened to her talk about books, her reading habits, and read her written responses, she lacked *substance*. Most of her replies were phrases that represented what students often think they should say such as, "I really liked the book because it had interesting characters." That was it. To be honest, she didn't need to read the book to come up with that answer.

Unbeknownst to her, Angelina sent me a signal, a hint that invited me to "visit the well," so to speak. Even if she achieved standards this year, it was only a matter of time before she began to struggle with the very subject she was always "good at" and praised for. While Angelina was nothing like Richard from a behavior and attitude standpoint, when it came to their test scores, they could have been identical.

So it came to be that during a conference with Angelina I shifted my chair a bit so I could make eye contact, looked directly at her, and said, "So, Angelina, tell me about you as a reader."

I wasn't sure what to expect when I asked that question. I'm not even sure what I hoped to learn. This was a wholly new experiment for me.

I guess it was for Angelina, too, so I was a bit surprised when she answered almost immediately, with absolute confidence and, I think, some pride, pronouncing, "Oh that's easy. I'm a level 50 reader!"

In our district, level 50 meant reading at a fifth-grade level. It meant that Angelina recognized that she was on grade level. It clearly meant to her that she was doing what she should be doing, that all was right with the world.

To say I was dismayed would be an understatement.

I thought about all the effort, resources, and hard thinking that had gone into the "expertise" I had developed, along with the elaborate curriculum I had mastered and was now offering to her and others. My focus had always been on critical thinking, strategic reading (Barnhouse & Vinton, 2012), and fostering a reading life outside of school. Yet, in spite of all my efforts, it was clear to me that the major lesson Angelina had learned was how to perform—for us.

We asked her to identify a strategy, and she identified a strategy. We asked her to recall facts and key details, and she produced them. We asked her to engage in independent reading, and she dutifully chose a book, read enough pages a week, wrote about it in her journal, then abandoned the book before finishing, and chose another.

It's no wonder Angelina thought of herself as a level 50 reader. We thought of her that way, too. Her answer to my question that day forced me to see this hard truth about what I was doing all day as I focused on fulfilling what I thought I was expected to do. I was teaching a curriculum, not students.

It's no wonder Angelina thought of herself as a level 50 reader. We thought of her that way, too.

Pedagogies and Implications: The Ubiquity of Shame

When I started this book, I began a serious inquiry into students' experiences. I let myself be led by my curiosity into their thinking about their own learning. As I began to actively question and urge them to reflect, I learned that I, as an educator, had made a choice, a choice that was undermining the students' sense of self and stunting their development as readers and active agents of their own learning (Aukerman, 2007). I had chosen curriculum *first* and rather than building strong and healthy relationships around reading and learning, in the process, I was building a culture of resistance, defiance, disengagement, and—the word none of us want to hear—shame.

I was building a culture of resistance, defiance, disengagement.

Shame is a strong word. I don't use it lightly. I'm not arguing that we as teachers use shame as a tool to control students. Nor am I saying every student experiences shame because of how we teach reading. I am contending that to fully understand the effects of our practices on students' identities, it's useful to consider how shame infiltrates our classrooms: what I'm calling *the shame factor.*

Alice Miller, the author of the quote displayed by the principal at the faculty meeting in the opening vignette and whose research into and writing on shame is considered by many to be foundational, is one of the many thinkers on the topic who have driven my understanding of the complex workings of shame in the classroom. Her thinking has helped me navigate the important work of considering what it means to make this critical shift from teaching a curriculum, to teaching students, to teaching maturing people with real emotions and perceptions that stimulate their motivations, concerns, ambitions, life stories, fears, and hopes and dreams.

In the *Pictures of Childhood* (1995) and *Drama of the Gifted Child* (1997), Miller explores how children develop an identity under the influence of parental values. Of course, teachers and schools are not parents, and thus we are not concerned here with Miller's conclusions about the trauma children can experience under parental dominance. But her work has important insights to offer about how adult authority figures can impact identity development in children and use their authority to manipulate children into embracing the adults' worldview and values. According to Miller, this is where the shame and fear of shame can undermine a child's identity and autonomy, making it impossible for a child to cultivate and express their unique gifts. It's important to note that Miller's view of giftedness has nothing to do with the particular kind of cognitive capacities educators associate with the gifted. Giftedness is instead a function of a child's development of the self. Manifesting a whole, authentic self, according to Miller, means fully expressing their gifts. This giftedness is thwarted when children are asked to dissociate from and stunt their developing identities to serve their adult-imposed values. The result is shame and shame-based behaviors.

For the purpose of this book, shame is a negative sense of self, an internalization of faultiness or unworthiness.

What is shame? This word, and others like it such as *shamed* or *shaming*, is tossed around a lot in different contexts but is often different from other emotions like guilt and embarrassment (Newkirk, 2017; Tangney et al., 1996). For the purpose of this book, shame is a negative sense of self, an internalization of faultiness or unworthiness. Shame is an abstract noun, not a verb. More, I define shame as the inability to manifest as ourselves because what we represent is not accepted or what others desire. We have all felt it in various situations, maybe instances when we let someone down or didn't measure up to expectations. But Miller is concerned with something even more profound and pervasive—the emotional consequences of a shame-based identity. When someone lives in shame, they feel they will never truly measure up. Their lives revolve around trying to prove their own worth to the outside world—*to be the person someone else expects them to be.*

While there is much nuance in the literature about the sources of shame and its effects on the self and identity, researchers agree on the following:

- Shame alters a person's perception of "what is" from "how I see it," to "how am I *supposed* to see it" (Rizvi et al., 2011).
- Shame is detrimental to the self, interfering with an individual's ability to develop a functional and healthy self-image; highly individualized (Brown et al., 2011; Middleton-Moz, 1990; Monroe, 2009).
- Feelings of shame occur when the perceived flawed parts of the self—the parts you want to hide from others—are revealed or exposed (Tangney & Dearing, 2002).
- Shame is relationally based. It grows out of relationships and social contexts (Gilbert, 2000).
- While it is in the same family of emotions as guilt, embarrassment, and humiliation, shame is different and distinct from these (Kaufman, 1993; Nathanson, 1992; Potter-Efron, 2002).
- Shame has received only limited attention from researchers in psychology while student mental health (psychopathology) is a rising concern in primary, intermediate, and secondary schooling (Ang & Khoo, 2004; Muris, 2015; Muris, et al., 2014; Thomaes et al., 2007; Welford & Langmead, 2015).
- Shame can result in the following dysfunctional behaviors in both children and adults (Dearing & Tangney, 2011; Gilbert & Andrews, 1998; Nathanson, 1992; Potter-Efron, 2002):
    - withdrawal and avoidance
    - grandiosity and putting on a false front
    - perfectionism
    - expressing contempt for others' values and actions
    - unhealthy dependency on others or on substances
    - confrontational and oppositional tendencies

Shame in the Classroom

If you have noticed in your students one of the behaviors mentioned in the last bullet above, it's not necessarily because these students are products of shame-based families. Shame grows and thrives in social and relational contexts (Gilbert, 2003; Muris & Meesters, 2013; Tangney & Dearing, 2002; Tracy & Robbins, 2004). Interpersonal relationships have a significant impact on our motivations (Baumeister & Leary, 1995). It's within relationship to others that shame manifests itself. In fact, if a human never encounters another person, shame can never be experienced. This, of course, can never happen; we are biologically engineered to rely on our caretakers and other relationships. For many generations, the act of shaming in public and parochial schools was used to "encourage" students to reform, academically or socially, for the better. But as medical social worker Dr. Ronald Potter-Efron (2002) relates, "Problems occur . . . when individuals feel too much shame for too long a time or when they conclude that they cannot change their ways and so are doomed to a lifetime of *perpetual failure* (p. 1; emphasis added). The perpetual failure part is our link to reading development. How many struggling readers do we see, day in and day out, who self-identify as failures, maybe perpetual failures? Our readers internalize the idea that they are not as valued or as talented as their peers, or capable of the expectations placed before them. In short, they may believe they are bad or defective. That is no inspiration to read, nor is it motivation to even try. And I'm afraid this is what many of our struggling learners have come to learn about themselves.

How many struggling readers do we see, day in and day out, who self-identify as failures, maybe perpetual failures?

Where does this occur? Within relationships. We are prone to basing our self-worth on our own perceptions of ourselves in relation to others or in relation to the social constructs, attitudes, and beliefs that dominate our culture. Beliefs that others hold about us, whether we're rewarded in our attempts to gain favor, acceptance, or even recognition, influence how and what we believe about ourselves. When a relationship is broken because of deficiency, ineptitude, or because the relationship is contingent on one's ability to rise up to someone's expectations, it can trigger shame. Many shame researchers relate that "it takes a relationship to experience shame. It takes a relationship to get out of shame" (Gilbert & Andrews, 1998; Mordrcin, 2016; Tangney & Fisher, 1995). Whether trauma-based, from feeling rejected or abandoned, or simply desiring someone to see you as you, it's very true. And that's where our role as teachers, as mirrors, makes a difference—to help students "get out of shame."

In the reading classroom, too often the focus is on performance indicators imposed by an adult or authority. As you read through the list of common shame-based behaviors described in the next section, it may be tempting to think, "This is what students *do* in school," "This is personality-based. Some students are just like that," or "This is developmental. It's our job to teach students how to behave."

You might be correct. But I would urge you not to dismiss the role shame may be playing in your classroom. Instead, push your thinking a bit further. Why is it that this is what students *do* in school? Does the same student who dysregulates during reading demonstrate this same behavior in other contexts? On the playground, at home, or in different subject areas? And finally, if this behavior is developmental, is the structure of the reading classroom and the delivery of the curriculum promoting developmental growth or impeding it?

1. ***Withdrawal.*** Students distance themselves from the demands of the classroom, using different strategies to remain unnoticed and stay under the radar. In a small group, for example, a student might respond to a question about what they think by pointing to a group member and saying, "I think the same as him." This is a pretty standard self-protective move used by students who don't want to risk saying the wrong thing and exposing their ignorance to the group.

2. ***Grandiosity.*** In reading, grandiosity appears in those students who have no clear understanding of their abilities yet believe and contend they can perform nearly impossible tasks. Grandiose readers often "read" 500-page (fantasy) books in a single night. Some truly are reading the pages, some are putting on a false front and mostly pretending to read, but none of them are engaging with the content in a substantial way. Grandiose readers are motivated by the outside validation and recognition they get for completing the book. Note: It is important to distinguish grandiose readers from those students who are passionately driven by reading, particularly an interest in a genre or an author.

3. ***Contempt.*** Expressions of contempt can involve actions as simple as directly ignoring a teacher's request by pretending not to hear. It also can be expressed more overtly by routinely pushing back and calling the teacher's methods into question, responding to instructions with such comments as, "This is stupid," "This is boring," and "None of my other teachers made me do this before." These expressions and actions are efforts on the part of students to define their own terms and assert power and identity in the face of threatening change.

4. ***Perfectionism.*** On the surface, perfectionism in students can look like a good thing. Perfectionism is accompanied by a range of behaviors, including, but not limited to, feelings of anxiety and an obsessive desire to get everything right. Perfectionists might also avoid tasks so as not to lose stature. Others put all their efforts into maintaining an acceptable identity by appearing "smart" and are reluctant to receive feedback and admit mistakes. Many perfectionists are students whose self-worth depends heavily on external praise of their intellect and ability. This "problem" may not manifest as directly as a problem in the classroom as the other shame-based behaviors. Indeed, these students' reading scores may be a teacher's pride and joy, but at what cost to the student's long-term development and sense of identity?

5. ***Compliance and Dependency.*** Some students cope by becoming overly compliant and even dependent on the teacher for help and instructions. Unlike students who resort to expressions of contempt, compliant students do exactly what they are told, trying to follow directions in the hopes that this will be enough. Some students, like Angelina, the student who identified as a level 50 reader earlier in the chapter, have used this strategy to "get by," but without internally driven confidence and purpose, their engagement in reading often remains on the surface. So when higher demands are made of them to think critically about their reading, their reading success suffers; scores go down when compliance isn't enough.

6. ***Refusal of Responsibility.*** Feeling unworthy or experiencing failure, many students avoid feelings of shame by turning away from their own actions to focus on other people's failures. Students might point out the inadequacy of other readers or compare themselves to struggling readers to avoid responsibility, feedback, or otherwise disconcerting realizations about themselves.

7. ***Expressions of Anger.*** Some students move quickly into anger when their sense of self is challenged. Students who haven't developed the capacity to protect themselves through such seemingly socially acceptable behaviors as withdrawal, contempt, or blame express their frustration and fear of shame through bursts of anger. This can look like loudly slamming a book shut, throwing something across the room, slamming a door, or even, at another end of the anger spectrum, going silent.

8. ***Avoidance.*** Our first signal that shame is internalized is avoidance. We tend to fear what we don't know or what we've consistently failed at, which in my opinion is the opposite of a growth mindset. (However, telling a student to have a growth mindset could create further shame because a teacher is ignoring the student's authentic feelings about how they see themselves or their potential in a given setting.) Avoidance is meant to preserve ourselves, to avoid being reminded (again) of what we can't do. I've found students who avoid reading aren't doing so out of defiance, but a sheer lack of understanding of how a middle-grade novel works and what they should take away from the experience.

From "Good Readers" to Authentic Readers

While the behaviors above may look very different, they all are signs of the same thing: students coping in an environment where they are challenged to define themselves in relationship to a fixed external identity. Reading, maybe more than any other subject or skill taught in school except perhaps writing, is tightly tied up with individual development and self-worth. We know that when students read and write they are also carrying on a conversation with themselves, or they should be. (We discuss this in Chapter 4.) Reading can allow students to explore ideas, feelings, and subjects they may learn to love or already love. Reading will be the medium through which they discover themselves and the world. This is what authentic reading is, and it is what most of us want for our students.

Perhaps you tell your students, as I have done, over and over, what an amazing gift learning to read is, how it will make them powerful, and give them options. Maybe you share your own experiences about how much you loved reading, how it changed your life when you were a child and continues to enrich your life. Maybe you put up posters in the classroom like these:

On the surface, these messages are positive and certainly benign. Until they aren't.

To a student who doesn't really like to read, a student who hasn't yet established their own connection to reading, a student who wants to please but may not be fully mastering the range of skills and strategies we are teaching, what messages do these sentiments send?

- "Read to Imagine" Does *that mean I can't imagine if I don't read?* (Alternate: *Was I supposed to imagine something?*)
- "I cannot live without books"—Thomas Jefferson *Well I can!*
- "I Read" *Well I don't. And maybe I never will.* Or *Sure I read. I'm at a level 50. I'm on grade level, which means I don't need to read much.*
- "There is no such thing as too many books." *Really? Have you seen my teacher's classroom?*

We have become very sensitive as a society to messages and images that present unrealistic ideals to young people, in particular, unrealistic ideals about what their bodies should look like. We call this body shaming. But what about the intellectual and educational ideals we dangle in front of our students on a daily basis? How are these different? Just because we value reading doesn't mean that students aren't sensitive to how they don't measure up.

Nowhere is this more apparent than in the language we often use when we present reading strategies to students. Let me first say, I teach the strategies. They are invaluable. Developing productive and effective reading habits, and learning to be active readers, is critical. But so is how we position those strategies with readers (Fisher et al., 2020). When we tell students, "This is what good readers do," we are telling them:

- there are good readers (and this means there are bad readers),
- they are not good readers if they cannot do these specific things,
- the path to becoming a good reader is narrow and specific, and
- good readers love reading (like there's nothing else to do).

When searching for posters to use as examples, I came across this one. It stands apart as certainly less benign than the others, but I'm including it because I think its stark and unforgiving message reveals the dark side of elevating good readers while emphasizing the moral failings of the "bad readers," who, it is implied here, are lazy and entitled.

Vulnerability as a Path to Authentic Reading

A strong and powerful path to authentic reading can be forged using the literature on shame as a guide. Many of you may be familiar with shame researcher Brené Brown. Her books on shame, vulnerability, and courage are regularly on the bestseller lists. Brown describes what she discovered in her more than a decade of research on shame. It's our fear of shame, says Brown (2017), and struggle for worthiness that causes us to retreat from complexity by making "everything that's uncertain, certain," to seek perfection in ourselves and work hard to make our children perfect, and to retreat into blaming and an insistence on our own invulnerability. It's no surprise then that Brown positions a willingness to be vulnerable as the antidote to shame. In her talks, she identifies vulnerability as the birthplace of joy, creativity, belonging, innovation, and change. As teachers, we know that the most profound learning happens when we can embrace what we don't know, risk making mistakes, and open ourselves to uncertainty.

Brené Brown positions a willingness to be vulnerable as the antidote to shame.

The reading poster on page 13 says, "Good Books Make You Ask Questions. Bad Readers Want Everything Answered." Ignoring, for a moment, the destructive underlying messaging to students that they fall into one of two camps, the enlightened readers of good books or bad readers, it is no surprise that the poster associates bad readers with wanting all the answers. If bad reading is about wanting certainty, then good reading is about moving into uncertainty. While this is not something we want to tell students—it's the telling part that is truly destructive—it is a message that can inform and drive the choices we make as teachers and the way we frame the challenge of teaching reading.

To help students move away from certainty, we need to help them be *vulnerable*, removing students from the burden they carry because of complex relations, or the multiple intersections between the teacher (e.g., personality and pedagogy), curriculum (e.g., standards, programs, and hidden agendas), and the student (e.g., personality, experience, and abilities), which are all well beyond the control of the student (Jaeger, 2015). Promoting vulnerability requires more than simply following the guidelines for creating a safe space to learn. Vulnerability cannot be nurtured in an environment that insists on defining success in terms of performance and measurement against an ideal. Instead, we as teachers need to make critical shifts in how we view our job as teachers of reading.

Vulnerability cannot be nurtured in an environment that insists on defining success in terms of performance and measurement against an ideal.

As I indicated earlier in this chapter, we need to put the curriculum in the background and put students squarely in the foreground. What does this look like? It means changing what we privilege, value, and choose to emphasize in every interaction with students, in every decision about how we structure our classrooms, in how we plan for the year, in how we assess students, and in how we develop instruction. In this book, you will find practical, if not *disruptive*, advice on making these shifts. You will find specific ideas for language to use and ways to productively scaffold traditional reading curricula. But these are ideas, illustrations, and models. They represent what has worked for me in my practice to focus on preparing students to learn, take risks, be vulnerable, or, as Brown (2015) suggests in the title of her book, *Daring Greatly*. I wouldn't presume to offer these ideas as ideals of practice that you should judge yourself against. That would subvert the very thinking that informs what I am presenting here. Instead, I hope they show you that there is a different way and that they spark the thinking that will allow you to also dare greatly when it comes to reaching out to your students.

Changing Our Priorities: Five Critical Value Shifts

The shifts I describe here didn't come fast, and they didn't come easily. Years of training, my own struggles, fears, and my concern with my professional reputation often got in my way.

As I mentioned early on in this chapter, I was once a successful reading teacher—according to reading achievement scores. My students' (state test) scores always improved, and most met standards. My identity was wrapped up in these scores, and I didn't want to lose that. Then things went wrong. Terribly wrong. As I started reading shame research, I became aware of the limits of their engagement in reading, mostly associated with self-perception and self-efficacy. The more I became aware that their high test scores did not coincide with a real interest in reading or ability to deeply comprehend text, the less tolerance I had for business as usual. So slowly and gradually I began to experiment, taking risks, and changing things up. The more I experimented, the more my students saw themselves as readers. The more my focus and priorities shifted, the more I focused on the uniqueness of the readers and the students' needs rather than my own self-interest, the more I was able to let go of pressures like the need to get high test results. In short, I became more invested with my readers through the interpersonal bridge, which formed my new pedagogy. And quite frankly, the more I saw the reading attitudes in my readers shift and our relationships improve, the more our classroom reading culture improved. Did I mention that our benchmark and achievement scores improved, too?

As you read through these shifts, I urge you to think about your own practice, values, and priorities and where you might begin your own journey.

CRITICAL SHIFT #1: PRIORITIZING STUDENTS OVER CURRICULUM

If someone asked you, "What do you value more, your students or the curriculum?" you would likely answer, "Why my students, of course." But ask yourself, what drives your planning for the year? The district-mandated program or your students' emotional, developmental, and cognitive needs? When you are preparing to teach any particular lesson, are you thinking, "How can I present this part of the curriculum as effectively as possible?" Or "Is this what my students need to learn right now?"

We are taught and expected to prioritize both the curriculum and students, finding some "sweet spot" where they meet and working to make that meeting as effective as possible. But even if such a sweet spot can be found, is it worth the effort? Is the prescribed curriculum a sacred text we are meant to honor and serve? The shift I am describing here flips that assumption on its head, positioning the curriculum as something that should be serving the student and the teacher in a mutual effort to help the student grow and learn. It is a tool, not a goal. As Jane Wellman-Little, literacy instructor at the University of Maine, once told me, "**You** are the silver bullet, not the program."

In practice, this means:

- Holding off on teaching particular strategies, skills, or texts until you truly know your students are ready.
- Creatively implementing district pacing expectations when necessary.
- Not letting program or district assessments solely define student capacities and needs.
- Getting to know students as unique, independent readers.
- Helping students establish their own, authentic purposes for reading.
- Working one-on-one with students to help them learn how to engage in authentic assessment of their own reading capacities and determine areas for growth.
- Helping students be the authors of their own reading lives.

CRITICAL SHIFT #2: PRIORITIZING INTERPERSONAL BRIDGE

We all work to establish good relationships with students. We learn about their personal lives, listen to their stories, read their essays, hear about their fears and hopes, and meet with parents and sometimes siblings and other family members (Daniels & Pirayoff, 2015). But deliberately building the interpersonal bridge is entirely different and is a critical tool in building an authentic reading classroom where the shame factor plays little or no role. Remember, shame is rooted in relationship to others, so it's not a surprise that one of the biggest factors in mitigating it depends on relationship building.

My professional beliefs further altered when I read about Kaufman's (1993) concept of the **interpersonal bridge** in his landmark text,

Shame: The Power of Caring. Noted psychologist, professor at Michigan State University, and a pioneer of shame research, Kaufman explores the critical relationship between adult and child and the consequences when authority is prioritized over trust. He introduces the interpersonal bridge as a mechanism for building trust, mutuality, and amending relationships. One important feature of the interpersonal bridge, which is not often supported or valued in teacher-student relationships, is *mutuality of response*. Kaufman defines mutuality of response as "one is in a real relationship with another, in a word, to feel wanted for oneself" (p. 13). In other words, the relationship is about the student and the student alone. The reader is not a tool for providing data or evidence of growth but is a maturing reader who deserves guidance to incorporate reading into their lives based on the uniqueness of their individuality and with respect for their sense of self-efficacy and perceptions.

Kaufman later adds that this is the "basis for trust" within a relationship.

Now, this doesn't mean we are on equal footing, or that I give up my role as teacher in an effort to "be a student's friend." In fact, just the opposite. Mutuality of response is about an open and authentic recognition of our shared needs and concerns. I need to teach and evaluate and guide, and the student needs to learn. But more important, I need to recognize the child as an individual first. I need to recognize that reading will not come just because I studied the data and applied the right intervention; it will come because the student had a trusting relationship with an adult who provided an avenue by which to become a reader. By focusing on where our interests meet and negotiating solutions, we build and strengthen the interpersonal bridge.

I need to teach and evaluate and guide, and the student needs to learn. But, I need to recognize the child as an individual first.

In practice this means:

- Listening to students from a place of humility and good faith, withholding suspicion and judgment, and not making assumptions about a student's motives.
- Providing opportunities for open and clear communication about obstacles to learning.

- Soliciting and listening carefully to student feedback.
- Setting clear expectations and being willing to change them when they aren't working.
- Communicating my purposes and motivations as a teacher.
- Being careful not to impose my own or others' interests and enthusiasms on students.
- Being willing to ask students hard questions when necessary.
- Sitting side-by-side with the most apprehensive of readers, reading stories and engaging in "real talk" about what it's like to be a reader and struggle with reading.

CRITICAL SHIFT #3: PRIORITIZING STUDENT AUTONOMY OVER STUDENT DEPENDENCE

In a reading classroom focused on performance, test scores, and teacher appraisal, either in the form of praise or judgment, it is all too easy for students to become so dependent on external markers that their relationship with reading becomes distorted. We as teachers might work hard to offer choices when we can, but these choices, often in the context of independent reading, feel incidental and peripheral compared to the performance demands made of students daily. Making this shift doesn't necessarily mean ignoring performance demands, lowering expectations, or giving up authority in the classroom. As I once described (Stygles, 2014) in "Losing Control to Gain Readers," I had to let go of managing every aspect of a reader's development because I'd broken the cardinal rule, "never work harder than my students" (Jackson, 2018). I had to shift the accountability and adopt a relationship-based, student-centered approach (Cornelius-White, 2007), finding age-appropriate ways to give students ownership over their perception of competence (Gilbert, 2004) and performance, including assessment.

In practice this means:

- Teaching students about assessment—the different kinds, and their purposes and limitations.
- Helping students learn to assess and evaluate their own performance and make decisions about what to do in response.
- Using interactions with students—whole class, small group, and one-on-one—to reinforce where they have choices.

- Asking questions that put the responsibility back on students.
    - What do you think you should do next?
    - What is your intent?
    - What are you planning on doing?
    - What are your next steps?
    - What can you or do you need to do differently?
- Cultivating your own comfort with student discomfort as you make these shifts.
- Helping students develop their own goals and purposes.

CRITICAL SHIFT #4: PRIORITIZING VULNERABILITY OVER COMPLIANCE

No one likes feeling vulnerable, but as Brené Brown (2007) found in her research, the people who were the most courageous in their lives were the ones who had made friends with their own vulnerability. Reading requires courage. And learning to read requires that students and teachers both are willing to take risks, make mistakes, cultivate judgment and the courage to act on it, and finally communicate honestly about the whole enterprise—together. Student autonomy is dependent on students' willingness to look honestly and clearly at what they need to learn versus simply following teachers' directives. For instance, every year I struggle with one student. The student always follows the same pattern. In previous grades, the student was considered gifted. Through compliance, punctuality, and saintly behavior, they gained the favor of the teachers. Terms like responsible, respectful, and sweet were words used to describe them. Yet never once did they have to prove evidence of their reading or comprehension. They had high test scores, designations, and completed work that portrayed an image of their "giftedness." But after 2 months in my class, the same student was seemingly anxious. They felt they had "fallen out of favor."

And every year I wondered why, until my research uncovered the answer. This student forsakes involvement in the development of their own identity by becoming a people pleaser (a shame-based manifestation). The student also develops anxiety (also a shame-based manifestation), not out of fear, but because any previous understanding of success was irrelevant in my classroom. Since their internalized identity as a "good" reader was borne from compliance and perfect-score worksheets, they now felt and experienced "failure" because they had to demonstrate something unfamiliar—revealing their perceptions—which they didn't know how to do. In this, I realized I had to teach them.

It's safe to think if we comply with all the district's mandates and train our students to complete their work based on these programs and mandates, things will go smoothly. There's less mental anguish for us, and we don't fall out of favor, meaning we secure the validation we desire from our leaders. But who does this really help? Where does this leave our readers?

What I've come to learn is that the responsibility of learning to read (or failing to)—that is, managing a reading life, strategically reading, and developing a reading identity—often falls solely on the student. In other words, they are often left alone to figure out what this "love of reading" or "lifelong reader" thing is all about. It's no wonder they quit. For one, why would you do anything nobody notices you for? Worse, what if you do it and you're still not accepted? Or the student might think, "Plainly I have other things to do that I enjoy that don't require someone else's judgment." These then force the hand of compliance.

It's safe to think if we comply with all the district's mandates and train our students to complete their work based on these programs and mandates, things will go smoothly.

Directives and compliance are not conducive to authentic learning and reading. Compliance will not create lifelong readers out of struggling ones.

Compliance will not create lifelong readers out of struggling ones.

To shift away from compliance in practice means doing the following:

- Modeling healthy vulnerability every day in your role as teacher. "Oops! I blew that, didn't I? Okay, kiddos, let's try that one more time."
- Creating a classroom culture that values vulnerability by allowing kids to share their perspectives, embrace inquiry, and acknowledge error with the opportunity to amend behavior rather than be punished or "held accountable."

- Sharing your learning and mistakes, using personal stories as appropriate. I'm never afraid to tell kids about my failures in school or struggles. This creates empathy and connection while modeling resiliency.
- Gently and respectfully insisting on student risk-taking in whole-class, small-group, and one-on-one discussions. Encouraging students to model self-expression and support peers.
- Guiding reluctant students into class discussion.
- Letting yourself be vulnerable enough to listen to student feedback and change plans accordingly.

CRITICAL SHIFT #5: PRIORITIZING LONG-TERM STUDENT DEVELOPMENT OVER SHORT-TERM MASTERY

When I teach my students, I don't ignore the importance of mastery of discrete skills. However, I do prioritize teaching and learning that invests in long-term development over the immediate measurement of discrete skills. Discrete skills, while important, are not the overall mission. Developing an authentic purpose to interact with a text is. And it takes time.

Where does that leave you? My answer is that you are left with the classic paradox: Sometimes we need to do less to achieve more. Building the kind of classroom culture that allows and encourages vulnerability and risk-taking, autonomy, and strong relationships through the interpersonal bridges with students may not look at first like progress. But progress can be deceptive. Remember Angelina, the student who identified as a level 50 reader? She was a master at fulfilling expectations; that is, she completed the assigned tasks and mastered specific skills outlined in our curriculum, yet she didn't know how to engage with a text. Her comprehension was narrow and fleeting. Working with her required starting from scratch and going backward for a while before we could go forward.

Window or Mirror?

Before we talk about how to begin this work with students and what the critical shifts, previously discussed, look like in practice, I'd like to pause and encourage you to reflect on your own views about reading.

As educators, we can be very fond of metaphors. One of the most popular metaphors about readers and text is *Windows, Mirrors, and Sliding Glass Doors* (Sims, 1990).

At first blush, we often talk of reading as opening a window into discovering ourselves through text and characters (Johnson et al., 2017). On the surface, this sounds exciting, but in emphasizing what is external, the world outside the window, what are we inviting students to think and do? It's great to see ourselves in reading, but what happens if we come to believe we are not good readers in the first place? What if our first barrier is the question, "Am I valued as a reader by my teacher?" In this case, I am offering a slant on the metaphor by suggesting that "windows and mirrors" is more than seeing oneself in a text through characters. It's also about seeing oneself as a capable, competent reader in the way that a student interacts with text and how they are seen by peers, teachers, and parents. Our thoughts or perceptions about what others believe we can do has a resounding impact on our ability to engage in relationships, and ultimately, to learn. Here, I want students to see themselves as readers. We are the mirrors that reflect that image back to students.

While I agree that learning can prepare students to meet and know the wide, wide world beyond themselves, by emphasizing the value of this world for students, by telling them what they should be seeing through the window, we run the risk of turning this window into a negative and destructive mirror of themselves. Let's consider Angelina.

Mr. Stygles:	"Angelina, what do you think of yourself as a reader?"
Angelina:	"I suck at reading!"
Mr. Stygles:	"Wow! What makes you say that?"
Angelina:	"My reading teacher told me in fourth grade."
Mr. Stygles:	"What do you mean? You had a reading teacher?"
Angelina:	"Yeah. She came and took a few of us out of the class because we were bad at reading."
Mr. Stygles:	"Did she tell you that you 'sucked'?'"
Angelina:	"No. I just knew because I was in a special reading group. We were the ones who couldn't keep up with the other kids in the class."

(Continued)

(Continued)

Mr. Stygles:	"What makes you think you don't read very well?"
Angelina:	"I'm slow. I get some words wrong when I read."
Mr. Stygles:	"How do you know you are slow?"
Angelina:	"Every time I go to her class I have to read aloud. She makes these marks on the paper. When I am reading, I look over to see what she is marking down. She crosses out the words I have a hard time with. I don't read perfectly like the other kids. I just suck at it. It's boring."
Mr. Stygles:	"Is there any other reason you don't read well?"
Angelina:	"I don't get to read a lot. I have a baby brother at home so there is no time. We live in a small apartment over by the gas station. He's crying all the time, and there is no place to read. I want to read; I just can't."

If we pause and consider what Alice Miller (1997) teaches us, do we respond to Angelina's "legitimate need to be noticed, understood, and taken seriously?" If we do, we can find a wealth of information—the data points that we're really looking for and the ones that will help prevent shame in the future.

On the surface, Angelina describes a situation in which she's been defined as a reader and where her perception of the teacher's view of her defines her self-worth. She is looking into the mirror at her own performance. Further, she's denied the capability of looking through the window the text might provide. Through this simple interaction of Angelina's reading, the window has been transformed into a mirror, a mirror of the teacher's making, which reflects back to Angelina a vision of herself as someone who "sucks" at reading.

But let's say the teacher takes a different approach, and instead, reflects back to Angelina praise for her work. What if the teacher were writing things like, *Well done! Excellent work! You really managed to read that one line very well.* Is that better? I would say no, it isn't. Approval comes from the teacher, not necessarily from within because this is still a mirror of the teacher's making. This is where shame thrives and where student agency, self-assessment, and motivation go to die.

So what are we to do? My answer is both complex and deceptively simple: We need to alter how we serve as a mirror for students and focus our teaching on guiding students to find their own mirror, one in which they recognize who they really are as readers.

> **We need to alter how we serve as a mirror for students and focus our teaching on guiding students to find their own mirror, one in which they recognize who they really are as readers.**

I haven't found all the answers. Teaching students to read, let alone developing independent readers, is a complicated process, part art, part science, and full of mystery. But I have learned some things about helping students see themselves clearly as readers and develop confidence and agency, while not sacrificing rigor, which I share in the following pages.

Reflect and Act

Use these reflection questions to consider the information shared in the chapter and how you can apply it in your own classroom.

1. How has this chapter altered your thinking about what shame is?
2. What critical shifts have you sought to make, and how does this chapter support your thinking?
3. Think of a student who challenges you. What is it they might really be looking for or signaling to you about?

2

MENTORING READERS

Why You Matter Most of All

iStock.com/monkeybusinessimages

Have you ever felt like you're doing all the work for a reader? You've set up small groups. You've met in reading conferences. You've even walked by, tapped the kiddo on the shoulder, and said, "Keep reading. Stay on task. You're doing great!"

Every day, you work to build relationships and positive connections. In a sense, you've responded to your readers, but why aren't they responding to you? You wonder, "If they aren't responding to me, what's happening while they read?"

You make a few calls home. You ask some colleagues for advice, yet nothing seems to change. You feel at a loss. No matter what you do, there seems to be a barrier between you and the students.

What happened? Why are things like this? You ask yourself, "What can I do to make it better?"

The Costliest Mistake of All

From my days working in daycare through teaching upper elementary during the depths of school reform, evaluators noted my relationships with students. One performance review mentioned, "The kids would follow you into the fire." At that point in my career, I only had one goal. This was even before I'd become obsessed over test scores and data points. I wanted every kid to love me and be their favorite teacher. Until I wasn't.

I didn't know the first thing about relationships. Instead, I was focused on me and being the "best" teacher every student loved. Think Michael Scott, manager of Dunder-Mifflin Paper Company on the hit-comedy *The Office*. Most kids had a great time. In retrospect, I'm not sure they learned much. Then, in the era of school accountability, a shame-based policy on multiple levels, a devastating reckoning occurred in my approach.

> I didn't know the first thing about relationships. Instead, I was focused on me and being the "best" teacher every student loved.

I grew up with a strong expectation of conformity and outright compliance. I'd excelled and gained favor, nay, respect because of it. I didn't budge from this for fear of *everything*. I made my way through college and the first decade of my teaching career relatively devoid of the concept of relationships, or what educators call mentoring, for one simple reason: I'd spent my life trying to be who everyone else wanted me to be. I had to do what others said, or be like others, or else I was worthless.

Turns out, I treated my students the same way. I'd lost my focus because of my success with test scores and benchmark assessments. I became all too aware of my error when this happened:

I'd just started teaching fourth grade. One student was very excited to be in my class. However, day in, day out, he sat and did nothing. He always said he loved to read, but little evidence suggested he did so (e.g., He read the same book for a month straight and made very little progress during independent reading). My guess is that he claimed to "love" reading attempting to gain my favor or attempting on his part to form the interpersonal bridge.

He'd been placed in my class because of my "good connection with struggling readers." Everyone thought he would be a good fit with me because he needed a strong male role model. I was too immature to recognize he was begging me to notice him, to be his friend. I needed kids meeting reading standards to maintain my reputation. And that's what I went after, whatever the cost.

One day, out of deep frustration about his laissez-faire ambivalence, I figured I'd "motivate" him. I peered down at him saying, "You're lazier than fungus on a rotting log."

The room went silent.

He looked at me with all the courage and strength he could muster. Not a tear fell.

If I ever thought shame worked to correct a student's motivation and interest, his affect told me I was dead wrong. His face showed me how much of a fool I really was. And for what? Test scores, reading levels, and reputation. I'd just sacrificed my integrity for superficial representations of what the student desired most—to be noticed and taken seriously.

So much for being the teacher who "got kids to read." I had failed beyond words. Looking into his hollow eyes, I thought to myself, "I just broke a child." Rather than taking the time to learn right alongside him, I turned away from him, knowing I had destroyed his soul.

Looking into his hollow eyes, I thought to myself, "I just broke a child."

Later, I called his mother, but there were no apologies that could make this right. At no point could I rectify the situation. I had done my damage.

Misidentification of Students as Struggling Readers

What did the young reader I destroyed struggle with? A lack of attention. It's reasonable to consider that our struggling readers don't feel they've been given the same attention as their successful peers. I confirmed that for this student. Not only did I ruin a rare interaction between the two of us, but he also had proof to justify that I wasn't joyful and positive with him like I was his classmates.

Too many readers don't identify as good readers. Their reward for being a struggling reader is a label. If they're lucky, they are invited to an intervention, a dubious distinction. Just as much as they are seeking our attention, they are failing at *what we want them to do.* No matter what, though, there always seems to be an impenetrable barrier between the student and the teacher.

And here's why: The attention these readers receive is linked to an imposed, and eventually internalized, deficit. Readers struggle because of the context we create for them or because they've entered into a reading experience that is generally unfamiliar. The burden of reading struggles falls on the student when they are otherwise *alone*. Furthermore, struggling readers come to realize they are different from their peers. Lesser than. So how do these kids survive? They withdraw from the whole process. They dissociate from who they are to who they need to be or create an appearance that they are in line with the image of being a reader.

Struggling readers come to realize they are different from their peers. Lesser than. So how do these kids survive? They withdraw from the whole process.

Dissociation—The Reason to Reframe Relationships

Struggling readers have a conflict with reading in the context that exists. Whatever the struggle might be, they can adapt through dissociation. Dissociation, in this context, is when a person develops a persona to adapt to an environment, which is different from the actual person, or authentic self (Block-Lewis, 1990). When we've (unintentionally) sought more from the student as a reader than as a person, we should consider how the student is responding and, if needed, chart a different trajectory.

Generally, the signal behavior for dissociation is something we are all familiar with: apathy. Essentially, the reader couldn't care less about reading; they are more likely to demonstrate compliance—doing enough to get by because the teacher said so. A dissociated reader hates reading but loves you. At recess, before school, or anytime other than reading, the reader thinks you're the greatest person in the world. They may even revisit you in later years. But when it comes to reading, they are a completely different person. A split self if you will. This reader believes they must be a particular person as a reader, and that person is not themselves. If they are authentic, they risk the exposure of deficits; they feel they must comply to adhere to the expectations we set forth, be they pedagogical (e.g., volume reading) or curriculum-based (e.g., biography units).

Dissociation can be resolved. The answer: The reader and I must push into the discomfort of reading deficits and enter a world of vulnerability. The essential nature of our relationship is predicated on the reader's feeling that I value them as a significant player in the relationship and that that value is not based on their achievement of a particular reading level. Harkening back to chapter one, Kaufman (1993) calls this the *mutuality of response*.

The essential nature of our relationship is predicated on the reader's feeling that I value them as a significant player in the relationship and that that value is not based on their achievement of a particular reading level.

Thus, within the classroom or intervention setting, the relationship between the reader and the teacher must be grounded in the reader's merits as a person—a person who engages as a reader—and a thinker—full of their own perceptions, epiphanies, and evaluations. Over time, I learned to see readers as unique individuals with unique experiences and different ways of reading. Now, when facing a resistant reader, I ask myself, "Is this relationship strong enough to push into discomfort? Do they trust me to help them?" It's at this juncture, the initiation of the interpersonal bridge, that can make or break a reader. We must show our readers that we are available and willing to join them on their journey as maturing readers.

- Are we willing to listen without judgment or speaking for the reader, to their story, their struggles, and their worries, above our own data-satiated goals and expectations?
- Does the student realize that we will be there, forgiving and learning from mistakes, treating every transgression like a new beginning?
- Does the reader believe that their struggles will end because of our partnership?
- Does the reader believe they can stop saying "I hate reading" because we opened new avenues for them to experience in their journey to become a reader?

Or will we simply suggest the next book and send them on their way?

Enter Delaney. Age 10, Delaney faced many struggles as a reader, including decoding. She stated several times that she didn't like reading. Nor did she read any more than she had to. I could tell by observing her as an independent reader that she didn't really understand what "reading" meant.

I turn to Delaney in our conference, asking, "Hey, do you want to talk about your book some?"

She shakes her head. "No."

Mr. Stygles:	"Really? What's going on?"
Delaney:	"I don't want to talk about the book. You're gonna make me read it out loud then tell me all the errors I made or that I didn't read fast enough."

Mr. Stygles:	"Hold on, are we doing an assessment or talking about a book?"
Delaney:	"I don't know. Probably both. You know I'm bad at reading. Why should I talk to you about it?"
Mr. Stygles:	"Ok. Fair point. But I'm tellin' ya, I just want to see what it's like to be you, as a reader. I want to see how you think."
Delaney:	"What? That's dumb. That's what everyone says I need to do."
Mr. Stygles:	"What are your thoughts on that?"
Delaney:	"What do you mean?"
Mr. Stygles:	"I mean, 'everyone' says *you* need to do something different when you're reading. What does that mean to you?"
Delaney:	"I don't know. I never really thought about it. I just do what they say. I don't care. All they will do is tell me I didn't do good enough, again, so why bother."
Mr. Stygles:	"So let me go back to my question, 'Can I talk to you about what you're reading, to see what's going on in your world?'"
Delaney shrugs her shoulder.	"Maybe. How are you different than anyone else? I mean, you can try. Why would you care about what I read?"
Mr. Stygles:	"Because, Delaney, the only way you're going to believe in yourself as a reader is if we look at how you think about reading. I want to know you as a reader. Is that okay?"
Delaney:	"I guess."

Carrying the burden of the student whom I crushed in the earlier vignette, I worked to shift my approach when I noticed Delaney sitting at her desk during independent reading, quiet as can be, doing almost nothing. Her eyes scanned the room a few times before fixating on the scene outdoors. The most recent book she'd chosen, *The Queen Bee and Me* (McDunn, 2019), didn't capture her interests like the ebbing tide of the tidal river she could see out the window. Did she know her book was upside down?

I didn't need to snap at her. I didn't need to tell her to read. I wasn't about to tell her to stay on task. I wasn't about to tell her she was lazy. I pulled my chair right alongside her desk. She faced the front of the room. I faced the back. Together we sat side by side, facing each other. She corrected the position of her book. Delaney read hers, I read mine. Proximal. Just before our time was done, I asked Delaney if she liked what she read today. She returned the courtesy by asking about my book, *New Kid* (Craft, 2019), thus initiating our relationship.

REBUILDING SECURE, TRUSTING RELATIONSHIPS WITHIN FAILINGS: THE ROLE OF READING MENTOR

One of our most human desires is to have someone around us when we are failing. We don't want to feel alone and abandoned. While we don't want to be seen as failing, it sure is better for someone to be there than to be left alone—even if we're busy pushing people away. Our readers' failing is their plea for proximity. Do we leave them to their devices, or do we have an opportunity to walk alongside the reader in their trials?

> **Our readers' failing is their plea for proximity. Do we leave them to their devices, or do we have an opportunity to walk alongside the reader in their trials?**

Naturally, I am concerned about readers who display unresponsive, disengaged, resistant, withdrawn, and/or avoidant behaviors. Whatever negative shame manifestation is present, I need to notice and respond—not fight and argue. Shame intensifies if I tell a reader to engage with their book regardless of their present emotional state or confidence level. If I say such things, I'm asking the reader to shut down completely. To avoid creating a compromising situation for my readers, I use a structure (Figure 2.1) that helps them portray their perspectives and develop identify as a reader.

I have the responsibility to notice the reader's actions and inquire, in a more private environment, one-on-one. This is especially important for my shy, timid, anxious readers. Small groups are not always their scene, at least not until confidence, maybe even social capital, is present. The security of the interpersonal bridge is where I can support the reader outside of the uncomfortable environment that inhibits interactions with text. I fulfill this mission by serving as a reading mentor.

2.1 Framework for Reading Conferences

Action Step	Example	Purpose
Clearly set the intention behind the conference.	Strategic Reading Conference	Even though I am setting the purpose, students have the option to discuss what features of this topic appeal to them. Generally, I'm available for students to share what they are reading during my "free times."
Dive deep for the reader's perspective.	Does the reader enjoy using _____ (reading strategy)?	I have to be very careful not to assume or judge. The student's narrative is the most important perspective to consider because it represents where they are at a moment of vulnerability. What I think is secondary to their viewpoint.
Restate what the reader says and ask a clarifying question.	I heard you say you're not a big fan of using ______ (reading strategy).	Students need to know they are heard and understood. When they aren't, they can feel undervalued, or they might concede to whatever we think to end the discussion.
Pose guidance as questions or suggestions.	Do you think _______ (e.g., Do you think pausing for a second just to make a quick note, to place a landmark of your thinking, might help you recall more details?)?	There's telling and then there is questioning. Telling means I have the power and I direct the learning. Questioning allows the reader to consider options and wonder what could be, which promotes versatile thinking.
Negotiate the challenge or task to discuss at the next conference.	I'm curious, what are you interested in trying next? Next time we meet, let me know how that goes!	Accountability is compassion. I need to send a clear message that I have a vested interest in their reading development. If they go away knowing they matter, they will come back (sooner than later) to share. If they don't, that's telling in and of itself.

What does mentoring look like? That's hard to answer for every teacher; however, I've learned over time that there is one key practice that enables us to strengthen the interpersonal bridge and invite students to develop as readers: conferring.

Atwell (2015) wrote a single statement that reminded me of my role as a reading mentor with respect to conferring, "The key to handover is that it draws on adults' knowledge" (p. 15). What I take "handover" to mean is that I can't just demand reading because I expect it. Instead, I have to hand over my knowledge about being a reader to the reader so that they have keys to establish themselves as *lifelong readers*.

Kaufman (1993) contributes to my conceptualization of a reading mentor. He writes,

> The relationship . . . must be a real one. Each must come to know the other as a real, very human person. And the relationship must be honest. In these ways the [teacher] will increasingly gain the [student's] confidence and the [student] will permit the [teacher] increasingly to enter his or her experiential world inside. The **onus** to gain entry resides solely with the [student]. . . . [O]nce let in, not only can the [teacher] provide some healing for the wounded self, but [the teacher] can also literally "see" the current inner functioning or life of the [reader]. (p. 134)

In what might feel contrary, sometimes we have to push our readers to face challenges that might otherwise go ignored or they don't want to face (e.g., close reading instead of pleasure reading). Therapist and shame consultant Matthew Mordrcin (2016), LCSW, acknowledges that we must push into the discomfort to release the shame that inhibits development. This has implications in reading as well. We too must lean into discomfort with our readers, which can be done in several ways:

- We cannot make reading easier to avoid, or ignore, the reader's struggle.
- Nor can we patronize a reader by saying, "Let's go with an easier book" and interaction that could potentially leave the reader more vulnerable to shame in the future.
- On the other extreme, we cannot create experiences that lead reading to be a constant frustration, dealt with by the reader alone. This only invites readers to quit reading or make excuses for not reading.

Rather, we have an implicit responsibility to engage readers with "productive struggle," a challenge that, in a mentorship, the reader and teacher undertake collaboratively. In my classroom, I use a framework to recognize the interplay between me and my readers, based on trust and mutuality, within the interpersonal bridge (Figure 2.2) This is how we become *reading mentors*. In doing so we become the mirror that reflects back the confidence we have in the reader and the glorious feeling that comes with embracing vulnerability and tackling challenges successfully.

We become the mirror that reflects back the confidence we have in the reader and the glorious feeling that comes with embracing vulnerability and tackling challenges successfully.

2.2 Interplay within the Interpersonal Bridge

Stage of Interpersonal Bridge	Intention Within the Relationship	Description
Entry Point	Story of Safety What I know about "me"	"Story of Safety" is a therapeutic term used here to know the reader's story. What is it that helps a reader feel safe, secure, confident, and competent enough to read, which informs the teacher and the student what is known about "me"?
Conferring	More targeted instruction occurs Inner defenses are more likely to manifest	Students are best instructed in smaller settings. This makes the reader more vulnerable than in a larger group. Unless the relationship is considered safe, the student is likely to exhibit an array of behaviors to impede either learning or portrayal of more authentic character.
Defense Strategies	Brain Activates (Mal)adaptive process of "self-care"	We are more apt to recall "shaming" because our brain has been activated, albeit negatively. Students engage in (mal)adaptive behavior to protect themselves against exposure. Self-care manifests in the form of compliance (e.g., nodding yes to every statement), withdrawal, or rage, which leads to dissociation, the reader they *need* to become rather than who they *can* become.

Acknowledging the Reader's Vulnerability With Trust and Respect

Delaney, as described above, was one of the readers I noticed. Her face was riddled with confusion.

I paused, commenting, "You look confused."

She concurred.

I said, "Let's talk a little later, ok?"

She approved.

Rather than pulling Delaney from her peers, making a scene so to speak, I made an appointment with her during independent reading.

"Delaney, can you tell me where you started to be confused." She pointed to a place in the text. "Great! Can you etch a question mark in the margin? After you've done that, reread the section."

After rereading, she indicated what made better sense. I instructed her by saying, "Any time you feel confused, stop. Mark a question mark, then reread. Can you do that for yourself?"

Note the last word: Yourself.

I'm informing Delaney that reading is for her, not for my appeasement or satisfaction. I'm merely a support in her quest to improve her reading comprehension. I invoke the interpersonal bridge to address vulnerabilities with the aim of instilling confidence and improving self-perception.

Can I Read a Book With You?

Have you ever caught yourself telling students to read? Do you have that insane feeling of agitation that you're crying out to your students "Read!! Please!! It's good for you!!" Or worse, "Read, or it's gonna make me look bad!" Yet there they sit, motionless, affectless. And it's almost always the same students who don't read at home and for the most part can be a bit incorrigible.

Truth be told, I'm not one to blame a student for not reading. However, there was a time this was not true. A critical shift for me was when I realized that children are not in complete control of their lives outside of school. I'm now very aware of the struggles some readers face at home (Payne, 1998) and what many students have been through before they reach my classroom. When well-being and a personal sense of security are either at risk or nonexistent, where does reading fit? Whenever in the life of many readers has the act of reading provided a sense of purpose, accomplishment, or enjoyment? Delaney was one of these kiddos. She had a busy schedule outside of school. Add in a distaste for reading and a high level of self-consciousness about her reading, and there was no way she wanted reading to interrupt her security and sense of self within in her own sheltered world at home.

During the first few months of school, I seemed to have nagged Delaney about her reading day after day. It was one constant reminder to read after another or asking her why she didn't read.

Every day at dismissal, I got the same reply, "I will." The next day . . . nothing.

My research into shame made me realize the dual nature of my error. For one, I was telling Delaney to read. There was no relationship. Just an expectation; more a demand. A barrier existed between us because I was the authority in the power dynamic. All she had to do was appease my request with a compliant reply. She knew what she was going to do. Why change? If she was not valued or heard as a reader, why did she need to comply?

Second, at that time, nowhere was there evidence that *I* read. Herein lies the shame inducing, "Do as I say, not what I do." Delaney had no reason to read. It's not like I went home and read. I was hypocritical. I mentored Delaney as a reader by sharing books or talking about characters. Why didn't I read? Ironically, like Delaney, I had no one to talk to about books or I believed my thoughts weren't welcome. For Delaney's sake, I had to get my act together. I looked at Delaney one day as she trolled through baskets, and I asked, "Delaney, have you read *Family Game Night and Other Catastrophes* (Lambert, 2017) before?"

She replied, "What's it about?" No doubt, gauging whether or not she was (or could be) interested in it.

I replied, "I don't know. I only heard about it a few days ago. I'm kind of interested. Want to check it out with me?"

"Sure." She stated, almost as if conceding. (I'm not sure she wanted to keep looking for books, which means I gave her an out.)

I could tell she wasn't excited about the proposition, but at least she was willing to try.

Regardless of the outcome, I was trying to create a bridge between Delaney and me, focused on reading, but ultimately with Delaney as a person. Her lack of "book love" (Kittle, 2013) was not likely due to disdain but rather from unfamiliarity. I'm sure she'd been told to read for years, by several people, but with no one to read with, she was abandoned as a reader. My continual demands didn't inspire her; they drove her away. I should have known better from my own experiences (and desires).

> **My continual demands didn't inspire her; they drove her away. I should have known better from my own experiences.**

So I read with Delaney. While you will learn more about inviting students into reading in the next chapter, it's imperative to realize that the genuine nature of the interpersonal bridge starts by sitting side-by-side with the student, with the same purpose. In this case, we were learning about a new book; neither one of us knew if we'd be interested in it or not.

Day after day, we checked in with each other. Some days were more successful than others. At times she read more pages than I did, and vice versa. Some days we sat together and read (on days I didn't sit with her, I was doing the same with other students). Nonetheless, we built a relationship by talking about the book, setting reading goals, and asking each other questions, both to clarify misunderstanding and to speculate.

While I couldn't do this with every book Delaney read, or with every student simultaneously, for that matter, it established a sense of security for Delaney. Someone would be there to talk about books and understand that sometimes, reading isn't joyous, nor is it easy to take time to do. I removed the power dynamic in favor of mentoring. Gone was punishment or lectures for not reading. In exchange, she learned about me; I learned about her. All because of a book.

The Importance of Prioritizing the Reading Conference

Here's something I don't want to admit. The most difficult aspect of my reading instruction is making time for reading conferences. Conferences are easy to deprioritize when racing against time and curriculum expectations. Yet there is no more crucial component of a workshop model—and nothing more important when it comes to building the interpersonal bridge. Reading conferences demand time, presence (mindfulness), and authenticity.

In the past, I had shirked my own responsibility to initiate and engage in reading conferences and misplaced my irritation, putting it on students by telling them to "show you are a maturing reader and take responsibility for your own reading lives." On a really bad day, I would simply use a status of the class to find out who didn't read, then keep those kids in for recess to somehow absolve myself of the guilt I felt for not engaging with readers frequently enough to promote and scaffold their reading interests. It was counterproductive.

Conferences can take on a variety of styles and purposes. A reading conference can be, for example:

- An informal conversation between a reader and teacher when a student first arrives at school
- A 5-minute conversation during independent reading
- Kneeling next to a student who is working on close reading in a shared reading activity.
- Giving feedback on something a student has written about reading

The larger purpose of a conference is to demonstrate a genuine interest in the child. A reading conference fosters the mutuality of the relationship, through instruction and an interest in the reader's development

Over the years, I've learned that if I don't confer with readers, I essentially abandon them. The implication being that reading, or their reading, is not valued on my agenda. Readers respond in kind: They stop reading. When I skip reading conferences, I convey to students that their ideas and experiences are not important. Then I wonder why they don't read, or read them the riot act, as if angry words could create the resiliency to overcome my abandonment. To "dive deep" and best support the reader, I hold an array of reading conferences.

2.3 Types of Conferences

Conference Type	Function	Frequency
Interim Assessment	• Gain a sense of the reader's self-evaluation and rationale • Seek clarification and understanding of perceptions and narrative • Determine actionable goals to incorporate in the reader's process	Trimonthly
Book Selection	• Rationale for selection and goals • Consider prior knowledge about the topic, author, theme • Establish boundaries for successful reading experiences • Consider possible challenges and approaches to persevere	Whenever Possible
Reading Passport	• Create self-awareness and self-efficacy around daily reading habits • Negotiate boundaries that will support successful reading • Observe and consider trends	Monthly
Strategic Reading	• Support recognition of affective response while reading • What actions are you taking to monitor your comprehension and what is the evidence? • How is strategic reading improving engagement, joy, and overall opinion of a book?	Biweekly
Comprehension	• Evaluate what's happening in the book that makes you think about yourself and the world around you • Consider the lessons you're taking away and why are they meaningful • Celebrate reader's perceptions about the text and improve self-perception	Biweekly

Conference Type	Function	Frequency
Reflection	• Acknowledge the reader's process. What's improving? What adjustments are being made to create more successful reading experiences? • Support metacognition. How do I know I'm improving? What can I do to make shifts? • Discuss and consider opportunities for reading habits	Monthly
VOWELS Checklist	• Create self-awareness and self-efficacy around reading habits • Seek clarification and understanding of perceptions and narrative • Celebration of the reader's improvements and identification of target areas to discuss later	Weekly

Consider a child who has made a discovery. They cannot wait to express their joy to a loved one. However, when the discovery is shared, the sentiment is discounted or rejected. In turn, the child feels a sense of unworthiness and abandonment. The interpersonal bridge is shattered, and the child internalizes the sense of abandonment (Claesson & Sohlberg, 2002).

This is what happens when we do not prioritize the reading conference. A reader who has no place to share their reading discoveries recoils from reading. Further, by suggesting to a maturing reader that they are solely responsible for their reading requires that the maturing reader assume the role of an adult reader. The student is denied the mirror though which to see themselves in the eyes of a valued person. When children do not receive feedback, they often presume the worse.

I've since learned that my students, maturing as readers, deserve my attention. They deserve feedback and encouragement. I can give them this by prioritizing the reading conference.

Teacher Credibility

In recent years, Hattie (2012, 2016) and authors Fisher and Frey (2016) have discussed the importance of teacher credibility. Teacher credibility has a .90 effect size (Fisher et al., 2020)—meaning it has the potential to more than double student learning. Teacher credibility might be what is known as the *it factor.* While the charisma or dynamism that a teacher brings to a classroom is important, teacher credibility is more than that. It is also the belief on the part of students that they can learn from this person; that is, students need to view their teacher as competent. Finally, there must be a foundation of trust, and what the authors call *immediacy,* for a teacher to be fully credible in the eyes of their students. Immediacy "focuses on the perceived, and even actual, distance between the teacher and his or her students" (Fisher et al., 2020).

When I think about my journey as a teacher, I had dynamism and affability, but I didn't have credibility. A big part of credibility, as I said earlier, is defined as the perception that a student can learn from a teacher. In the past, readers in my class may have liked reading, but I didn't convince them that reading was worthwhile. I didn't exactly hear them say things like, "He makes you interested in reading." No, what I heard was, "He's fun! But he makes you read a lot." The negative association students had with reading displayed my lack of credibility. Readers enjoyed my classroom, but I wouldn't say they believed I would be the one to eliminate their reading ills. I had to do more. Yes, more. I had to knock down the wall between my readers and me.

Kaufman (1993) notes, "Being in a relationship to a significant other of necessity conveys to children that they are loved as persons in their own right and in some fundamental way that they are special to that significant other." Here's when I knew Delaney trusted me enough to be able to become a reader:

Mr. Stygles:	"Do you want to become *a reader*?"
Delaney:	"Yeah."
Mr. Stygles:	"What does that mean?"
Delaney:	"Yeah, I want to read better. I don't like how it's hard to figure out words. I don't like how it literally takes forever to read a book. I don't like that other people can read better than me."
Mr. Stygles:	"Man! Sounds like your carry a lot of angst. Do you know what angst means?"
Delaney:	"No."
Mr. Stygles:	"Angst is like negativity, worrying a lot, or feeling anxious."

Delaney: "I guess so."

Mr. Stygles: "What do you think it takes to become a reader?"

Delaney: "Reading more books?"

Mr. Stygles: "Do you know how to read?"

Delaney: "Huh? Duh? You read the words on the page."

Mr. Stygles: "Maybe," I say, smiling because I'm apologetic for slightly patronizing Delaney's intelligence. "I mean, do you know how to manage yourself as a reader, meaning explore your book options as a reader, use strategies as a reader, make time, or use time successfully to read?"

Delaney: "Huh? I only read 'cause I have to. I just read what the teacher tells me to read."

Mr. Stygles: "Let me ask you again, 'Do you think you can become a better reader in this class?'"

Delaney: "Mr. Stygles, you're confusing me."

Mr. Stygles: "Why?"

Delaney: "I already read what I have to. I may not read every night, so what else do I have to do?"

Mr. Stygles: "Well, it's not necessarily what you *have* to do, it's how you do it and what you do for yourself. You see, despite what everyone says about 'Mr. Stygles makes you read forty books,' the truth of it is, it's not about me making you read, it's about *you* making the choice to say, 'I want to read.' Sure, I'm going to get a bit upset if you don't read. Yes, I might 'pester' you about your reading, but I only do it because I want to see you become a reader. Then again, it's not what I want—I can't force you—but I will ask you what you are doing to take care of yourself as a reader."

Delaney: "Umm . . . are you saying you're trying to trick me into reading?"

Mr. Stygles: "Ha! That's kind of funny. I didn't look at it like that."

Delaney: "Then why do you want me to read?"

Mr. Stygles: "Like I said, it's not about me *wanting you* to read, it's about adding a special dimension to your life that will help you gain knowledge and experience and give you something to believe in about yourself."

(Continued)

(Continued)

Delaney:	"Whoa, dude. Now you're kinda creepin' me out."
Mr. Stygles:	"Why?"
Delaney:	"'Cause no one's ever talked to me like this before. They always just say, 'Here's what you're going to read,' then they make me read aloud. Not even my mom cares if I read. She just signs the reading log so I don't go to detention."
Mr. Stygles:	"Well. Let's change this. Let's make this about you."

Final Thoughts

If we consider the role of shame in reading development, we must look beyond defining students through superficial descriptions. Readers—like other people—change over time. Identity cannot be "fixed," it has to be nurtured. Acceptance cannot be conditional (e.g., "I like you because you do this . . ."); it must be shared freely with every student.

The question is, can we accept a reader for how they think rather than defining maturing readers by superficial qualities (i.e., "I like mystery books" or "I'm a level ___ reader"), which will undoubtedly change over time?

Our identity evolves through our experiences, perceptions, and perceived acceptance. Superficial qualities have their role in an identity. "I like . . ." for example, is one of the ways we begin to connect and associate with others. We are attracted to people with matching interests. But the rise of a reading identity originates in strong relationships based on acceptance.

A reader's self-perception is built on what is seen, heard, and felt, from an array of sources including parents, schools, media, and other experiences. Not to mention our impact. No matter how hard we try to control factors such as poverty, language development, and equal access, the fact remains, even if we were able to establish equality for all, not one of us can control how another human being internalizes the world. Internalizations form our self-perception far beyond the speed in which we can teach. It's in this that we have to value and prioritize our relationships with our students. We can control our interactions and the feedback we provide to students. More, we have the great fortune of helping readers, reflecting back the image they can see of themselves as maturing readers.

For as long as I have taught, reading policies have overlooked the potential of students who incorporate reading as part of their identity. Standardized test scores and reading levels continually define our readers, whether by identity, or the trajectory of the reading instruction they are *bound* to receive. In turn, readers do not evolve into thinkers but rather identify by the labels assigned to them, with little or no choice to the contrary. Again, I cannot blame any reader who displays apathy because their outcome is seemingly already determined for them. We can change this by providing a classroom in which a reader can articulate their voice and by honoring their perceptions, discoveries, and awareness.

Reflect and Act

Use these reflection questions to consider the information shared in the chapter and how you can apply it in your own classroom.

1. Consider your conferring practices, what shifts are you interested in exploring based on this chapter?
2. Consider a negative interaction you had with a reader. What was it that upset you? What could you do differently next time?
3. What assessments are you currently using? How do they inform your instruction based on the student's voice, experience, and perspective?
4. What challenges do your students display that you can "lean into" with them and connect with your readers?

3

GETTING TO KNOW THE READER

Identity, Experience, and Mirrors

iStock.com/SDI Productions

At the beginning of the school year, we are all, to some degree, teacher and student alike, blank slates. We don't know the students and the students don't really know us. This is an exciting opportunity to begin anew, and we feel that excitement as we usher the students through the door and to their desks. What will this year hold? What breakthroughs can we all make? At this moment, all is potential.

In an effort to welcome and orient students, we might spend the first weeks doing ice-breaker exercises, introducing students to classroom routines, and we also likely begin assessing their skills, administering our formal assessments, trying to obtain a sense of where students are at. We want to know what their interests are, what strategies we will need to focus on, and we consider the formation of small groups to maximize learning.

What's at the forefront, what's most important at the start of the year, is our attempt to develop an understanding of who our readers are and *what* they come from. Without this knowledge, we run the risk of not providing the most targeted instruction possible. Moreover, we need to find the means to connect and empathize with our readers. Whatever information we collect at the start of the year, we are sending a powerful message to students about what is and isn't important. We might implicitly send a message that performance is everything. We may reveal to our students that the celebration of their being is the greatest gift. It depends on what we value most.

Many of us regularly experience the pressure of early (and intensive) benchmark and summative assessment to obtain the data that suggest how we should design our instruction. It's not that district-mandated tests and various reading assessments don't have value. They do. But it's not the student's story. It's someone else's. Aside from sending powerful messages about what we value most (test scores), the assessments can also obscure more than they reveal, much like the moon, so small in the sky, can blot out the sun during a solar eclipse. I like to think of students as being as big as the sun. This means we need to control how we position the data so that it doesn't blot out their light.

Test scores and assessments can obscure more than they reveal, much like the moon, so small in the sky, can blot out the sun during a solar eclipse.

Before any mandated assessment, we have to place our students first. We need to "read" their story. The first step in building student ownership, independence, and agency in reading is putting the student, the students' stories about themselves as readers, first. Research has been pointing to the importance of student agency for years (Johnston, 2004; Vaughn et al., 2020). Henk et al. (2013) explain, "Students who do well in school have developed self-efficacy; that is, they believe they can perform an academic task. They have also internalized a high-level of self-regulation, believing that they can control the factors necessary to perform the task" (p. 4).

The first step in building student ownership, independence, and agency in reading is putting the student, the students' stories about themselves as readers, first.

This is our target.

This is how we help readers overcome shame. The assessments I prioritize scaffolds the reader's autonomy, inviting students to become what Frey et al. (2018) call *Assessment Capable Learners*. My aim is to wean them from defining themselves through someone else's mirror (Learned, 2016; Mueller, 2001; Muhammed, 2020), which can be the source of so much shame, self-consciousness, and negative feeling. The best way to start is by introducing them to the idea of introspection, to explore and take ownership of their reading lives (Appleman, 2006; Tatum, 2009). Perhaps more important than our getting to know them, they need to know themselves, and it's our job to help make it happen (Roorda et al., 2011).

In this chapter, I describe in detail how I engage students in the work of leaning into who they are as readers. One of my favored assets is an extended and in-depth version of a reading autobiography. Because it is so important and serves as a launching pad for my yearlong interactions with students, I devote almost this entire chapter to the steps I take to make this a meaningful and productive process. There are, however, other tools I use as well that help me see how students see themselves, to paint a broader portrait and misrepresentations (Jones, 2020). These instruments, or interim assessments (Valencia, 2011), take little time to administer but provide my students and me with critical information to help us both zero in more precisely on student perceptions of their own learning:

- Reader Self-Perception Scale (Figure 3.8)
- Reading Process Self-Evaluation (Figure 3.9)
- Index of Reading Awareness (Figure 3.10)

I describe these later in the chapter.

The goal of the reading autobiography is to recognize the reader and validate their experiences, positive or negative, successful or damaging. The autobiography is a mirror—one that reflects a sense of identity as a reader, albeit temporary, and documents the legacy of learning to read, setting the stage for resiliency. We can differentiate most effectively when we know who the reader is as a person.

The reading autobiography is imperfect, but it's a catalyst to the *reader's* narrative—their perspective of learning to read. Although our maturing readers cannot recall every reading scenario, setback, or accomplishment, nor are they developmentally capable of completely expressing their viewpoints or recounting every landmark on their reading journey, thankfully, we have additional tools that extend the reader's voice and provide a further window into their perceptions. These are affective assessments (Stahl & McKenna, 2010), and I use the three listed earlier, four times each, over the course of the school year. From these assessments I can gain insight into what Stiggins and Popham (2010) call "academic efficacy," or "a student's perceived ability to succeed and the student's sense of control over her or his academic well-being" (p. 1). This is important because a lack of control over one's own actions engenders shame. Further, renowned assessment expert Peter Afflerbach (2016) adds, "If we do not regularly assess the development of students' motivation and self-efficacy for reading, we cannot make measurement-based inferences about the development of these critical factors." Affective assessments provide more voice for maturing readers to share their perceptions about reading that cannot be discerned from benchmark assessments or even the reading autobiography. In other words, we cannot assume everything from a benchmark assessment. Since a reader's sense of competence has a significant impact on motivation (Cambria & Guthrie, 2010; Guthrie & Wigfield, 1997), we have to dig deep to find the factors that hinder our readers. There are a few interim assessments I like to use throughout the year to uncover different "internal" aspects of my readers (see Figure 3.1). The three measures you will find in this chapter do just that.

3.1 Assessment Pacing Guide

Beginning of the Year	Late Fall/Early Winter	Early Spring	End of Year
Reading Autobiography			Favorites Bookshelf
• Reader Self-Perception Scale • Reading Process Self-Evaluation • Index of Reading Awareness	• Reader Self-Perception Scale • Reading Process Self-Evaluation	• Reader Self-Perception Scale • Reading Process Self-Evaluation	• Reader Self-Perception Scale • Reading Process Self-Evaluation • Index of Reading Awareness

We start with the reading autobiography, then consider each of these instruments in the context of this larger effort to help students develop a maturing self-awareness of their own agency as readers (Vaughn et al., 2020).

The Reading Autobiography: So Much More Than an Ice Breaker

You may be familiar with the reading autobiography. Indeed, you may assign it at the beginning of the year to your students. Many teachers, like Katherine Solokowski, Paul W. Hankins, and Penny Kittle, and numerous preservice literature professors have students develop autobiographies as an ice-breaker exercise to help them learn about each other and form connections and, of course, to help the teacher learn about their students (Barone & Barone, 2015). Muhammed (2020) speaks to the relevance of identity and the influence of that identity on self-concept and the desire to read. If we consider the reader's history first, we can set a course for the reader to consider how they will include reading into their lives.

The practice I describe below may differ from that of other teachers in the amount of time and importance I attach to this autobiography. I don't just see this as an assignment. I see it as a critical first step in building student agency, responsibility, self-knowledge, and competence. In short, this is the first step in helping students develop a strong, shame-resilient sense of themselves as readers (Parsons, 2009).

A 3-Week Exploration of Students' Reading Lives

I spend at least 3 weeks taking students through a careful exploration of their reading lives. They brainstorm, share, and interview parents, teachers, and even each other. They write their reading autobiographies, get feedback, and revise. While this is going on, we are establishing routines, expectations, and beginning conversations about reading.

I see this process of delving deep into their struggles and challenges, points of excitement and points of boredom, their fears, and victories as readers, as the first step to developing student agency for their learning. Perhaps shame researcher, clinician, and author DeYoung (2015) says it best,

> Narrative fosters integration, not because the stories told are accurate histories, but because they enact the teller's agency and capacity to tell. When the telling is freely chosen, it can integrate pain and joy, pain and regret, relief and resignation. (p. 112)

In other words, students begin to own their story, not the one we create for them through assessments. Students in upper elementary, indeed most students of any age, are typically surprised to learn they have reading lives, and they are certainly not thinking of it as something they can take the lead in nurturing. This reading autobiography opens up that possibility to students.

Through reading autobiographies, students begin to own their story, not the one we create for them through assessments.

The work sets in motion two processes that are critical for shaping an authentic and powerful relationship to reading and reading instruction.

1. The process of developing and maturing a reading identity.

2. The process of building an interpersonal bridge with their teacher.

To mature, versus becoming resistant, reluctant, or compliant, students need to make sense of how they learned to read, understand their own story, share it with us, and trust us with it. As instructors, we need to be respectful, curious, and open to students' narrative. We need to take them seriously, probe deeply, and then when the assignment is over, not put them in a drawer and move on, but work cooperatively with students to continue to build this narrative and make sense of it. In doing so, we initiate our interest in the reader and the development of the interpersonal bridge: a representation of our respect and understanding toward the student.

> **We need to be respectful, curious, and open to students' reading narrative.**

The students are writing more than an assignment; they are creating a legacy, a living document that initiates their involvement in their reading development and creates a milestone to be built on. I do not prescribe a length, but I do ask that every grade level be accounted for, from preschool up through a student's most recent grade level. Next, I outline how this 3-week process unfolds.

Days 1–4

WRITING PROCESS: INFORMATION GATHERING

I typically devote the first week to information gathering using a matrix I developed that I call, "My Reading Life—Memories Matrix." For that week, our whole class reading lessons involve introducing students to each column of the matrix and modeling how to fill it in. It is important to do both these things and not just hand students the form and expect that they will be able to fill it in. I usually give them at least a week to finish this process as they talk with parents, teachers, and other family remembers and check in with each other to prompt their memories.

3.2 My Reading Life—Memories Matrix

	Favorite Books	Positive Reading Memories	Negative Reading Memories	What I Remember Learning About Reading
Before School				
Kindergarten				
1st Grade				
2nd Grade				
3rd Grade				
4th Grade				
5th Grade				

DAY ONE: FAVORITE BOOKS IN EVERY GRADE

On the first day, I start by asking students to remember their favorite book(s) in every grade. I ask them about books that teachers read aloud. *What books did you enjoy in small group reading with Mrs. Smith in third grade? What books did you read on your own that were your favorite?*

To help students out, I allow them to consult their teachers. Some prefer to look in the school library. Most students take time to review my classroom library in hopes this will help them remember titles read from grades three and four. Students are also encouraged to collaborate with peers with whom they shared previous classes to walk down memory lane together. Finally, all students are encouraged to take the My Reading Life—Memories Matrix home to work with parents. But I tell them I prefer they try hard to recall on their own, which is an indication of which books left the biggest impact.

DAY TWO: POSITIVE READING MEMORIES

On the second day, I ask students to focus on positive memories. Like the first day, students spend the lesson brainstorming positive events in their reading history. I want students to recall, unaided. I want to know what jumps out at them first. Such memories are likely the most impactful, the most memorable that have led readers to where they are.

Ashlyn, for example, wrote:

Preschool: *My preschool teachers read two picture books a day.*

Kindergarten: *We read the Gingerbread man and made Gingerbread men.*

1st Grade: *I liked reading sight words.*

2nd Grade: *I read a bit of books.*

3rd Grade: *I read a thick and hard chapter book in two weeks.*

4th Grade: *I started a good book.*

My guess was Ashlyn would have written more if she had had more space. But I wasn't sure. Moreover, I grew concerned that she couldn't remember much about her books in third and fourth grade, or her overall reading experiences. I made a mental note that my expectations might create unwanted vulnerability for Ashlyn in the weeks to come. She is a student I would later confer with to gather more information than just single memories. As I discuss later, conferring with individuals and groups in a flexible process based on student responses to the My Reading Life—Memories Matrix is a critical part of helping students make this a meaningful activity.

DAY THREE: NEGATIVE READING MEMORIES

Our third experience with the memories matrix can be a bit more difficult. I ask students to begin exploring negative memories. There are several reasons students might be reluctant to share such memories. One reason I'm seeing more and more often is a concern that "my parents will say that is not true" or "my teacher will say it didn't happen that way." Such responses only confirm that students have not been allowed or perhaps adequately encouraged to honor their own perceptions, distorted or not. Students who are less apt to share might be looking for approval, like Nicole, whose memory matrix (Figure 3.3) after day three, included only a few positive memories and favorites. They may also feel like turncoats or unsafe. After all, students are taught not to talk negatively of others, which, while generally a good character trait to develop, can sometimes stand in the way of developing true self-understanding. To what extent will a student disguise or contain negative experiences to protect an authority figure because they are "supposed to show respect"? But, as I mentioned above, we aren't necessarily searching for the absolute truth. We are searching for the students' identification with their own stories. Even though I may have my own understanding of what brought a student to the place they are in, it's not my place to determine or dictate what that story is.

We aren't necessarily searching for the absolute truth. We are searching for the students' identification with their own stories.

DAY FOUR: REMEMBERING LEARNING.

Despite curriculums, expectations, and in some cases, explicitly stated learning intentions, I find students often don't remember what they learned. Mainly, I look for what students have learned in the past about using strategic reading processes. Students who demonstrate the most shame-resilience are those who are aware of their reading process, more so than students who only remember the books they have read. I am looking for responses that point to this awareness—for example, saying something like, *"My teacher thought I could learn more if I made a connection to the reading,"* or *"I learned how to summarize or how to break apart words."* But it is rare that students display such insight and awareness. Jason's rudimentary and cryptic responses are more the norm.

Before School: I learned to listen to people read.

Kindergarten: I learned to stop crying in reading time and liked looking at picture books.

1st Grade: I learned to READ.

2nd Grade: I learn to read better.

3rd Grade: I learned to like reading tests.

4th Grade: Listened to first graders read.

If anything, his compliance, "learning to listen to people read" and "crying," invited further inquiry. The story behind these events might be a reason why Jason's reading level lingered well behind his peers, especially with these limited reading experiences. Otherwise, the lack of specifics begged for clarity. I definitely wanted to know more about "I learned to like reading tests."

Completing the Memory Matrix

Throughout this first week, I want to encourage students to move into a more mature and productive relationship with their own strengths and weaknesses, their own success and, yes, their own failures. Doing so requires digging up memories, both negative memories that may be hard to face, as well as positive memories, which can easily be drowned out by negative experiences. Thus, as we move through the first week's work of completing the memory matrix, I model for students how to think about and access both kinds of memories. By sharing my own negative experiences, not only am I modeling the kind of vulnerability students need to embrace to become self-motivated, shame-resilient learners, but I am also working to build trust and mutual empathy. This means I share memories like this one:

In third grade, I had an assignment to find a book in the library, read it, and do a book report on it. Back then, books didn't have appealing covers. I let the librarian choose a book for me, a mystery since that was the genre we were studying at the time. The book was horribly boring. So instead of reading it I copied parts of the text into my report. I got a C+ on the assignment. I'd thought I accomplished something—getting a reasonable grade for doing little work.

Hopefully, throughout the year we can help students build a foundation of more functional and productive and positive experiences. But for now, to mitigate the dysfunction created by shame—the grandiosity, perfectionism, avoidance, and acting out when it comes reading—we need to face the beast and guide students through the process of doing the same.

DAY FIVE: SHIFTING FROM MEMORY GATHERING TO MEMORY ORGANIZING

After Day Four, I shift the focus. I let students know that I'm not looking for every memory but rather those of special significance, ones that may have influenced their attitudes toward and experience of reading (Jang et al., 2015).

I give them a handout that prompts them with the following questions:

Reading Prompts

- Was there a book everyone had to read? Did you feel like you had a choice?
- Was there an assignment or expectation from a teacher that you found helpful?
- What were the moments that made you want to stop reading?
- Was there a moment when maybe you realized you were different? Maybe you felt like you were falling behind or not measuring up to the other readers?

My deeper dive into the readers' backstory, what some could consider "pushing into discomfort," is meant to recognize the reader for all that has happened, good and bad. We can create resilience through acknowledgment rather than repression. Here, I am digging deeper to encourage trust, respect, and empathy, within our newly forming relationship by attending to their narratives (Vlach & Burcie, 2010).

Week 2

DAYS 6-10: WRITING PROCESS: DRAFTING AND DIGGING DEEPER

Day Six: After 5 days of brainstorming and filling out their memory matrix, students are ready to begin composing their initial drafts at the start of the second week (the sixth day of our work). The finished autobiography needs to include separate sections on each of the grade levels represented on the memory matrix, but I encourage students to begin where they feel the most comfortable, which is likely the previous year. I model how I approached writing my reading autobiography by starting with fourth grade, my most successful year as a reader. As I described earlier, I included an anecdote that I remembered clearly. I give them typically 45 minutes in total to work on their drafts. I collect these to get more insight into who is truly struggling with their memories and where students will need extra support to create meaningful narratives.

Days 7-10: While we have already spent over a week on the reading autobiographies, in many ways I see the real work beginning right here. I recognize that I am asking students to write a relatively expansive piece at the start of the year. Some students may not be "warmed up" to recall educational memories even after a week with the memory matrix. To help students, in addition to doing group and individual conferring, I supply them with a handout listing the following set of explicit questions that can be applied across every grade level. I use these questions to get students to dig deeper.

Questions to Support Student Writing

1. What was the first book you read alone?
2. What was the best book you read in each grade?
3. What were the titles you liked that were read to you?
4. What was the worst book you ever read?
5. What books do you recall looking at the most? Or spending the most time with?
6. What books did you enjoy listening to your teacher read aloud?
7. What phrases do you remember being told about reading (positive or negative) that have stuck with you?
8. What phrases do you remember being told about you as a reader (positive or negative) that have stuck with you?
9. What memories or experiences do you have about reading in small groups?
10. What do you remember about reading being hard? Why? What grade?
11. What do you remember about reading being enjoyable? Why? What grade?
12. Did you ever choose to stop reading? Why?
13. Was there ever a time, or times, when you didn't feel like you could read? Or were told you couldn't? Please explain.
14. What is the most important book in your life? Why?
15. Who were some of the most important people who helped you read? Why?

Now that they are wrestling with the act of writing, students typically welcome the prompts.

Knowing When to Probe for Memories

Undoubtedly, there are students who can think of nothing to write. To a point, I have to decide what the student can recall on their own.

I don't want to stifle autonomy, foster compliance, or weaken a reader's self-perception. However, there comes a time when I need to intervene. Thinking compassionately, I recognize some students may need their educational memory "warmed up." That's when I might engage them in conferring, either individually or in small groups. (I include more on conferring at the end of this chapter.)

3.3 Nicole's Memory Matrix

My Reading Life—Memories Matrix ***Nicole***

	Favorite Books	Positive Reading Memories	Challenging Memories	What I remember learning about reading?
Before School	Hungry hungry Capital the old lady how to sword a cow.			How to listen to a story
K	Five little monkeys jumping on a bad	Why was Read Aloud positive?		
1st Grade	Animal books			
2nd Grade	Dog books	History books plant books		How to find a quiet place to read so you don't get distracted by people.
3rd Grade	Upside Down maging	Forest books maging books		How to write about reading in complete sees
4th Grade	Untechbols and little house on the prairie	Finch books nonfiction books I was getting better at reading		Read big chapter books

Note: The responses

With students like Nicole, who was from day one asking for affirmation ("I'm doing this right, aren't I, Mr. Stygles?" or "See? I did it right.") I might tread lightly and not push too hard to force negative memories. But with other students, it can be worthwhile to probe and learn more. Take the case of Bry, whose completed autobiography is shown in Figure 3.4. The negative memories Bry initially recorded on her matrix were cryptic and hard to decipher and invited some questioning in a one-on-one conference. But beyond that, I couldn't help noticing that they weren't really focused on the experience of reading as much as on her experience of teacher expectations of reading behavior. In this figure, you will notice numerous writing errors. This is evident of a student's work and initial data collection as the student is still learning language conventions and their applications across subjects. Here is what Bry wrote:

Before School: had to be a short story (her exact words)

Kindergarten: Understanding what I read.

1st Grade: Remembering what to bring home for homework.

2nd Grade: Reading what I didn't want to read.

3rd Grade: Didn't want to read chapter books.

4th Grade: Reading what I could write without copying a sentence.

Of course, Bry's memories didn't exist in a vacuum. Even though it was the beginning of the year, I had had enough casual conversations with her to suspect that she read more than her reading matrix let on. For this reason, I made a point of conferring with her to learn more (Barnes, 2020). Reviewing her matrix, I was intrigued by her self-awareness in kindergarten. I wanted to know more about what she meant by "understanding what I read." (Her explanation would later be the more in-depth and insightful version she used in her completed autobiography.) Further, I was curious about her feelings on reading things she didn't want to read. What slowly emerged via conferring was that Bry was an avid reader, but a private one, which is also revealed in her final autobiography. Why hide this? We can never be sure, but one interpretation is that her "shame" wasn't related to reading so much as insecurity about her capacity to get the reading behavior just right. This is important, because it helps us as teachers understand how a focus on external reading behavior can create dysfunction within many students, even a strong and motivated reader like Bry. The experience of probing negative memories and crafting an authentic autobiography allowed Bry to better connect her private and her classroom reading. The result, over the course of the year, was that I could approach her with new texts, challenging her to take on texts she might have otherwise been resistant to.

3.4 Bry's Reading Autobiography

Hi, if you want to learn about my life in past grades, then you should read this. I don't know why you would want to read this, oh, wait, I do know why, you would want to read this because it says things about my past grades that will make you think of your past grades too. Anyway, if you want to read this, go ahead!

Kindergarten:

In Kindergarten, I remember Ms. Degrasse reading a book I can't think of to us on the rug, back when she had strawberry-blond hair. I do not have the least idea what the book was though.

I also remember trying to learn my ABCs while secretly drawing on my page. It was not so secret when Ms. Degrasse looked down on my paper, was not that fun either, because she sent me to a "time out" for five or ten minutes. Those were the longest five or ten minutes of my life.

I remember my favorite book was *The Peanuts.*

I think my first book I read was *give a mouse a cookie,* but I'm not sure.

I do remember reading some type of picture book, although, I don't remember what it was though. Well, whatever it was, I think I liked it, I wish I knew or remembered what it was about though.

I remember Ms. Degrasse and Ms. Treasure reading *Goldilocks And The Three Bears* to us on the rug back at the old school. THAT WAS A NIGHTMARE!!!!!!!!!! I remember being SO bored while they read it, but honestly, I feel bad for them, because I bet I was such a pain to them while they read it to us.

I also remember boasting at recess because I read a "Tough book," apparently.

First Grade:

In First grade, I remember making my own books, and feeling so proud reading them to the class. One took two months to make, The books were about a cat named Lilly, in several problems. I decided to make books about Lilly, because I liked cats a lot. I also remember me getting mad at Ms. Sweetwater because she said I could not make books right at that moment. I remember reading so much *Bad Kitty* you could spit cloth hangers. I remember crying while reading because I missed my auntie Kattie who had just died at that time.

I remember reading about bees and how they save plants and what there jobs were inside the beehive.

We had a Butterfly in our classroom, I remember Ms. Sweetwater making us read about Butterfly's so we could know what our butterfly does and why. I liked the teacher read to. It's weird, but First grade is one of the grades I remember most. I don't know why, I just remember this grade a lot, I guess.

Second Grade

In Second grade, I remember reading *Greedy cat* to Ms. Swale so she could grade my reading level, In where she could tell where my reading level was. I remember learning what the word "Greedy" means while reading about a greedy cat who took all the cat-food for all the other cats. I remember being caught drawing under my table. I regret that, because Ms. Swale made me sit out for a bit. My favorite book was *Warriors*. I had just started to read those types of books, and when I started reading the book I just couldn't put down. I remember my favorite book was *Warriors: Fire and Ice*.

I don't remember much about reading in Second grade, and to be honest, I didn't like reading in Second grade either. Because I remember being so bored reading a really boring picture book on our I Pads in class.

I do remember reading about insects, and how they help our Earth In class.

Ms. Swale read *Grumpy Cat* to us on the rug, I remember how happy I was to have Ms. Swale read that book to us.

Third Grade:

In Third grade, I remember reading a cool chapter book, I don't remember what it was though. I also remember learning more about capitals, punctuations, and expression in reading, as a result, I wanted to have a break with Ms. Bluegrass instead. I got distracted by a friend instead of reading a lot, then I had to talk to Ms. Winterniz for me not to talk out of turn.

"Stop talking!" I remember her repeatedly saying.

I could never forget how much I really disliked my reading homework. My favorite book was *Warriors: Midnight*. Because of this, I read *Warriors: Long Shadows*.

I remember reading some of *Dark Stories To Tell In The Dark*, but I didn't get to finish it though.

I remember Catherin, Ryleigh, and I think Shannon, all loved reading about horses.

I can't remember much books I read in Third grade. I really wish I could though.

Fourth Grade:

In Fourth grade, I remember reading a lot of poems and reading the book *Sisters*, *Ghosts*, and *Smile*. I also remember trying to find more chapter books to read. I read a lot of graphic novels, then trying to read some chapter books as well, and I remember feeling so confused on which book I should read. I also remember book club, I remember reading *Charlie And The Chocolate Factory* and me and Brycen making a poster of it, I still have it at home. I remember Ms. Frame sending out book club books for us to read, and me being the only one that chose *Inside Out and Back Again*, the only book club book that was in poem form. I felt a little happy that I was the only one that chose that book. I'm glad I read it to. Because that was a great book, I really loved the story. I also remember Ms. Frame getting mad at me for a reason I don't remember. As you probably know, THAT WASN'T FUN AT ALL.

Ending:

Knowing of my past grades, I feel that I can improve this year, better than the past years, at least. Well, that's my story anyway, I hope you liked it! To be honest, I don't know if I will make another writing piece or not, but I think so. Was your grades like mine, or different?

Referring back to DeYoung (2015), it's not so much the accuracy of the story she told. I know this wasn't the full story. I know this from other teachers and other stories Bry told me. However, it is what she is ready to open up to me about. Now she is taking steps forward on the interpersonal bridge because of her sense of security, trust in me, and my validation of her narrative, her perceptions.

When Negative Memories Dominate

Every year, there seem to be a few students who are more than ready to release their unspoken contempt for learning and reading. Their autobiographies are accusatory and dominated by negative memories. These students may also be the ones who actively express contempt, anger, and rage about reading in other contexts. While it can be useful in small-group or one-on-one conferences to engage them in brainstorming to locate some positive or neutral memories, it's important to keep in mind that we likely have more to gain by taking their stories at face value, accepting them, and not forcing students to find something positive when their personal experience feels so negative. For example, take Landon, whose autobiography is shown in Figure 3.5. It is tempting to dismiss his negative memories as a kind of complaining and a refusal to take responsibility for himself as a reader. But doing so is simply imposing on Landon an ideal or image of what he should be remembering or choosing to share. To the extent that he is willing to reveal himself in these early days of the semester, he is offering the information he feels is most relevant to the conversation. To build trust, I must acknowledge and respect what is presented to me.

3.5 Landon's Reading Autobiography

In kindergarten, I read *Green Eggs and Ham* by Dr. Seuss. My teacher read the book out loud to the whole class, and we really liked it. A person in a Cat in the Hat costume came to visit our classroom. He read the book, and then we ate green eggs and ham.

In first grade, I read nothing because my teacher didn't make us. She didn't have any books in her classroom. All we did was math, math, math. She read us books to the class, but she wouldn't let us read book on our own. One of the subs let us read, but just barely. All our subs let us read.

In second grade, I had nothing but **bad experiences**. I forgot my own teacher. We had to recommend books to our classmates, and I really didn't read any books I liked so I couldn't recommend books.

Also, my teacher assigned us books, so we had to read them. I don't like assigned books because I might not like them and take forever to read them.

In third grade, I had a tough teacher and **that was not that good of a school year**. We had to do book for bikes thing. I did very bad and didn't get that many books done. There weren't many chapter books in her room.

In fourth grade I had such **a bad school year** I forgot my teacher's name. It was such a bad school year because I went to the school near my house and did HORRIBLE with my grades. My reading was the worst out of all my grades. Writing was alright, I think. Math was pretty bad, too. But I'm pretty sure I didn't read much books, and I had a hard time sitting still. I had to walk around in the class a lot because the school didn't have an upstairs so I couldn't walk around that much if I did I would have gone to the lunch room.

Week 3

WRITING PROCESS: COMPLETING THE FINAL DRAFTS

The third week is dedicated to students completing their drafts. I use this time with them to work on the clarity of their writing and expanding the details in their narrative. The final draft is a word-processed document.

At the same time that we are about finishing the reading autobiography, I also administer the Reader Self-Perception Scale (see page 80), the Reading Process Self-Evaluation (see page 84), and the Index of Reading Awareness (see page 87) with the students for the first time. See page 57 for more information about these assessments.

The Role of Conferring: Scaffolding Brainstorming and Drafting

My involvement with readers during the brainstorming and drafting process is an important scaffold (Anderson, 2000). My role as a scaffold builds the foundation of the interpersonal bridge. I engage in frequent and targeted conferring (Allen, 2009) with students, both in small groups and one-on-one, depending on their needs.

I prefer to work with students in small groups during brainstorming because they can often feed off one another in positive ways. But if I have good reason to believe that a student's skills might be strikingly different from the other students, and that working in a group might put them at risk for exposing serious deficits they might be self-conscious about, or painful memories they might be harboring, I will work with them one-on-one. I find the drafting process, when students are struggling with how to translate their memories into coherent stories, can require frequent one-on-one conferences. To give you an idea of how such conferring can unfold both during brainstorming and drafting, I provide the following two examples.

Example of Small-Group Conferring: Brainstorming

During the first week of brainstorming, I noticed that three students needed more help digging for meaningful memories. Over the previous week, I had observed each of them looking around the room or sitting quietly saying, "I'm thinking." Their thoughts never made it onto paper. Each of them had asked to visit a previous teacher or go to the library, but no memories could be unlocked.

When I called the three students over and asked about fourth grade, their most recent grade level, they seemed to have no problem remembering favorite books or how much they enjoyed reading aloud. Two of them mentioned how reading assigned books in small groups agitated them. Third grade was similar. This opened the door for Nicholas, the lone boy, to report how he grew tired of always having to be in the same group, reading "easy" books that were boring because he wasn't interested. I asked him, "Why do you think that happened?"

Nicholas replied, "I've always been a low reader. We have to read the same books with the teacher. We take turns reading aloud. She marks what we get wrong when we are reading. Sometimes we talk about what happened, but I don't see the point."

I made a mental note that Nicholas deserved different peers to work with and he deserved to work with challenging texts.

I noticed all three seemed to have a "blank spot" in second grade. I asked what class they were in. All three shared the same classroom. This was interesting to me. Natasha piped up, "We didn't do anything in second grade." I inquired further.

"We weren't allowed to take any books home."

"Yeah," Marita followed. "All she [the teacher] cared about was math. We did math problems all the time. She never read a book aloud to us."

I asked, "Would you call that a negative memory?"

Natasha asked, "Why? Why would those be negative memories? She didn't let us do any reading. Why would that be a bad thing?"

I said, "Well, is it maybe a good thing? Did you like that you didn't have to read?"

Nicholas smiled. "Yeah! I didn't have homework, and I was able to play my video games at home."

Marita added, "I don't know. Is that why we are behind everyone else?"

I wondered with her, "I can't say. I know that reading more helps boost your level and should help you be more interested in reading."

Marita continued, "I never know what I am interested in reading. Most of the time, I just sit down to look at the words on the page. My teachers do a lot of the talking when we meet."

"Okay, I want you to decide. Where would you place these on your memory matrix?" All three added them under negative memories.

To finish, I turned to Natasha and asked about her placement. She said, "Maybe we could have learned other books. It seems like we were ripped off."

Students who internalize shame can feel alone. They might say, "I'm the only one" or "No one likes me." We have to be mindful to listen, not negate or discount what they say (e.g., "that's not true" or "lots of people like you"). A shame-bound person clutches on the evidence that they are different, not liked, and/or unvalued. Organizing small groups has to be deliberate, with a goal in mind. In this case, a small group like this one opens up opportunity for students to see that they are not alone, at least provide some *evidence* that is contrary to their internalized perceptions. It can normalize their experience while at the same time giving them a safe place to share, away from the gaze of the whole class. Typically, if I can get one student to begin opening up, then the others will follow. There is no exact science for how to form such groups. In this case, their empty memory matrices were a good enough rationale to try them together in a group.

Example of One-on-One Conferring: Drafting

There are many reasons to confer with students on their writing. At times it can be something as simple as spelling errors or difficult-to-read handwriting, or it might be to address something more complex, like organizational structure. With Eric, for example, I had to work closely to help him unpack his memory matrix (Figure 3.6).

3.6 Eric's Responses to Reading Autobiography Prompts

1. What was the first book you read alone? *Smile*
2. What was the best book you read in each grade? *Sisters, Smile, Ghost, Amulet 1, Amulet 2, Amulet 3*
3. What were titles you loved to have read to you? *Ghost*
4. What was the worst book you ever had to read? *Amulet 5*
5. What books do you recall looking at the most? Or spending the most time with? *Smile*
6. What books did you enjoy listening to your teacher read aloud? *Rules*
7. What phrases do you remember being told (positive or negative) that have stuck with you? *Had it on the tip of my tongue*
8. What can you recall about the experiences in reading groups or book groups? *Reading together The Sandstorm*
9. When can you recall about times you were frustrated or angry about reading? *When I lost the Thieves book*
10. What do you remember about reading being hard or enjoyable? *All the Amulet series*
11. Who were some of the most important people who helped you with reading? *Mom*
12. What is the most important book in your life? Why? *All chapter books*

For many, there can be other areas of resistance. Take Ian. He was able to complete the memory matrix without too many problems. However, when it came time to draft his autobiography, he preferred to joke and tussle with peers at his table rather than focus on his writing. He made a few attempts at drafting his third-grade experience but preferred not to. The drafting process was complicated by the fact that during that week, he left his Reading Response Journal with his memory matrix either in his locker, homeroom, or for some strange reason, at home (I say strange because Reading Response Journals don't go home). In short, Ian seemed to restart his writing every day. Eventually, because of his missing matrix, scattered initiated drafts, and continual avoidance, I called Ian over to redirect his efforts. Ian explained that being called over to the table, based on previous experiences, meant he wasn't doing well.

He said, "The whole class knows that anytime a person has to go to the table it's because 'they don't get it.'" That might be his truth, but I also observed Ian had insecurities about revealing or expressing his thinking. Ian also said, "I just write what people tell me to think. That way I can just be done, and I won't be wrong."

Rather than scolding Ian or levying some negative consequence or trying to instill some enthusiasm that he certainly wasn't feeling, I wanted to convey to Ian that his story mattered. That meant listening to him and for the time being, jotting down all that he said. I started by asking the question from the autobiography prompts listed.

I asked him, "What was the first book you read alone?"

"I don't remember the title."

"That's fine for now. What can you recall about the book?"

"There was a slot thing that had wooden cup characters. The next page people were doing stuff, like 'I spy.'" Then it dawned on him. "It was *Beauty and the Beast*."

Within our first few conferences, I observed that Ian had a habit of disparaging himself, a defensive move I recognized from my own childhood behavior. By undercutting his merits, he managed to preempt any judgment that might come from his teacher or others. In this case, he tried to communicate that if he didn't read much he could just be ignored and left alone, that there was no problem here. However, he eventually revealed how much he enjoyed listening to *Beauty and the Beast* for the first time, in second grade. I later learned he enjoyed fairy tales, or stories with joy.

Using our momentum and developing trust, I asked Ian to consider his favorite books in each grade. He mentioned *Cat in the Hat* for first grade. He added, "I liked the book because of the rhyming." He couldn't readily recall second grade, or third, but when we got to fourth grade, he named the Animal Ark book, *The Puppy Place: Shadow*. I would later find he favored books aligned with his interests: dogs.

"*Juicy* was the worst book ever read to us," he added. "It was soooo long! It took us a long time to read, and there were so many words." Kids around the class overheard his comment and agreed with him.

After about 10 minutes, we worked through the first six questions. Ian had some information he could use to begin constructing his autobiography. What had I learned most? Ian's preferences were largely based on books read aloud to him. When I asked him about reading *The Puppy Place: Shadow*, he said, "I read some of it. Most of it I read with my teacher. She read one page; I read the other."

My dedicating a bit of time to Ian daily was annoying to him, but sometimes a persistent approach is what is needed with students who are buried under protective barriers.

From there, Ian could take my notes on what he told me and use them to draft his autobiography. I'd meet with Ian twice more before the deadline. His ideas could be drawn out orally, but he was still hesitant to write anything. As he said, "I'm sure you don't want to hear everything that happened." That's where I latched on to two new ideas about Ian. For one, he spoke with "extreme language" as indicated by the word "everything." Extreme language is represented by words like *never, always, everyone, or everything*. There is no distinction; *everything* is generalized, which is merely a signal that the student is overwhelmed and off-center. Second, he was again diminishing his value. He was assuming I didn't value him or his voice, or if I did, he was doing me a favor by not divulging his "tragedy." Little did he know, I was more curious than ever. Moreover, I realized he needed a partner in learning—someone who valued him as a student, as a reader, and as a person.

My dedicating a bit of time to Ian daily was annoying to him, but sometimes a persistent approach is what is needed with students who are buried under protective barriers. Ian always had a massive gap between what he articulated to me in conference and what he was willing to make permanent on paper. We worked in chunks by talking through specific grade levels to bring some memories to the surface and setting micro-goals, such as to complete Grade 3 on the memory matrix. I would sit with Ian as he drafted an initial paragraph. From there, I would provide feedback (Grade 3 negative memories) then encourage him to write the next paragraph (Grade 3, positive memories) alone, only calling me over when he had finished. And so Ian's autobiography unfolded, bit by bit.

In the end, I had to be comfortable with the limited information Ian provided. He either wasn't ready to let me into his world and share his memories, or he was essentially withdrawing from the whole process of trying to identify them for himself. Ian is an example of the kind of maturing reader who needs us most.

At the end of the reading autobiography, I collect all the typed versions. I then take a highlighter and pen to every manuscript, noting important moments of students' reading histories, so I can use them as reference points when planning later instruction or when in conversation with students. It is well worth the time; students love when I later reference the information they provided. That's when they begin to feel that they are really seen by me. Additionally, I am reflecting back to them not my vision of who they should be, but the first view of themselves in a mirror of their own making. Our work together is just beginning.

Students do not print a copy and take it home at this time. Instead, we revisit them at the end of the year when we add on memories from the current school year. Then students can take them home to cherish forever. The reading autobiography becomes the cornerstone of their reading legacy. Besides, who knows when they will write their next one?

Other Interim Assessments

As I mentioned earlier, periodically throughout the year I administer other interim assessments. These assessments help me better understand the readers in my classroom as well as provide me with valuable information to use during conferences and as I work to build the interpersonal bridge.

3.7 Assessment Overview

Assessment	Duration	Interval	Reading Function	Instruction
Reading Process Self-Evaluation	< 30 minutes	Quarterly	Reading Process Strategic Reading Executive Function Transactional Reading	Conferring • Strategic Reading • Affective Annotation • Self-Monitoring • Small Groups • Reciprocal Teaching • Notice and Note • Literature Mapping
Reader Self-Perception Scale	< 20 minutes	Quarterly	Reading Process Self-Concept	Conferring • Reading Passport • Reading Visa • VOWELS Checklist • Physiological State • Small Groups • Observational Comparisons • Social Capital • Social Feedback
Index of Reading Awareness	< 20 minutes	Quarterly	Reading Process Strategic Knowledge	Conferring • Reading Interests • Small Groups: Purpose for Reading

The Reader Self-Perception Scale

This assessment is administered four times throughout the year. The first time I give students this assessment is during the first few weeks of school. I administer this assessment three additional times during the year—midway through the year, in the spring, and at the end of the year—to determine how much students have become their own reader.

What Is It?

The affective survey, the Reader Self-Perception Scale (Henk et al., 2012), measures students' beliefs about themselves as readers and their attitudes about reading. The current version contains 47 items, statements that are answered using a Likert-like scale, choosing one of five options (strongly agree, agree, undecided, disagree, strongly disagree). Self-perception and self-efficacy carry significant implications for reading (Ortlieb & Schatz, 2020). To mine this information, I introduce some ideas about where their own perceptions of themselves might originate. For example, one of the questions asks them to rate the truth of this statement: *My teacher thinks I read well.* This is likely the first time they've been asked to consider their teacher's view of themselves separate from their own.

The Reader Self-Perception Scale consists of four subcategories:

- **Observational Comparison** reflects how students see themselves as readers in comparison to others, asking students to rate such statements as, *I read faster than other kids.* Student responses reveal just how many kids see themselves as slow readers compared to their peers.
- **Progress** reveals how students perceive their own growth and improvement as readers, asking students to rate such statements as, *I understand what I read better than I could before.* What such responses often reveal is how deeply their perceptions of their own learning can differ from what I observe: their ratings are often considerably higher than I would imagine. This makes me curious and spurs me to learn more. It provides an opening to work with students.
- **Social Feedback** determines the reader's reliance on or self-assessment regarding external influences. Asking students to consider statements like, *People in my family like to listen to me read* can reveal the attitudes and degrees of support that may influence students' self-perceptions.
- **Physiological States** informs teachers about how comfortable, or secure, the student feels when reading. We also can begin to see how students view reading as gratifying. Students are asked to rate such statements as *Reading makes me feel happy inside.* Not many students rate this very high, revealing the huge gap between what educators are telling students they should be feeling and what they are really feeling.

3.8 Reader Self-Perception Scale

Listed below are statements about reading. Please read each statement carefully. Then circle the letters that show how much you agree or disagree with the statement. Use the following scale:

SA = Strongly Agree

A = Agree

U = Undecided

D = Disagree

SD = Strongly Disagree

Example:

I think pizza with pepperoni is the best. SA A U D SD

Response Guide

If you are really positive that pepperoni is the best, circle SA (Strongly Agree).

If you think that it is good but maybe not great, circle A (Agree).

If you can't decide whether or not it is best, circle U (Undecided).

If you think that pepperoni pizza is not all that good, circle D (Disagree).

If you are really positive that pepperoni pizza is not very good, circle SD (Strongly Disagree).

Questions:

1. Reading is a pleasant activity for me. (PS) — SA A U D SD
2. I read better now than I could before. (PR) — SA A U D SD
3. I can handle more challenging reading materials than I could before. (PR) — SA A U D SD
4. Other students think I'm a good reader. (SF) — SA A U D SD
5. I need less help than other students when I read. (OC) — SA A U D SD
6. I feel comfortable when I read. (PS) — SA A U D SD
7. When I read, I don't have to try as hard to understand as I used to. (PR) — SA A U D SD
8. My classmates like to listen to the way that I read. (SF) — SA A U D SD
9. I am getting better at reading. (PR) — SA A U D SD
10. When I read, I can figure out words better than other students. (OC) — SA A U D SD
11. My teachers think I am a good reader. (SF) — SA A U D SD
12. I read better than other students in my class. (OC) — SA A U D SD

13. My reading comprehension level is higher than other students. (OC) SA A U D SD
14. I feel calm when I read. (PS) SA A U D SD
15. I read faster than other students. (OC) SA A U D SD
16. My teachers think that I try my best when I read. (SF) SA A U D SD
17. Reading tends to make me feel calm. (PS) SA A U D SD
18. I understand what I read better than I could before. (PR) SA A U D SD
19. I can understand difficult reading materials better than before. (PR) SA A U D SD
20. When I read, I can handle difficult ideas better than my classmates. (OC) SA A U D SD
21. When I read, I recognize more words than before. (PR) SA A U D SD
22. I enjoy how I feel when I read. (PS) SA A U D SD
23. I feel proud inside when I think about how well I read. (PS) SA A U D SD
24. I have improved on assignments and tests that involve reading. (PR) SA A U D SD
25. I feel good inside when I read. (PS) SA A U D SD
26. When I read, my understanding of important vocabulary words is better than other students. (OC) SA A U D SD
27. People in my family like to listen to me read. (SF) SA A U D SD
28. My classmates think that I read pretty well. (SF) SA A U D SD
29. Reading makes me feel good. (PS) SA A U D SD
30. I can figure out hard words better than I could before. (PR) SA A U D SD
31. I think reading can be relaxing. (PS) SA A U D SD
32. I can concentrate more when I read than I could before. (PR) SA A U D SD
33. Reading makes me feel happy inside. (PS) SA A U D SD
34. When I read, I need less help than I used to. (PR) SA A U D SD
35. I can tell that my teachers like to listen to me read. (SF) SA A U D SD
36. I know the meaning of more words than other students when I read. (OC) SA A U D SD
37. I read faster than I could before. (PR) SA A U D SD
38. Reading is easier for me than it used to be. (PR) SA A U D SD
39. My teachers think that I do a good job of interpreting what I read. (SF) SA A U D SD

(Continued)

(Continued)

40.	My understanding of difficult reading materials has improved. (PR)	SA A U D SD
41.	I feel good about my ability to read. (PS)	SA A U D SD
42.	I am more confident in my reading than other students. (OC)	SA A U D SD
43.	Deep down, I like to read. (PS)	SA A U D SD
44.	I can analyze what I read better than before. (PR)	SA A U D SD
45.	My teachers think that my reading is fine. (SF)	SA A U D SD
46.	Vocabulary words are easier for me to understand when I read now. (PR)	SA A U D SD

Source: Henk, W. A., Marinak, B. A., & Melnick, S. A. (2012). Measuring the reader self-perceptions of adolescents: Introducing the RSPS2. *Journal of Adolescent & Adult Literacy, 56*(4), 311-320; figure on p. 315.

While I hope that students' self-perceptions improve over the course of the year, I often find that they don't change significantly or even are often lower. But what do change are the comments students offer and the questions they ask. I always let students put questions and comments in the margins. By the end of the year, the comments reveal a higher level of student confidence in their ratings, revealing a stronger comfort level in their own assessment of themselves. This is significant.

The Reading Process Self-Evaluation

I first administer the Reading Process Self-Evaluation during the third week of school. This assessment is administered to the entire class and takes about twenty minutes. I administer this assessment three additional times during the year: midway through the year, in the spring, and at the end of the year.

What Is It?

I use an adapted version of the Reading Process Self-Evaluation (Burke, 2012) to explore a reader's comfort or competency using various strategies that support how they interact with the text. I also use the questions to scaffold the language readers will need when it comes time to introduce explicit instruction around reading strategies. I'm trying to gain an understanding of the reader's awareness of unique processes and interactions with the text. The questions fall into the following categories:

- **Before Reading:** I'm looking to see how students strategically engage in self-selection and preparedness to engage in a reading process. For example, one question asks students about whether they "gather any materials" that might be needed (book, pencil, highlighter, etc.). Almost always students indicate they never engage in such preparations for reading, a sign that they are accustomed to pleasure reading and/or have not yet experienced efferent reading (Rosenblatt, 1995).
- **During Reading:** I want to know how students employ their "unique reading process" and use their process to interact with a text. For example, students are asked to rate this statement: "I make connections to myself, the world, and other texts." I often find that because students don't have to show evidence, many make grandiose claims in response to these questions. For example, I read the entire Percy Jackson series in second grade. I'm not going to doubt that the student, in some capacity, experienced the entire series (audio book, read alouds, etc.), but I am nearly certain the full extent of their ability to comprehend these books has not been maximized. My aim is that by the end of the year, students will have developed a more realistic view of themselves as readers, as well as the confidence to bring more honesty and integrity to their self-assessments.
- **After Reading:** I'm seeking to learn how students consolidate their learning after reading. Overall, I am attempting to gain a sense of the reader's agency and their valuation of meaning-making processes that support engagement and enjoyment. Students consider statements such as, "I evaluate all that I read to determine what is most important to remember in the future." My students commonly choose "usually" as their response. I interpret this not just as a lack of self-knowledge (because most students don't approach their reading this way initially and may not even do so at the end of the year) but also as a need to project an image to me that doesn't fit with reality.

As I noted previously, students tend to rate themselves overly high on the reading process indicators at the start of the year, in an effort to present themselves as "good readers" who consistently engage in the strategies they all know they should be using. As the year goes by, as we authentically engage in reading and the strategies become more meaningful actions than abstract ideas, their self-ratings tend to decline. By the end of the year, students' responses are more accurate, perhaps honest, representations of what reading processes they actually employ as well as their own assessment of what weaknesses still require attention.

3.9 Reading Process Self-Evaluation

Before Reading (Previewing)					
I ask myself what I already know about this subject, story, or the author.	Always	Usually	Sometimes	Rarely	Never
I preview the book to see what it's about by prereading random pages and to see what kind of challenge the book will be.	Always	Usually	Sometimes	Rarely	Never
I preview a book to make a plan of how long it might take to read.	Always	Usually	Sometimes	Rarely	Never
I make predictions about what I will read before beginning.	Always	Usually	Sometimes	Rarely	Never
Before Reading (Preparing)					
I gather my materials that I will need to read (highlighters, notebook, sticky notes, etc.).	Always	Usually	Sometimes	Rarely	Never
I chose a place without any distractions to do my reading.	Always	Usually	Sometimes	Rarely	Never
I go over any directions for my assigned reading.	Always	Usually	Sometimes	Rarely	Never
I consider what reading strategies I might use to help me understand.	Always	Usually	Sometimes	Rarely	Never
During Reading (Making Meaning Challenges)					
I gather my materials that I will need to read (highlighters, notebook, sticky notes, etc.).	Always	Usually	Sometimes	Rarely	Never
I chose a place without any distractions to do my reading.	Always	Usually	Sometimes	Rarely	Never
I go over any direction for my assigned reading.	Always	Usually	Sometimes	Rarely	Never
I consider what reading strategies I might use to help me understand.	Always	Usually	Sometimes	Rarely	Never

During Reading (Ensuring Comprehension)					
I make connections to myself, the world, other books, or other things I have studied.	Always	Usually	Sometimes	Rarely	Never
I track the main idea and supporting details when I am reading.	Always	Usually	Sometimes	Rarely	Never
I use what I learned from other books or my own experiences to help me understand new information I read about.	Always	Usually	Sometimes	Rarely	Never
I make predictions while I am reading and track what happens later in the reading.	Always	Usually	Sometimes	Rarely	Never
During Reading (Note Taking and Monitoring)					
I take notes or annotate a text when I read.	Always	Usually	Sometimes	Rarely	Never
I summarize what I read at certain points in the text (like the end of a chapter).	Always	Usually	Sometimes	Rarely	Never
I use "fix-up" strategies when I am confused or am trying to figure out new words.	Always	Usually	Sometimes	Rarely	Never
I ask questions about what I read (to explore ideas later, as I am reading).	Always	Usually	Sometimes	Rarely	Never
I write down questions at the end of the chapter to leave for future readers.	Always	Usually	Sometimes	Rarely	Never
After Reading					
I take a few minutes to review taking some notes or writing my thoughts in a journal entry.	Always	Usually	Sometimes	Rarely	Never
I make a few predictions about what will happen in my later reading.	Always	Usually	Sometimes	Rarely	Never
I make a plan of what I will read the next day.	Always	Usually	Sometimes	Rarely	Never

Source: Burke, J. (2012). *The English teacher's companion* (4th ed.). Heinemann. Adapted by Justin Stygles.

Index of Reading Awareness

I administer this at four points over the school year; the first time is by the third week of September. The 20-question assessment is given in a whole-class setting and takes no more than 30 minutes. Typically, students require less than half that time.

The assessments are not timed, but generally they need no more than 20 minutes. Should students find a question unclear, I'll work one-on-one with readers or in small groups (e.g., reading aloud questions and responses) to ensure validity. Also, readers are invited to write clarifying comments on any questions for which they might have more than one answer, no answers, or variations of the suggestions provided.

What Is It?

This tool helps answer the question, *"To what extent does a student manage their reading process?"* When I use the Index of Reading Awareness (Jacobs & Paris, 1987), I am looking to determine how well a student knows how to use a text that is suggested, self-selected, or assigned. This assessment provides potential challenges a reader faces when they say a book is "boring" or "not very interesting."

The Index of Reading Awareness covers four domains:

- **Evaluation:** Like previewing a book, I am curious to discover how the boundaries or parameters (see Chapter 6) the reader sets either permits or inhibits access to text regarding comprehension.

  Here's an example. "What is the hardest part of reading for you?" Of the three options, students normally select, "When you don't understand the story." While at first glance this might look like students are pointing to a simple problem of understanding the words on the page, my experience has shown that it actually often represents a lack of ability to make meaning beyond the words.

- **Planning:** In this subsection, I am looking for insight into how well a student accesses information for general comprehension or recall, a preliminary look into the student's reading process. For example, a question asks, "When you tell other people about what you read, what do you tell them?" When given the choice between the most important parts or all the parts, students often choose all the parts, reflecting a lack of intention or understanding of how text operates, like distinguishing important details from finding every detail important, which would help them appreciate what they need to take away from their wording.

- **Regulation:** Here I get a brief look into the reader's process or skills necessary to maintain interest in reading. Consider the question, "What parts of the story do you skip as you read?" Students tend to respond by moralizing, "You never skip anything," yet don't understand the difference between the "skip-it" method and skimming a text to narrow a focus.

- **Conditional Knowledge:** In the last category, I am looking at how a student processes information in a way that produces meaning or knowledge useable for later tasks. Here we can determine if a student is still "learning to read" or using the text for higher-order thinking. For instance, in response to "Which of these is the best way to remember a story?" many kids respond, "Thinking about all of it." Most avoid "Write it down in your own words," which tells me students will need to learn the benefit of consolidating and summarizing information after reading.

3.10 Index of Reading Awareness

Please read each question. Select the answer that best fits what you do when you are reading.

1. What is the hardest part about a story for you?
   a. Sounding out hard words.
   b. When I don't understand the story.
   c. Nothing is hard about reading.
2. What would help you become a better reader?
   a. If more people would help me when I read.
   b. Reading easier books with shorter words.
   c. Checking to make sure I understand what I read.
3. What is special about the first sentence or two in a story?
   a. They always begin with "Once upon a time . . ."
   b. The first sentences are the most interesting.
   c. They often tell what the story is about.
4. How are the last sentences of a story special?
   a. They are exciting action sentences.
   b. They tell you what happened.
   c. They are harder to read.

(Continued)

(Continued)

5. How can you tell which sentences are the most important ones in a story?

   a. They're the ones that tell the most about the characters and what happens.

   b. They're the most important ones.

   c. They're all important.

6. If you could only read some of the sentences in the story because you were in a hurry, which ones would you read?

   a. Read the sentences in the middle of the story.

   b. Read the sentences that tell you most about the story.

   c. Read the interesting, exciting sentences.

7. When you tell other people about what you read, what do you tell them?

   a. What happened in the story.

   b. The number of pages in the book.

   c. Who the characters are.

8. If the teacher told you to read about a story to remember the general meaning, what would you do?

   a. Skim through the story to find the main parts.

   b. Read all the story and try to remember everything.

   c. Read the story and remember all the words.

9. Before you start to read, what kind of plans do you make to help you read better?

   a. I don't make any plans. I just start reading.

   b. I choose a comfortable place.

   c. I think about why I am reading.

10. If you had to read very fast and could only read some words, which ones would you read?

    a. Read the new vocabulary words because they are important.

    b. Read the words that I can pronounce.

    c. Read the words that tell most about the story.

11. What things do you read faster than others?
    a. Books that are easy to read.
    b. When I've read the story before.
    c. Books that have a lot of pictures.
12. Why do you go back and read things over?
    a. Because it's good practice.
    b. Because I didn't understand it.
    c. Because I forgot some words.
13. What do you do if you come to a word and you don't know what it means?
    a. Use the words around to figure it out.
    b. Ask someone else.
    c. Go on to the next word.
14. What do you do if you don't know what a whole sentence means?
    a. Read it again.
    b. Sound out all the words.
    c. Think about the other sentences in the paragraph.
15. What parts of the story do you skip as you read?
    a. The hard words and parts I don't understand.
    b. The unimportant parts that don't mean anything for the story.
    c. I never skip anything.
16. If you are reading a story for fun, what would you do?
    a. Look at the pictures to get the meaning.
    b. Read the story as fast as I can.
    c. Imagine the story like a movie in my mind.
17. If you are reading for science or social studies, what would you do to remember the information?
    a. Ask myself questions about the important ideas.
    b. Skip the parts I don't understand.
    c. Concentrate and try hard to remember.

(Continued)

(Continued)

18. If you are reading for a test, which would help most?

a. Read the story as many times as possible.

b. Talk about it with somebody to make sure I understand it.

c. Say the sentences over and over.

19. If you are reading a library book to write a report, which would help you the most?

a. Sound out the words I don't know.

b. Write it down in my own words.

c. Skip the parts I don't understand.

20. Which of these is the best way to remember a story?

a. Say every word over and over.

b. Think about remembering it.

c. Write it down in my own words.

Subtest Score	Interpretation
8-10	No significant weakness
6-7	Some instructional support needed
0-5	Serious need for instruction in this area

Source: Jacobs, J. E., & Paris, S. G. (1987). Children's metacognition about reading: Issues in definition, measurement, and instruction. *Educational Psychologist, 22*, 255-278.

At the beginning of the year, students score rather low on this assessment. Regulation and conditional knowledge are typically the lowest scoring categories. A deeper look shows students working to understand text at a decoding level more than comprehension. The Index of Reading Awareness is the one interim assessment that reveals significant shifts in metacognition in the readers' process over time.

Final Thoughts

I spent much of my life reading the *Daily Racing Form.* In sixth grade I began handicapping horses using the *Form*, which meant I used various data points to evaluate horses in a race to determine what horses would win. My ex-wife, on the other hand, is a natural horsewoman and couldn't care less to look at the "data." She knows how to read the physical signs on a horse and the best way to respond, or work with the animal.

When the movie *Secretariat* came out, we took our daughter, Rhiana, to her first Belmont Stakes. We stood at the paddock watching horses parade for a turf race on a rain-soaked day. My ex-wife turned to me and claimed a horse would win because the horse had wide feet, which meant the horse could handle the wet grass better. After I studied the data, I completely disagreed. The data suggested as much. About 10 minutes later, I was left empty handed. She'd chosen the winner.

That moment forced me to face a brutal recognition amidst some two decades of data-based decision making. Numbers simply do not tell the whole story. Numbers cannot account for the other layers of information that can be sourced from a reader (or a horse). My ex-wife had managed to undermine nearly a decade of strategy creation through one simple means: looking at the horse. We must consider this same scenario when working with students.

As a teacher, I became obsessed with controlling the interpretation of my instruction through data. I had stopped looking at readers, their behaviors, and processes. I stopped noticing them, let alone listening to their stories. Tom Newkirk (2017) wrote, "We simply cannot translate bare numbers into recognizable human reality; our eyes glaze over." He's right. My ex-wife proved this with one simple concept: consider what's in front of you before you consider what the data says.

Data has an integral role. Just because I lost didn't mean I stopped looking at data. It meant I had to look at data differently. We need to look at numbers to notice trends and use assessments to help students communicate in ways they cannot. We can use data to notice our students, but until we hear their story, the data is meaningless. When making instructional decisions, we marginalize students through their reading levels, fluency rates, and accuracy.

We can use data to notice our students, but until we hear their story, the data is meaningless.

The best way to assess is through trust; the student's ability to be vulnerable and confident lies within the interpersonal bridge. When considering shame, if we don't look into the soul of the reader, we are already on the way to disenfranchising their reading lives. What does this mean for the relationship between shame and reading? We need to spend more time looking into their eyes, side by side, heart-to-heart, listening to their stories and answering their questions. This builds the trust required for the interpersonal bridge.

Reflect and Act

Use these reflection questions to consider the information shared in the chapter and how you can apply it in your own classroom.

1. Take time to generate your own Memory Matrix. What memories stand out for you? Why might these stand out the most?
2. In what ways could interim assessments provide information that compares and contrasts with that of benchmark and standardized assessments?
3. What interim assessment(s) would you like to try right away, and how can you consider the organization of your reading community based on that data?

4

READING FOR THEMSELVES

Helping Students Claim Their Reading Independence

Independent reading is a funny term when you think about it. The intended outcome for a *reader* is directly correlated with the *educator's* definition.

On one hand, *independent reading* refers to reading students choose for themselves, separate from any shared or guided reading done in class. Teachers and policy mandates vary in how they value or practice independent reading (Hudson & Williams, 2015; Kelley & Clausen-Grace, 2009; Sanden, 2012). Within various practices, some students are asked to keep a reading log, maybe a journal (Buckner, 2009). Others expect students to meet a reading goal of a specified number of titles or pages. We've come to accept the intent of wide and voluminous reading—that it will increase readers' interests and vice versa (Miller, 2010). We've also come to accept that the merit of independent reading lies in student choice and agency (Wilhelm & Smith, 2014)—that by reading what they want to read, students will learn to experience what reading can offer, thus becoming motivated to read and engage more fully in the reading process. Gallagher (2010) calls this the "sweet spot" in his seminal text, *Readicide*.

There's also the interpretation of independent reading that is influenced by semantics. What students can *read* independently. This definition stems from the now-institutionalized practice of benchmark assessments. A reading level, be it Lexiles, DRA, Fountas and Pinnell (2012), and so on, all indicate what a student should be able to read independently, without our support. But then we fall into the conundrum of what defines *support*; can a student really read a book of that level *independently*? For now, neither matter. There's something more beneath the surface.

In my experience, from schools, classrooms, and students I've worked with in diverse settings, one thing is evident among all others. One thing boils to the top, every time. A reading level is the identity of the reader. A reading level is the assignment of the child's reading capabilities, without any evidence or knowledge of experience with titles that support the claim. In other words, a level 50 is a designation. Seldom is a student designated a level 50 reader one who can truly engage with extended reading that employs strategic reading, which includes comprehension and self-monitoring, with a text within the ballpark of a level 50. Instead, what I consistently observe is that level 50 readers cannot distinguish between *Esperanza Rising* (Munoz-Ryan, 2002) and *Joey Pigza Swallowed the Key* (Gantos, 1998) and level 50 readers who haul out of the library *Harry Potter* and *Dogman* (Pilkey, 2016). All they have is a number, not a sense of orientation.

This is where shame is manifested and begins to hinder the progress of readers—nay, encourages the precipitous decline of reading interest we are all too familiar with.

Reorienting Ourselves to Orientate Our Readers

While most of us approach independent reading with great enthusiasm and intentions to motivate our students (Applegate & Applegate, 2010; Davis & Forbes, 2016; Malloy et al., 2010; Reynolds, 2004), this *sweet spot* that Gallagher refers to can be elusive. For many students the endeavor is not always as sweet as we hope it will be. As Chapters 1 and 2 have revealed, sometimes our greatest hopes for our students can be the source of their greatest shame and dysregulation in the classroom. *Let's see if you can read 40 books this year. Choose them yourself. Experience the joys of reading! Reading is the best!*

Would you like to guess how many students rebuke these sentiments?

Would you care to ponder why they are resistant, if not resentful about these attitudes?

Independent reading is a classic example of a window we try to open to students that can often turn into a negative mirror, for what students might see hidden there is their own failure to experience a love for reading—a lose-lose proposition for student and teacher alike. It's not all about struggling to read. Self-perception, previously instilled values (e.g., "We never had to read this much before."), or expectations (e.g., "You really expect me read a book in how long? I had my last book for a month.") can be strong influences on a reader's self-perception and self-efficacy. Students may want to love the activity, but they cannot experience it because their deficiencies or inabilities about reading are not accepted by those from whom they seek positive attention.

Independent reading is a classic example of a window we try to open to students that can often turn into a negative mirror, for what students might see hidden there is their own failure to experience a love for reading.

At some point in our careers, most of us have certainly experienced some level of frustration with our students and their attitude toward independent reading or their reluctance to adopt the practice so many of us cherish. It's for this reason that independent reading, which is often viewed more as a supplemental activity rather than something central, is worth the focused work of our teaching (Marcell et al., 2010). We actually have to teach children to become readers, which means we have to teach them how to incorporate reading into their lives and promote agency that leads to true independent reading.

Where the Independent Reading Crisis Begins

I've found that students who are inclined to read have no problem making the best of independent reading—even in classes outside of English language arts. Yet just beneath the student who is pouring out the details of their book to their overjoyed teacher is a student who withers away because they know they can never have that experience, or at least they think they cannot, until we help change that perception. Those who have a long-standing history of reading struggles don't adopt the same passion (Tovani, 2000), nor do they want to. In fact, that's where we begin to see shame emerge—through withdrawal and avoidance. They're angry about what they cannot do, or they perceive themselves negatively. Gilbert (2003) explains that we feel shame when we fail to live up to the expectations of what we enjoy or desire to be.

> **Just beneath the student who is pouring out the details of their book to their overjoyed teacher is a student who withers away because they know they can never have that experience.**

What they do make clear about reading is, forget it!

The crisis doesn't stop there. There are schools and classrooms that focus strictly on reading skills. The attention to skills, and ultimately testing, are so stringent that a contradiction often occurs. First, readers become fluency experts but struggle to comprehend (Applegate et al., 2009). Second, for all the skills taught and learned, students rarely have the opportunity to transfer the learning through experimentation of independent reading. What an irony. Readers at an independent reading level (where no support is required) don't independently read (which implies a *need* for support).

No matter what we teach, or how we spread joy about reading, readers can internalize any narrative about themselves.

Deeper beneath the surface, readers develop internalizations, or narratives, about themselves. Unintentionally, we scaffold these internalizations. Students then internalize the definition of "Good Readers," especially when it is linked to reading levels (Abodeeb-Gentile & Zawilinski, 2013; Hoffman, 2017). What I am saying is, no matter what we teach, or how we spread joy about reading, readers can internalize any narrative about themselves. We cannot begin to measure the time a student spends silently internalizing. Add in a negative or traumatic reading experience and the road to recovery becomes daunting—or easily ignored. This is why our students lose their enjoyment for reading, and reading declines precipitously (Beers, 1998; McKenna et al., 2012).

For all our efforts to inspire lifelong readers, for some, this is a complete nightmare. Our well-intended practices have an underbelly—a repetitive demonstration of deficiency and incompetence that doesn't seem to cease. When readers see themselves as incomplete through the "looking-glass" of independent reading, and with it, perceive negative valuation by peers and teachers, independent reading becomes exclusive, a privilege for certain students rather than a right or a beacon of hope for every student.

Throughout this chapter, we explore strategies that help readers determine how reading fits into their lives, to help them become resilient readers and uncover their "giftedness" (Barone & Barone, 2017; Miller, 1997).

Of course, the development of a reading life can happen with the interpersonal bridge, or support, something many readers have never experienced before. Later, you will see that something like the reading log, traditionally a tool to demonstrate evidence of responsibility or *accountability*, can be used to explore the diverse reading habits and interest of readers, as well as the integrity of the reader. From there, we look at strategies that invite even the most recalcitrant of readers back into the independent reading fold. It's at this juncture that we are bestowed the honor of partnering with maturing readers to establish the integrity and uniqueness of every individual, especially those to whom positive self-concept, self-efficacy, or agency as independent readers is completely alien.

When Well-Intended Independent Reading Goes Awry

First, I describe some of the pitfalls that can occur during independent reading. At times, we inadvertently encourage students to go through the motions of independent reading, as illustrated by a conversation I once had with Anthony. Anthony, age 12, was rather ambivalent to reading. He wanted very much to be a good reader but had lost faith along the journey. Nothing seemed to capture his interest. Even when it did, he didn't stay interested—not only in the book, but also merely in taking time to read. In previous years, according to his reading autobiography, Anthony shared that teachers gave him books about sports. He hesitantly informed me that he never really liked the books because they weren't really about sports. Anthony acknowledged that he pretended to read them so he wouldn't upset his teachers and that he made it look like he was reading.

"Mr. Stygles, this book is boring." Anthony calls out to me from his table, while I transition from one reading conference to another. He's rarely quiet.

"Are you still reading *Tale of Despereaux*?" I answer back, writing a few more notes about my previous exchange with a reader.

Anthony:	"No, I quit that two days ago. I'm reading *The Adventures of a Girl Called Bicycle*."
Mr. Stygles:	"Come on over here for a second."

Anthony jumps out of his seat and comes over.

Mr. Stygles:	"What's going on?"
Anthony:	"I don't know what to read. Do you have any book recommendations?"
Mr. Stygles:	"I can certainly give you some ideas. What are you interested in?"
Anthony:	"I don't know. Teachers just recommended books. I didn't want to get in trouble."

Mr. Stygles:	"Do you actually read them?
Anthony:	"Sometimes?"
Mr. Stygles:	"Tell me, honestly, what good is it if I give you a book recommendation and you don't read it? What happens if I unknowingly offer a book you aren't interested in?"
Anthony:	"I don't know? I don't read it?"
Mr. Stygles:	"Does that mean you are back in the library looking for a new one?"
Anthony:	"Yeah?"
Mr. Stygles:	"Would you find a book that interests you on that visit?"
Anthony:	"I don't know."
Mr. Stygles:	"Do you see what's happening here?"
Anthony:	"No."

Anthony, like many students, found ways throughout his elementary school career to successfully manipulate independent reading. During independent reading, he regularly walked into the class library. He stood, glancing down the shelves of books, and stared at the front cover of the first book in every basket. He took one, sat down and read during the allotted time, before repeating the process once or twice more that week. That was his book selection system.

Anthony basically worked overtime to disguise his greatest fear—he couldn't navigate independent reading. Despite repetitive instruction about how to select "just-right" books and strategies to preview a text (reading the back, the five-finger rule, and reading select pages), Anthony still hadn't learned how to select and stick with a book. No one turned over the rock to realize what he was doing. And why not? As early as first grade, students engage in independent reading. There is an implicit ideology that when students read at a level independently, they can also handle all the dynamics that constitute independent reading, independently (planning, safe sit spots, distractions, etc.). Anthony not only faced challenges with early literacy concepts, but he was also completely inexperienced with the idea of handling a book, alone, for a period of time. This was perpetuated, not for a session or two, but for years! How was Anthony supposed to believe that anyone really cared about him when he struggled alone, day after day? What Anthony chose to do was nothing short of survival and adapting to adverse circumstances—without drawing attention to himself!

Anthony basically worked overtime to disguise his greatest fear—he couldn't navigate independent reading.

His success? Compliance. He played the part and looked good doing it, or so he thought. In other words, he gained a lot of compliments and praise from his teachers by adhering strictly to what he was told to do. The consequences were manifesting.

And all the while, Anthony internalized negative beliefs about himself, and cherished independent reading time was rendered fruitless. No one really went eye-to-eye to apprentice him as a *reader*. He received redundant early literacy skill practice, but it wasn't what he needed. Instead, he paid the price for a responsibility he was not equipped to handle: a set-up for shame.

The behaviors Anthony manifested were a nonverbal response to what became apparent from Anthony's reading autobiography, reading engagement, and process inventory ratings, and then confirmed though conferences with him early in the school: He had no criteria for deciding what to read. Anthony's idea of *reading* meant grabbing the first book he saw only to abandon it after making a show of reading some pages.

See the Reader Self-Perception Scale, Reading Process Self-Evaluation, and the Index of Reading Awareness in Chapter 3 for more information about the interim assessments.

Too many readers feel lost and on their own during independent reading; worse, they never self-advocate because they are fearful of transgressions in social contexts (Piff et al., 2012). They live with the painful realization they are not the adept readers they think they should be and that favor from teachers will be lost because of their deficit. As we know, in the world of shame, there is always a price to pay for honesty. It's at this point we must start embracing readers' honesty—their narrative—to learn just what they are really thinking, what they need, and what they desire.

Reading Independence: Beyond "Getting Students to Read"

How do we support students like Anthony who are at a loss to select a book and stick with it? Do we step in and recommend specific titles? Do we model enthusiasm and excitement about recommendations? Do we fill our class libraries with graphic novels and "easy" books (i.e., *Wimpy Kid, 13 Story Tree House* series, etc.), or what I call "entertaining" books, to increase the chances that students will find a good match? Let's first look at some unintended consequences.

While recommendations and popular books serve a purpose, when students begin to rely on us and fail to expand their canon, students can potentially cloister their interests, placing them at risk of inexperience and the shame of ignorance or "what should be known" down the road. We can mentor our maturing readers to build capacity in these areas:

- **Selection**: How can we teach students to choose books to expand their reading experience rather than to perform an obligatory function?
- **Perseverance**: How can students face appropriate challenges to improve their competence and self-perception, without damaging their self-image and confidence?

Selection

Recommendations and Individuals: My discussion with Anthony points to how recommendations can backfire, so to speak. Recommendations can be assumptions about the reader that the reader doesn't wish to have assigned to them. We know our readers have preferences. We also know they can be on the fence about opening their worlds to new genres. A recommendation can be a test for us, the teachers, as to how well we know the child. It can also be an invitation to a reader to explore a new genre. I've made the mistake of saying, "Students loved this book in the past. I think you'll like it, too." It may not seem like much but by saying "students," I'm grouping Anthony into a population rather than attending to his interests or even the boundaries we've previously established.

Sometimes I've made the mistake of implicitly focusing on myself more so than the reader. I've said, "I just read this, and it was amazing. I think you might like this one." Or "This is the best book ever!" My error? I'm focusing on my opinions rather than inviting the reader to develop an opinion of their own. For one, I'm an adult. How I see the world is very different than that of my students. I may have thought a book was amazing, but that's based on my interaction. Am I really asking the reader to think like me or have autonomous thoughts? Then there is the word *best*. I could go on about shame and "shaming" caused by superlatives, but for now the best is a definitive statement.

Let's think about it: Is there seriously no other book that can be better? This recommendation here is the best? Of all time? To whom? I can tell you, it's not the reader. When I recommend a book as the best, I have unintentionally taken away the opportunity for a maturing reader to discover the quality of the book for themselves. I've potentially undermined the reader's perceptions, which obligates them to comply, if anything out of fear of thinking differently than me and, in their mind, falling out of favor with me. Students are inclined to impress their teachers or "not let their teachers down" because they have a contrary opinion. At worst, dissociation occurs—or "I'll be who you want me to be." We can avoid this by changing our language such as the following: "Anthony, I thought this book was great. However, I am very interested in what your opinion is. Would you like to give it a try?" Not only I am extending an invitation, but I'm also honoring Anthony's integrity as a reader.

Stereotypes and Interest: The term *interest* is multi-faceted. Does it mean "interested in reading," "reading interests," or is it a means to manipulate independent reading engagement?

For example, a student may acknowledge an interest in sports, which often leads to a fervent recommendation of books related to *any* sport. Unfortunately, there is nothing appealing about this approach. Despite the teacher's best intention to connect, the reader cannot be appeased—to no fault of their own. By nature, we are complicated beings and finding the sweet spot can be challenging. Consider this analogy. Some of us have very specific food interests. We want nothing else. Reading can be like this. Rather than take interest in the palate of books a teacher offers, we narrow into specifics. This can be considered a defense mechanism, in all honesty. In as much as the student is not opening up their interests (which will have an impact later), they are also insecure, not yet ready to risk vulnerability in expanded interests.

Typically, an interest in something is a generalization, not a deeper understanding. For me, for example, growing up my teachers pawned horse books off on me. I couldn't have cared less about equitation. I loved horse *racing*. Although shared with the best intentions, I never read their recommendations. For Anthony, he was fed up with hockey books. But he faithfully kept up appearances by opening the proffered dilapidated Matt Christopher novel. Again, compliance. Not authenticity. We can't assume students' personal interests translate to a reading interest. But more important, by emphasizing interest we risk setting up a false hope and false expectations for our students and ourselves. The false hope is that interest in a topic will be enough of an impetus to drag a reluctant reader through that window and out into the world of reading for pleasure. The false expectation for students is that books will and should hold their interest, and that the book, by holding their interest, will essentially do the work for them.

> **Growing up my teachers pawned horse books off on me. I couldn't have cared less about equitation. I loved horse racing. Although shared with the best intentions, I never read their recommendations.**

It's important to note that interest isn't just limited to students like Anthony. Even students who are independent readers can be falsely portrayed. Such readers repeatedly read *Smile* (Telegmeier, 2010) and *Wimpy Kid* or carry around *Harry Potter*. They're more apt to cite movies than text evidence. As I mentioned earlier, this narrow breadth of experiences leaves readers vulnerable in the future; they need opportunities to explore new reading interests. Reading football books in volume may move kids through reading levels, but it doesn't provide an "inventory of knowledge" (Redford, 2020) or expand background knowledge (Cervetti & Hebert, 2015; Hattan & Lupo, 2020; Lupo et al., 2018; Redford, 2020), the shame of which will be experienced much later in their formal or post-secondary schooling. Turning readers on to text can be done through explicit actions. These include

- Perseverance
- The Read Aloud
- Metacognition and Independent Reading (Reading Passports and Reading Visas)
- 30 Books in 30 Days

Perseverance

While recommendations work well for students who love reading, many students haven't developed a self-concept as readers, let alone self-monitoring skills (Blachowicz & Ogle, 2001; Johnson, 2006), or the capacity to persist when books present challenges. In the name of compliance, the shame-based, dissociative "teacher pleasing," avoidance (e.g., "I'm not interested anymore") maturing readers are afforded a luxury of opportunities to proliferate "fake reading" (Gordon, 2018; Tovani, 2000) or quit books rather than persevere to discover themselves as readers.

We are familiar with the students who profess boredom with books. It's not that they're bored or disinterested. Rather, the book's complexity increased, and they don't yet have a navigation system that permits them to access a text. Many times, we accept (tolerate) such sentiment without question, meaning we just let students quit books and move on. We downplay this as students making decisions about their reading lives. Sometimes there is danger with too much liberty. Even our highest achieving students can face perpetual abandonment. How often do we take the time to determine what's really happening? Please consider that tolerating students' actions is really appeasement. We're attempting to show empathy, but what's really happening is that we are keeping our readers at arm's length. Within the lens shame, the reluctance to take time with the reader equates to rejection.

We need to guide students into how to find pleasure in reading, including when things get tough.

In my experience, one sentiment is at the core of abandoned reading. Students, leaning on the trust built within the interpersonal bridge, have in one way or another admitted, "I don't really know how to navigate this book." Thus, even before conferring or small groups, we have the greatest opportunity to show, or teach, students how to really read a book. We need to guide students into how to find pleasure in reading, including when things get tough. Our job is to help all students take the risk of being bored, to explore and persist, to learn how to create (new) interests in reading through their own engagement. We start with our best friend the *read aloud*.

The Read Aloud: Modeling How to Select, Persist, and Get Engaged

When we read aloud, we have a golden opportunity to be vulnerable. To show our readers how we incorporate new interests, face our limitations, and push through parts that are confusing or for other reasons are commanding our attention, like complex text (McClure & Fullerton, 2017; Ness, 2017). The goal behind read alouds is to model the capacity to be interested (Brassell, 2006), sustain interest, and expand interest. With this type of read aloud, I'm modeling *how to fall in love* with a book and to face its ever-present challenges.

When we read aloud, we have a golden opportunity to be vulnerable.

This is why, in the first few days of school, along with building community and crafting reading autobiographies, I introduce the read aloud (Laminack & Wadsworth, 2006; Layne, 2015). My aim is to orient students to the dynamic nature of reading interests.

As with many of the critical shifts I've made in my teaching, I've had to consider what is about me and what best amplifies the perspectives of my students. For these reasons, I don't

- rely on books that are part of my own or widely accepted read aloud canon;
- engage in direct instruction about the processes and capacities I'm modeling;
- mention why students might find it interesting, or in any other way suggest I can anticipate how they might respond; or
- pretend to be confused or stumble over a word when I'm not.

As a result, I

- choose titles I've never read, but I know will be appropriate (see example below);
- make it clear to students that I haven't read the book;
- tell students how and why I chose it, focusing solely on my own interest and processes;
- share my authentic responses as I make my way through the book, including where I am confused or bored, as well as connections to my own life; and
- give my honest assessment of what I liked and didn't like about the book.

The deliberate function of my read alouds is to make reading visible. I want students to observe my initial reactions to a text, my confusions, how I navigate characters and mounting conflicts, and persevere through challenging parts. All this culminates in how I *learn* to take interest in a book. The reality is that many books, starting with middle-grade literature, develop slower than what students are accustomed to. This was the case with *Breadcrumbs* (Ursu, 2011), a book I had selected to show students how to take interest in expanded fairy tales. Since I was not overly interested in the book, this read aloud provided a good opportunity to model productive struggle, which involves patience and perseverance, as well as looking for opportunities to become interested through characters and making personal connections. Additionally, I wanted to show students that I could transcend the text, or go beyond plot, settings, and character's names, to see if the book would become a mirror—a means of finding a narrative much like mine. As my interest piqued, my students responded as well. Our patience paid off.

Here's the how the process unfolded:

As I expected, the first few days of reading, I wasn't all that engaged. I read a bit, demonstrating patience, but also sharing my desire for the book to pick up speed, making comments like, "I wonder if this book is going to get better." At the same time, I was actively looking for the point where I'd finally be interested—and what would promote my interest. About the fourth day, say page 60, I was picking up on a pattern of behavior between the two main characters, two life-long friends, Hazel and Jack. That sparked my interest. When Jack bailed on Hazel to begin making new friends, that conflict caught my attention. If there's one thing we know in life, it's that finding new friends can upset the apple cart.

"Hazel is treating Jack like he cannot function without her," I noted.

Later I speculated, "Is she jealous that he's moving on while she is left alone?"

This is not a question I pose to the class to answer, but to myself to demonstrate how the book and I were having a kind of conversation. The students were amazed!

My message to them wasn't, *"See how interesting this is?"*

Paying attention to the characters' interactions is helping me get engaged. That was the message I was sending. It also helped me demonstrate how to use the book as a mirror, since I started connecting events in the book to my own experiences as a student.

Of course, we all love well-plotted books. The hooks or desire to find out what comes next can keep us all turning the pages. (This is what students are often looking for when they describe their interest.) Sadly, many students believe *interest* is simply the desire to find out what happens next. Attention to characters is what I try to model and encourage because characters are mirrors that can reflect our behaviors and decision making; share joy and empathy for misfortune; in some cases, characters are representations of who we'd like to be (e.g., Ade Darcy).

In *Testing Is Not Teaching,* Graves (2004) urges teachers to attend closely to character. "Bypassing character also means bypassing the student who is struggling to grow up and make his or her own decisions" (p. 72). Rather than telling students that they need to be paying attention or even directing their attention to certain passages, the read aloud gives me a chance to demonstrate how I embrace characters, nay interest, with a book.

Successive Read Alouds

When we start our second read aloud, I practice a kind of managed choice with students. Here I display four books that I think students might otherwise ignore. I read the back or flaps first, since that is what students are familiar with. Next, I open the book to a random spot and read the two facing pages. Afterward, I distribute notecards and ask them to write down which book they recommend for the read aloud and why. Their reasons give me more insight into what factors they typically focus on as well as how much they may or may not have picked up from my first foray into modeling how I select a book.

For the remainder of the year, the read aloud is responsive to instructional needs (Morrison & Wlodarcyzk, 2009). If we are in a content unit (Jordan, 2015), for example, I might use two selections, one of fiction and one of nonfiction, that complement one another. I often give students the opportunity to provide input on the read alouds, but there are many reasons why I might decide unilaterally on particular books. On other occasions, I read books that I consider "annual" read alouds. These might be books the class deserves to hear, or are anchor texts for text-dependent question instruction. As the year progresses, I also permit readers' needs to determine how the read aloud evolves. Read aloud choices may be determined by

- newly released texts I want to introduce to the class;
- books students might otherwise avoid, such as books that "look" boring; or
- more complex nonfiction texts during content studies.

Book Reflection Choices

Breadcrumbs turned out to be a book the class and I *grew* from. But because I make an annual selection of a book I've not previously read, every once in a while, I wind up modeling how to engage with a book that is truly not very good. It was the thirtieth anniversary of the movie *Back to the Future* (1985). I found an original junior novelization of the movie (Gipe, 1985). I thought it might be fun to use at the school year, amid the hype of the highly anticipated 2015 release on YouTube of *Back to the 2015 Future*. We wondered what in the book (movie) actually came to be true?

Well, not only did *Back to the Future* fail to live up to fantasy, but also the book was beyond awful. The book was detailed, filled with embellishments to the movie. Was it a fail? Absolutely not. What this book allowed me to model was perspective about a singular reading experience. The value of the read aloud comes in modeling honest reactions to text; persevering to determine if we can expand our interests. I didn't hide my thoughts about how awful the book was. While I didn't solicit student responses, they offered them anyway. Many had seen the movie, and they were blown away by how a book could make the movie seem so much better. I made a point of telling students things like, "Well this book is awful, but I think I'm going to keep going just because I want to say I finished it. I think I can get through," or more pessimistically, "Now when I say a book is bad, I have something to compare it to!" I wanted students to understand that reading a (bad) book wasn't a waste of time. We had an opportunity to learn more about likes and dislikes and how they can inform our selections in the future. It's important that students see my integrity and credibility, which might allow them to be vulnerable with their own reading and brave books they might otherwise (albeit foolishly) ignore.

Metacognition and Independent Reading: Setting Readers Up in a Reading Community

After students have completed their reading autobiographies and we're entrenched in the routine of a read aloud, we immerse ourselves in independent reading (Moss & Young, 2010), our classroom reading community (Atwell, 2007). At this point, we're 3 weeks into the school year. I've taken steps to understand each student's reading history, favorite books, and *current* interests. Anthony, for example, was all about rereading *Wimpy Kid* and Raina Telegemier graphic novels. I'd gained some understanding of readers, but I wanted to learn a little more.

Up to this time, to build anticipation, I haven't opened the class library or allowed students to access those books. I've also placed orders either online or at my local books stores for newly released books and make a big deal about them as they arrive and are placed in the classroom.

My intention is to keep my library fresh since students tend to prefer new books. More, I can introduce them to hot new themes, topics, characters, and authors.

As an aside, I don't want it to seem as if I am barring students from reading for 3 weeks. For one, students are visiting the school library

4.1 and 4.2 Sample Classroom Libraries

and checking out books, which gives me insight into their boundaries and parameters. I also have a collection of books I've culled that students can access (and keep) before the library opens. The fact is, I want to learn about readers' preferences, habits, and approaches to reading before simply opening the library. The library is our most important classroom resource (Chambers, 1996). If used inappropriately, readers lose interest in the library, lose books, and in turn can be deterred from reading.

To that end, within this 3-week period, I start introducing book baskets (Sibberson & Syzmusiak, 2003). We talk about how to access baskets, sign out books, and find safe sit spots for privacy during independent reading. (The baskets in my library are organized by author, genre, theme, topic, etc.)

We then co-construct expectations that invite students to participate and support one another within our reading community and our reading lives (see Figures 4.3 and 4.4). The attributes that students inscribe are then turned into an anchor chart that can be referenced when students complete their weekly VOWELS Checklist (see Chapter 7).

Sample Co-Constructed Expectations:

- Read with students who are new to the language
- Be quiet while others are reading
- Every time they talk to you, don't mind them so they will see you don't want to talk
- Recommend books to others
- Help people find the type of books they like
- Respect other people's space
- Notice other readers and give compliments
- Recommend useful reading strategies to help them remember reading
- Tell them to persevere, encourage them
- Help with words they don't know
- Talk to them about their reading

4.3 and 4.4 Constructing Classroom Library Expectations

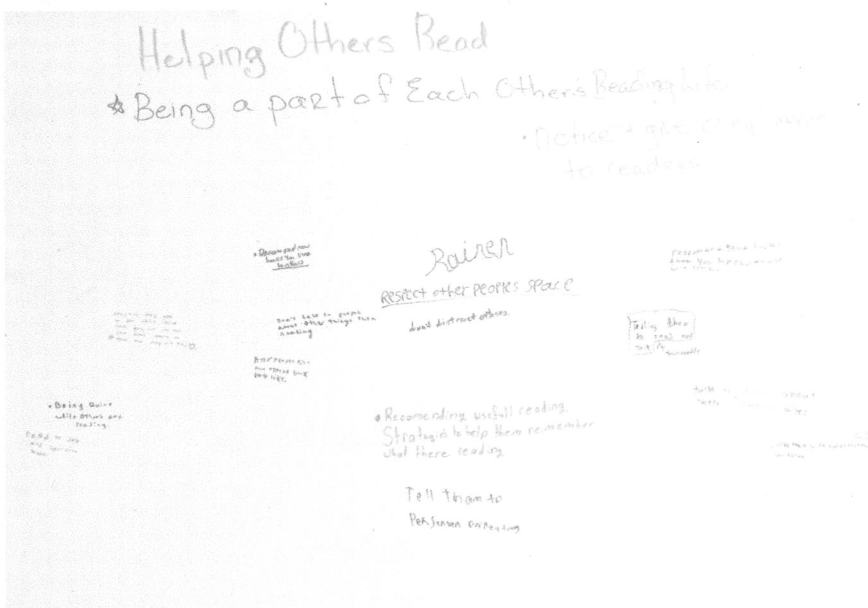

Before long we create the first of many Reading Passports (described later), a metacognitive tool for successful reading. Finally, I turn our attention back to the contents of the book baskets. This isn't done in a day, but I want to stoke their excitement. After all, one gift we can give our readers is to scaffold students for successful independent reading (Routman, 2003). I start with "hot" books and "legendary titles."

While this might seem contradictory to recommending texts, as I spoke of earlier, I frame these lists within the context of previous readers and what is currently trending. This doesn't mean readers are obligated to choose these texts. I offer them as a scaffold to spark new reading preferences and as a choice, an invitation that will always be open "if you're interested."

Independent reading, in my opinion, is about making the reading experience your own. That's the secret as those who have fallen in love with reading demonstrate. The reading experience is their own. In this sense, how we frame independent reading is of equal importance as the read aloud. Here's what I tell readers to kick off our reading community:

- They will read a wide variety of books over the course of the year. Forty chapter books is the target, but reading is far more fluid than that. You'll see!
- We will explore ways each of them can complete a book in a week. Graphic novels, biographical picture books, narrative nonfiction, *Basher* science—oh my! Reading is not always about 200-page fiction novels.
- They will have 25 minutes to read in class and challenge themselves to read for 30 to 45 minutes outside class. I tell them, "I ultimately can't make you read at home, but I am very interested to hear about how you are making reading a part of your life!"
- They will organize and monitor their reading lives using a Reading Passport.

Here are some examples:

Hot Books: *Stamped* (for Kids), *New Kid*, *Tight*, *Fish in a Tree*, *Night Diary*

Legendary Titles: *Hatchet*, *Rump*, *One Crazy Summer*, *A Long Way from Chicago*, *Granny Torelli Makes Soup*

I make it clear I have expectations of them as readers. To be frank, I tell them they cannot meet standards on the report card if they don't make the choice to read. This may seem harsh, but is not the goal *independence*? No accountability is the same as abandonment. If we don't follow through with accountability, what we are really saying is that reading is important, but I don't have time for you. Moreover, without accountability, there is no mirror—no means in which to reflect, see oneself grow. These accountability goals are established through the interpersonal bridge.

No accountability is the same as abandonment.

Reading Passports: Helping Students Evaluate Their Own Decision Making

Like many of you, I grew weary of reading logs. Nothing frustrated me more than seeing a turned-in reading log with one ink, one font, with the same amount of reading, beginning and concluding at the same precise time, seven consecutive days. Kids were lying to me, and they knew they were. I could further see evidence that reading logs weren't working when discussions within reading conferences didn't have the depth aligned with the amounts of reading recorded. Why do they misrepresent their reading lives? Over time I realized that students tell variations of the truth not out of maliciousness, but because they tried to cope with their internalized shame by defending what they couldn't control: their lives outside of school, including home and time spent reading.

See this book's companion website to download a full version of the Reading Passport.

The Reading Passport (Stygles, 2017a) is more than a way for students to keep track of what they have read. Students need and deserve an authentic means of evaluating their own reading progress. The intent is to help them become more aware of patterns and participation within their own reading life (not like traditional logs where parents historically were more in charge).

Within the pages of the Reading Passport, readers:

- consider what books they want to read and why,
- record what books they've read and why they were selected, and
- record title and page number on a calendar to monitor daily progress.

The Reading Passport is made of a single sheet of 12″ x 18″ paper folded in half. The front facing page is blank, which allows students to design their own cover containing three features:

- Name
- "Reading Passport"
- Month

On the flip side is a calendar (see Figure 4.7). On the left interior side, much like a traditional reading log, students list the books. I ask students to include the author, the date started, and the date ended. The information I really seek is the reason they chose this book, which is recorded on their reading log, inside the passport. Students who are "book grabbers," meaning they grab the first book in a basket or a book at random to play the part, are at risk of slipping through the cracks. This element of accountability, though annoying to students, is a hint to us both about how engaged or interested they are in either the book or participation in their reading life.

On the facing page is another list labeled To-Be-Read (TBR) list or Books I'm Thinking About Reading. Here, students jot down titles of books they are *interested* in reading. I prefer Books I'm Thinking About Reading because this is more indicative of a process. Anthony was notorious for writing books down following a book talk then having no idea what he'd read next. I'm certain he was "thinking" about what he wanted to read but was too overwhelmed to make a clear decision. Instead of rebuking him, he needed compassion and guidance, which meant we needed to utilize the interpersonal bridge to help him move forward.

Students who are facing challenges adopting reading into their lives tell variations of the truth.

The third page is a more traditional reading log. It's a slightly adapted version of Donalyn Miller and Susan Kelly's (2014) reading log. What's important to notice is that, once again, I ask students to state why they chose their books. As I mentioned earlier, students who are facing challenges adopting reading into their lives tell variations of the truth. What they write on the Reading Visa can often be different than the Reading Passport. This happens for a few reasons. Maturing readers:

- hurry to complete the ticket to read,
- include a response merely to complete the ticket, or
- aren't really sure why they are choosing a book, but they don't want that to be known.

Therefore, responding to the prompt a second time can either authenticate why a student chose a book or communicates a signal for me to intervene to find out what's really going on in the reader's life. Never do I compare information to call a student out. After all, the idea is to teach students to become readers, which means I need to check and double-check what's really going on in their reading worlds.

Additionally, I ask students to complete the reading log and the calendar, which might seem repetitive. To be clear, students fill out the reading log portion when they start and end a new book. The calendar is a daily update of what book was read and what page the reader finished on, which are both done as part of our class arrival routine. Once a week, students harvest thumbnails, which are pasted into a Google Doc for printing. After the pages are printed, students cut and paste the thumbnails on the date they started the book (referring back to the reading log and calendar). The result is that readers (and I) have two modalities in which to interpret the patterns within their reading lives.

4.5 Victoria's Reading Log Inside a Reading Passport

~~Books I Am~~ Thinking About Reading

Title	Did I Read This Book?	When did I Read This Book?	Why I want to read this book?	What do I expect to learn from this book?
Bad Babby Sitters			Beacuse This is the Babby Sitters club enimes.	I expect to learn to not Stell other Poples idays.
Wink	Yes	Jan 7 to Jan 24	I want to read it beacuse miss Ives read a little bit of it and it sound's good.	I exfet to learn That Pople with disabtleys can do anything.
Nupolen			I've ~~read~~ herd about him in music and I want to read it.	How wars were haped and how caned fo was mad.
The Adventurers Guilp			This sounds like a tail of magic and I liked that book.	A lot of magic and how it is done.
The Adventurers Guilp Twilite of the Elves			I want to read the secend book in the seares.	More magic and how it works.
Winny's grate war			this is about winny the Poo and I loved winy the Poo.	I exfed to learn how winny the Poo was made
Crashing into love			Mr. Styglass started to read the book but did't finish.	I want to lern how love works.
Summer and Juliy			I want to read this book because my firend told me it was a good book	I want to learn how two make opsits atrackt.

4.6 Ava's Future Reading—Books I Am Thinking About Reading

Reading Log

Title: The 47 people you'll meet in middle school	Date Stated: 1/3/2022	Ended: 1/16/2022
Why Did I Choose this Book? I chosed this book, because, when I saw the ... dy read	Rating:	

but then I readed in till the page 7 or 6 I think I wanted to read it so baddly.

	Date Stated: 16/16/2021	Ended: 19/1/2022
	Rating:	

	Date Stated: 1/19/2022	Ended: 1/26/22
Why Did I Choose this Book?	Rating:	

Title: lePold II butcher of the congo	Date Stated: 1-27-2022	Ended:
Why Did I Choose this Book?	Rating:	

Title:	Date Stated:	Ended:
Why Did I Choose this Book?	Rating:	

Title:	Date Stated:	Ended:
Why Did I Choose this Book?	Rating:	

Title:	Date Stated:	Ended:
Why Did I Choose this Book?	Rating:	

Title:	Date Stated:	Ended:
Why Did I Choose this Book?	Rating:	

My favorite element of the Reading Passport is the calendar. Interestingly enough, it's the calendar that tells the story. As morning work, I ask students to update their reading passport (which prevents parental interference). In the one-inch box, made from a 7 x 7 table, students record the title of the book read the day before and that page number.

When time, space, and resources allow, students print thumbnail images of the cover of the book contained on a running bibliography

4.7 The Reading Passport Calendar

Books I've Read
Libros que he leído
Livres que j'ai lus

using Google Docs. The result is a striking visual reality check. Students and I can note the patterns of their reading and possess a mirror of just what is happening in their reading lives. In turn, my job, through conferring and the interpersonal bridge, is not to judge a student's progress but to reflect back what is happening and assist them in making informed decisions about their reading interest and engagement. It's the calendar that tells the real story of a student's reading habits and prompts conversation!

Let's look specifically at Anthony. Anthony chose *The Night Diary* (Hiranandani, 2019) on one occasion, a novel about a preteen trying to figure out where she belongs as Hindus and Muslims are in conflict, forcing Nisha and her family to become refugees. I asked him, "What's your plan to read it?" I had his calendar in front of me; graphic novels dominated his reading, not a trace of a chapter book, let alone one this dynamic.

He returned, "I don't know. It's a big book so it'll probably take me a while." This is not what I call "an informed choice." He'd mentioned a friend had just read it. Somehow, Anthony believed if his friend could, so could he, which is not uncommon. Comparison fuels shame. We try to identify with others or see ourselves as equals without the context of the other person's experience. It didn't mean his selection was prudent, his *interest* well intended, or that it would serve a beneficial purpose. The idea isn't to deter Anthony despite the evidence in front of me. Doing so would invalidate his thinking and aspiration, showing him I didn't believe in him; he needs to experience trial and error alongside a trusted authority figure (Miller, 1995). Therefore, while finishing *The Night Diary* in a week seemed lofty (and it is!), Anthony's agency (Goldberg, 2016; Johnston, 2004) invited an exploration and a challenge, which required a plan. This is where the interpersonal bridge begins.

The Reading Visa: Nurturing Student Awareness of How and Why They Select Books

With their Reading Passports at the ready, the time arrives to make the library available to readers for an uninterrupted exploration of what books are available. After about 5 or 6 weeks of independent reading, during which I have been monitoring students' choices and persistence, I introduce the Reading Visa. Unlike the Reading Passport, which records what the student has read, stopped reading, or wants to read, the Reading Visa, as the name suggests, acts more as a kind of gatekeeper to reading. Students should complete a new Reading Visa every time they start a new book. To complete the visa, students must answer three questions.

1. *Why did I choose this book?* My purpose is to move students beyond relying on general and relatively superficial reasons, such as "It's about hockey." I'm challenging students to consider a reading experience that is focused on appealing characters and rich themes. What I don't want is students simply "book grabbing" or snatching the first book they see in a basket to say they are reading.

   As with all the tasks introduced here, the value resides not just in the student completing the visa as much as in how it serves as a springboard for my conversations with them. It's about accountability and involvement in one's progress rather than whimsical or passive compliance. When conferring, for example, I can use the visas as a starting point to remind them of their choices, reflecting back to students their reasons in their own words. This builds an awareness of themselves as decision makers and can be particularly useful when conferring with students who decide they don't like a book and want to abandon it. Together we can look at the limitations of choosing a topic and consider what other elements got in the way of the student sustaining an interest.

2. *Why will this book be a good selection for me?* Though a twist on the same prompt in the Reading Passport, this question asks students to consider how the book is a good match. What makes a good match could be any number of criteria depending on the student and their own reading goals. Is the reader trying to learn something specific? (Yes, this relates to topics and interests, but we're trying to build students' attention to what makes this specific book a good choice on this topic.) Perhaps the student wants a challenge: "I'd like to try a book that's more than one hundred pages," or "I read the first few pages and there were some challenging words, but I think I was able to figure it out." Or maybe a student wants to experiment by trying something new: "This book is good for me because I have not tried science fiction."

3. *What will I notice in this book?* This question drives at the reader's intention as well as awareness of what might be a pathway to engagement. It assesses just how well the reader previewed the book. Their response helps me understand what they are picking up from read alouds, conferences, and reading instruction, as well as recommendations, observations, and comparisons to classmates. Thus, I can consider the degree of agency they have formed from their selections. For instance, if a student who chose *Hatchet* (Paulsen, 1987) writes something like, "I will notice what the wilderness is like" or "I will notice if Brian is scared or brave," I know that they have truly made a choice based on information they picked up from the preview and used it to form an initial intent. If a student says something like, "I will notice how the characters get along with each other," I know that they are at least thinking about characters.

4.8 The Reading Visa

Reading Visa

Book Title: ______________________________

Why did I choose this book?	• Reason:
Why will this book be a good selection for me?	• Reason:
What will I notice in this book?	• Reason:

Expert responses to the Reading Visa do not appear overnight. It takes weeks, months, and for some it might be an entire year before maturing readers are able to, let alone adeptly, consider the whys and whats behind their reading choices. The tool is intended to promote metacognition and scaffold executive function, which every reader benefits from in varying capacities. In turn, the Reading Visa helps initiate the conversation about what it takes for an individual to be uniquely invested in reading, whether they are gifted, neurodiverse, or English learners.

In Anthony's Reading Visa, he wrote, "It was an age-appropriate book plus my favorite." He was dutiful in completing his task. His response isn't unusual for readers without a strong sense of their own purposes. But Anthony had a strong inclination to report what he thought I wanted to hear—another disguise to prevent me from seeing what was really behind the veil. Even before then, his habit was to enter the library, grab a book, brazenly hold it up, and declare to me, "Here, Mr. Stygles, I've chosen a book." Do you think he stopped to consider a Reading Visa? No. Anthony took months and persistent intervention to reach this point.

Anthony had a strong inclination to report what he thought I wanted to hear—another disguise to prevent me from seeing what was really behind the veil.

4.9 **Sample Reading Visa**

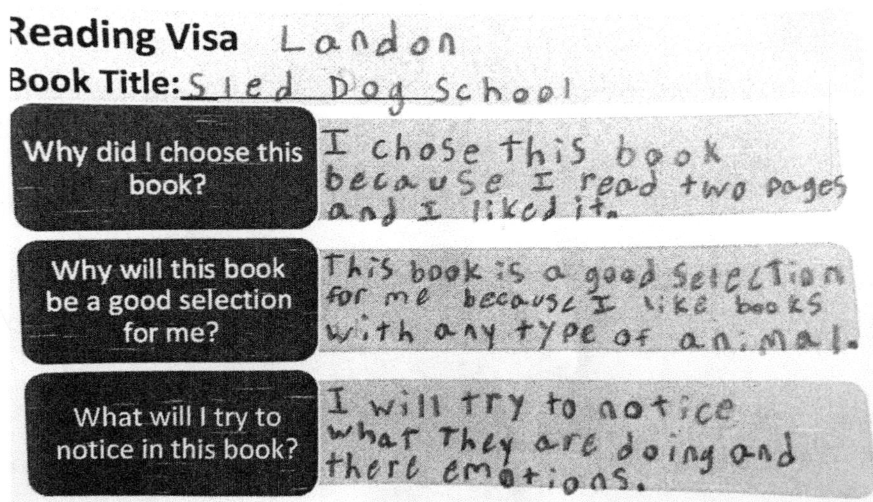

Reading Visa Landon

Book Title: Sled Dog School

Why did I choose this book?	I chose this book because I read two pages and I liked it.
Why will this book be a good selection for me?	This book is a good selection for me becausl I like books with any type of animal.
What will I try to notice in this book?	I will try to notice what they are doing and there emotions.

Accountability Is Love

What's the real lesson here? Brown (2010) points out that accountability is compassion. This won't be the first time I write this. When students see that we are invested in their actions, as evidenced by a Reading Visa or a Reading Passport, we reflect back how much we value their reading lives. That's not all. I find many readers, particularly neurodiverse readers, or those who are learning to cope with various executive functions, need the support—or boundaries—to learn what their capabilities are and how to exist within their current capacities. (See Chapter 6 for more information about boundaries.) My students often tell me that independent reading is not something they are overly engaged in. It's merely a function of a classroom. They get a book, they "read," and that's it. There's no rhyme or reason to what they read or why. They just do.

How do we keep such students accountable, while at the same time helping them find self-understanding about themselves as readers? Here, I describe what I do and don't do in these circumstances:

I DON'T

- assume student avoidance is motivated by apathy or refusal or
- communicate to them that they are doing anything wrong.

I DO

- interpret this avoidance as a sign of neurodiversity or intense interest,
- smile and acknowledge them when they show me their book but inquire about their Visa,
- make a point of conferring with them to help document this reading journey milestone, and
- focus solely on their thinking about their choices while conferring.

Now you will see how one of the early conferences with Anthony, our starting point, unfolded.

Anthony:	"I started reading *The Adventures of a Girl Called Bicycle*."
Mr. Stygles:	"Ok, Anthony, why did you choose it?"
Anthony:	"I saw it in the green basket. I thought it looked interesting."
Mr. Stygles:	"Why is this book a good selection for you?"
Anthony:	"I don't know. We had to read five books from the green basket. So I picked it."
Mr. Stygles:	"What page are you on?"
Anthony:	"Page six."
Mr. Stygles:	"So you just started that book today. What did you read yesterday?"
Anthony:	"Oh, I read a book from my bookshelf at home."
Mr. Stygles:	"And what book was that?"
Anthony:	"I can't remember. It was something I got back in second grade."

(Continued)

(Continued)

Mr. Stygles:	"Anthony, you're killing me. What's going on?"
Anthony:	"What do you mean?" He tries to giggle me away.
Mr. Stygles:	"You're not sticking with any books?"
Anthony:	"I know . . . Nothing interests me."
Mr. Stygles:	"Any ideas about how we should remedy that?"
Anthony:	"I don't know . . . You know I think reading is stupid and to read so much is dumb."
Mr. Stygles:	"I'm aware you feel that way. I hope we can rectify that eventually. So let's start now. What will you try to notice in this book?"
Anthony:	"Hmm . . . If I like it?"
Mr. Stygles:	"Anthony, do you by chance know what ambivalence means?"
Anthony:	"No."
Mr. Stygles:	"It's a fancy way of saying you don't know if you even care."
Anthony:	"Oh! I like that. I'm going to use that on my mom!"
Mr. Stygles:	"Awesome . . . but really, Anthony, you couldn't care less about this book."
Anthony:	"May . . . be."
Mr. Stygles:	"Well it's me and you on this one."
Anthony:	"What?"
Mr. Stygles:	"I mean, you and me. We're taking the next week to figure out how you are reading. Not what you are reading, but how you're reading."
Anthony:	"I'm confused. I already know how to read."
Mr. Stygles:	"I know. I've listened to you read. I've seen you answer questions after reading, but you're not really choosing to read, and that's what I'm thinking about."
Anthony:	"Huh?"

Mr. Stygles:	"I want to spend this week with you learning how and why you choose to read. I want to see what it's like for you, first to choose to read, then what it's like for you when you read. After that, I want to find out how you're attending to information while you read."
Anthony:	"You're so confusing me! I don't even know what you are talking about."
Mr. Stygles:	"Anthony, you'll see."

Our collaboration continues for months. This is the interpersonal bridge, an ever-persistent devotion to the reader's development through compassion, forgiveness, and accountability. By December, Anthony had chosen and completed his first book that year. But it wasn't until February that he had completed his first Visa. By the end of the year, he was making comments like this on his Reading Visas: "This is a good selection for me because it is a book I haven't read before, and I think I can finish it in five days." And he did!

30 Books in 30 Days

At some point every year, I replace the read alouds with a strategy I call "30 Books in 30 Days" (Stygles, 2017b). My intent is to encourage students to think outside of what has become their reading norm. Typically, the month falls somewhere in the middle of the year, but it varies depending on the need to respond to reading behaviors (e.g., waning interest, reluctance, complacency) I'm observing in students and the feedback I'm gathering in conferences.

Over the course of 30 days, I provide students short exposures to a wide variety of texts that they have otherwise avoided.

Over the course of 30 days, I provide students short exposures to a wide variety of texts that they have otherwise avoided. The purpose is to expand students' reading opportunities. We are all familiar with standards that indicate that students should read in volume across an expanse of genres and content. Yet quite commonly, students are not familiar with the possibilities of reading that can be subsumed within those standards. 30 Books in 30 Days is merely a tool to help introduce readers to opportunities that will help address those standards and improve the depth of their reading experiences and reading lives. This might include overlooked authors, avoided genres, and perceptually challenging text (nonfiction). I deliberately select books to target because I know the students, I know the books, and I want these overlooked books in their hands. Here's how it unfolds:

Each day, for 20 minutes, I read a segment from a different book. One day I might read the beginning of a book, the next day a random chapter from a different book from the same book basket. After I read, several things occur:

- I engage students in a discussion about what we have learned about the book, including setting, conflicts, characters, and archetypal roles that help us identify various characters. For instance, *which character if any might be the hero? Is there a villain or ally? Any character who seems to be in the role of apprentice?* These questions create pathways to engaging with and understanding the characters and scaffold identification and interaction.
- The students vote to decide if the book captured their interest immediately, a little patience is required before the book "gets good," or it just doesn't capture their interest. We record the class vote in the category "Potential Interest." We vote using the following guidelines:
    1. Yes! I want to keep reading this.
    2. Sorta? I need to be patient and let the book develop.
    3. No. This book just isn't going to work for me right now.
- Finally, we name *text features, content,* or *literary devices* that caught our attention under the column "Appealing Features" to clearly define what made each book interesting.

This discussion typically lasts 10 minutes. During that time, I jot notes on our "toteboard," which is really one of our free whiteboards that serves as a constant reference for students. While I read, students take their own notes on a note catcher to save their thoughts for the discussion. The note catcher (see figure 4.10) resembles the white board and contains enough space for five books (or one note catcher for each week). Later, I type up each board

4.10 Sample "Toteboard"

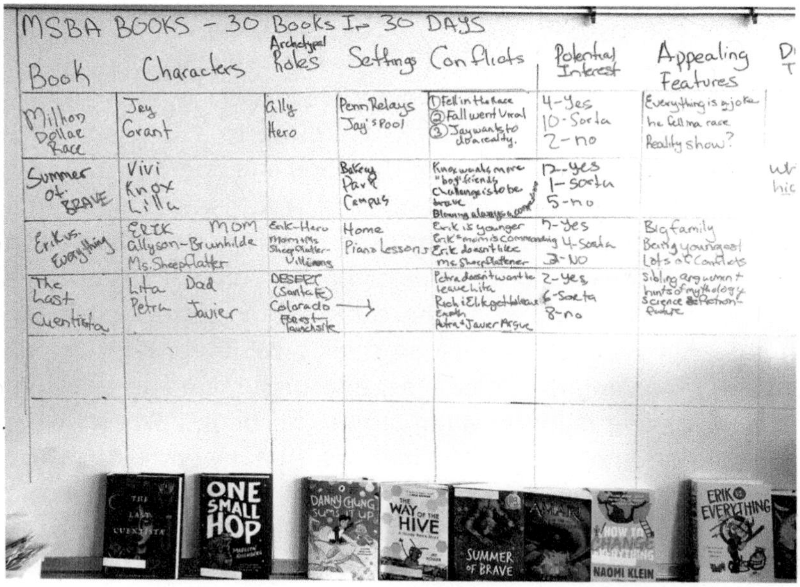

4.11 Note Catcher Template

Book	Characters	Archetypal Role	Setting	Conflicts	Potential Interest	Appealing Features

into a smaller anchor chart that students store in their Reading Response Journals.

Sometimes I devote an entire week to a particular genre or author. During one week of 30 Books in 30 Days, I introduced five Christopher Paul Curtis books. Long books, over 250 pages, tend to get overlooked, and many of Curtis's books are close to 350 pages. Beyond length, even if a student picks up the book and opens it, they might be overwhelmed by the sheer number of words, the length of paragraphs, and/or the types of words used. Curtis writes elaborate portrayals of characters and includes complex sentence structure, and his writing is richly layered. In short, his are more challenging books than students typically choose on their own. By previewing them extensively, reading long passages, and discussing the characters, I'm hoping to give students a leg up into his books. When I do so, I always take care not to send the message that my enthusiasm should be their enthusiasm. The message instead is, "Here is a book you might want to read to challenge yourself. Here is a preview of what is inside. I can help you enter this book. I can get you partway. You need to do the rest."

You might be wondering, do students end up choosing these books? Let's just say my basket of Christopher Paul Curtis books had been pillaged so badly that I needed to replace most of them. As Allington and McGill-Franzin (2013) noted, if you aren't losing books, kids aren't reading.

Final Thoughts

When I began teaching in 2002, I tried to hold students to a book every 2 weeks. My students thought I was wild. I found reinforcement (e.g., 40-book challenge; Common Core State Standards) for my rigorous expectations. But I continually found my readers underprepared and subsequently overwhelmed by my outlandish requirements (as more than one parent was happy to tell me). I came to discover that the trouble was a misinterpretation of independent reading. Every kid was an independent reader, but few read independently.

As we conclude, please consider the following—born from my former teaching style. A child might develop shame after repeatedly admitting they didn't read at home, unable to change the reasons they couldn't read. The student's sense-of-self, their self-perception as readers, their life circumstances, and my reaction to their transgression determine the extent of their shame. Let's consider possible reactions to readers who continually err in their *responsibilities*.

- Is our response to the student one of forgiveness? Or do we punish (e.g., loss of recess)?
- Do we leave room for the student to explain their circumstances or feelings?
- Do we believe students can develop their own habits? Or are they "like the rest of their family"?
- What supports can we offer? Or do we leave the student to figure things out alone?
- Do our responses leave open the possibility for future success? Or do we leave the reader feeling responsible for an existence they hardly have any control over?

Clearly, we need to help students find a balance between comfort and challenge, what a student can control and what they cannot. When a student tells me a book is boring, what's the real story? I'm not afraid of challenging readers to persevere through a book, provided there is support within the interpersonal bridge to navigate struggles rather than abandoning them to their own devices. I'll also consider the reader's circumstances to determine appropriate boundaries that scaffold the reader to maintain that same level of control in their reading life.

This support can take many forms. Most of it occurs during our conferences when we are negotiating expectations, exploring what is making the book difficult, as well as exploring ways to drive their interest and engagement. I might ask questions like, *"What is something interesting you are noticing in [such and such character]? Did any character do something that grabbed your attention?"*

Over time, we may have to agree that the student will not complete the book. It's important to help the student become aware of what they have learned about themselves as a reader, as well as what they have learned about what they can and can't do at this moment in time. How will this self-knowledge help them be successful at building a reading identity? By honestly framing it not as a failure but as an experience to learn from.

Shame is perpetuated when any shamed-based coping or defense strategy is inadvertently validated. Yet how often are readers able to disguise their deficient reading habits through compensating or masquerading? When we wantonly accept a student's reading behavior, we inadvertently validate their shame—not the reader—because we've placed our stock in what students have read, and their completed reading logs, establishing ourselves more as gate keepers of expectations rather than active participants in the interpersonal bridge.

Shame is perpetuated when any shamed-based coping or defense strategy is inadvertently validated.

Our students deserve to know more than compliance: efficacy, positive self-concept, and agency. There's a big world they are going into in which they must survive. That world is not even a close representation of the values we set forth, like reading compliance. We can change this by helping the reader establish a sense of reading within their lives and by creating boundaries they can continuously outgrow. We can help students manifest into the reader they never believed they could be and help them manage themselves when ever-persistent challenges come their way.

Reflect and Act

Use these reflection questions to consider the information shared in the chapter and how you can apply it in your own classroom.

1. What attributes define your classroom reading community? How does this chapter support or influence operations within the community?
2. In what ways does this chapter alter your thinking of traditional or widely accepted independent reading practices?
3. Which book could you begin reading aloud to your class, and what thoughts about your reading would be vulnerable enough to share with your students?
4. What steps can you take to enhance your independent reading practices?

5

PATHWAYS TOWARD COMPREHENSION

Using Reader Perceptions Strategically

At some point in a reader's life, comprehension can define them. When shame is considered, reading is not only about comprehension, it's about integrity—the desire to be perceived as a reader versus the painful reality the reader doesn't understand what is happening. To be fair, there are several different ways in which we consider *comprehension*, which means students can be labeled as various kinds of readers, none of which is actually within their control.

Since I started teaching, comprehension instruction occurred through an array of experiences within a variety of platforms (short texts, whole-class novels, small group reading, etc.) including close reading (Boyles, 2014; McLaughlin & Overturf, 2010; Robb, 2013), a means to revisit a text for specific information and multi-strategy reading (Palinscar & Brown, 1986) to scaffold maturing readers as they self-monitor their comprehension.

Can you imagine the weight maturing readers feel as the dynamic of what it means to *read* becomes increasingly complex? Many readers already struggle to

- recognize differences in reading experiences (from aesthetic to efferent), which has a strong potential to negatively influence a reader's perception of what it means to be a good reader; and
- make sense of reading in the first place, let alone complex text. Consequently, when previously effective strategies are no longer sufficient, readers are vulnerable to recognizing *deficits* that either didn't exist before or now risk increased potential to reveal challenges that currently or have existed for some time.

Therefore, shame must be considered at this critical juncture in a student's reading development.

Compounding these critical shifts in what students *perceive* to be reading is the notion that reading instruction doesn't guarantee success for every reader. Shame research notes that children are apt to assume responsibility for deficiencies when they fail or don't receive feedback about their learning (Kaufman, 1993). In other words, the shame-driven adage, "I taught it, they just didn't get it" has significant implications when considering appropriate instruction.

"They didn't get it." Just because we've taught close or strategic reading doesn't mean readers understand their purpose or function, nor do they automatically apply strategies intentionally or meaningfully. It definitely doesn't mean readers have assimilated strategies into their reading process to improve their perception of reading or comprehension.

"They didn't get it," means we have to ask ourselves, "How can we help students comprehend text?" That is, how can we invite maturing readers to engage vulnerably in what could potentially be considered a shameful element of reading (aside from the broader illiteracy)—comprehension, which is how one interprets and perceives a text. It's one thing for a reader to say, "I don't understand." It's even more intense to admit that you have no idea what's happening when reading. Meaning, comprehension is really about vulnerability and trust.

> It's one thing for a reader to say, "I don't understand." It's even more intense to admit that you have no idea what's happening when reading.

Uncovering Perceptions About Comprehension Through Affect

By November, I notice that readers grow frustrated, bored, and anxious about their reading. A bevy of assessments suggest to what extent my readers can decode and comprehend text, as well as provide insight into every student's perception about reading. However, data doesn't always determine who will demonstrate such behaviors. There are "high-level" readers who can't stay invested in any book, while "low-level" readers are more invested than ever. So when students start quitting books, or say that books are "boring," or begin to "misrepresent" what they've read, I start to wonder why. The answer resides in a maturing reader's *affect* or their physical and emotional responses that signal their comprehension.

It's at this turn, I start having more heart-to-heart discussions within the comfort of our interpersonal bridge, asking questions such as:

- Have you ever experienced excitement during reading? What was it like?

Pause for a second, please. Imagine what it feels like when "everyone" around you experiences variations of what is mentioned above, but you don't. When considering this perspective, we're beginning to explore the dynamic experience known as *comprehension*.

- Did you reach the suspenseful parts and nearly leap out of your skin?
- What about feeling so overwhelmed or over stimulated with information (perhaps content or rapid progression through a plot's development) that you have to walk around because your body becomes so amped you can't sit down?
- Did you ever feel like you connected with a hero—their trials and tribulations?
- Were you ever so compelled by an event, you had to find out more?
- Did you ever think something would be boring, and you found yourself wanting to learn more?

As we begin to go knee-to-knee, eye-to-eye, dipping our toes into the pool of vulnerability, I ask you to think of a time when you:

- couldn't stop reading because you couldn't wait for the next moment.
- read something that was a near example of an experience you had.
- read something that aligned with something you were experiencing.
- had to stop reading because you were frustrated or angry with the content.
- learned something from reading you didn't know before.
- read something that changed your mind about something.
- read something and realized your life couldn't be that way.
- read something that you didn't think you would enjoy.

What ensues can be heartbreaking. Most readers don't have answers, let alone believe such an experience could occur. The excitement of reading originates in comprehension (Zimmerman, 2011). It's impossible to enjoy anything about reading when you don't know what's going on. Readers need entry points, discernable access points to pinpoint and reflect back their monitoring (Beers & Probst, 2017, 2020; Serafini, 2004) and understanding of the text.

Acknowledging Perceptions of Maturing Readers

"I'm a bad reader! I can't read books like everyone else!" This is Lucia's introduction about herself in her reading autobiography. I didn't have a clear picture of what Lucia meant until our reading conferences. Originally, Lucia, age 13, received services for reading during the first trimester of the school year. She'd been retained and carried a "struggling" reader label. She once told me that she knew she was a struggling reader because in the room she went to there was a giant board with kids' names on magnets. She recognized her name on a magnet in the "second grade" category, while all her friends were in sixth grade. As I listened and took notes about her story, it became abundantly clear that comprehension made Lucia see herself in a negative light. That's what her reading experiences had been—a reflection of what she couldn't do. The lynchpin of the interpersonal bridge is the reading conference for this reason. Lucia opened up as we explored the abovementioned questions. She said, "I'm trying. I just read slow, and I don't know what's going on when I read."

> **"Lucia's reading experiences had been a reflection of what she couldn't do."**

Lucia was the kind of kid who represented a silent majority of students who drifted, socially and academically. Meek, sweet, yet withdrawn. She'd always carried a book and talked about what she wanted to read next. Before long though, she developed a habit of quitting books.

Lucia:	"Mr. Stygles, can I change my book?"
Mr. Stygles:	"What are you reading?"
Lucia:	"*Lucky Broken Girl.*"
Mr. Stygles:	"Why do you want to quit it?" *(Notice, I converted "change" to "quit.")*
Lucia:	"I don't like it."
Mr. Stygles:	"What do you mean?"
Lucia:	"Just because. I'm not really interested in it."

(Continued)

(Continued)

Mr. Stygles:	"Please, sit down. Let's talk a little more. First, when did you start the book?
Lucia:	"Three days ago."
Mr. Stygles:	"What page are you on?"
Lucia:	"10."
Mr. Stygles:	"Really? What's going on then? Is the book challenging?
Lucia:	"Not really. There's just so much happening, it's hard to keep up. I'm so confused."
Mr. Stygles:	"Tell me, you said, 'It's hard to keep up.' What are you doing to keep track of what's going on as you read?"
Lucia:	"What do you mean?"
Mr. Stygles:	"I'm talking about reading strategies. What are you doing to help you make sense of the book? Are you listing characters and determining who they are? Do you keep track of the conflicts and their outcomes?"
Lucia:	"Mr. Stygles, I don't know what you are talking about. I know you've taught us those things, but I thought you only meant we had to use those on the readings we did in class."

"I'm confused." There is no better way of appealing for help than admitting, "I'm confused." The vulnerability and risk-taking is a sign of trust as well as a plea. Lucia had several issues occurring while she was reading. I could have told her to get an easier text. Experience has taught me, though; there are more benefits to supporting readers through challenges than avoiding what will inevitably occur. Lucia was trying to remember everything she was reading, just as she had internalized from all her oral reading in short books years ago—not using strategies to help her. Times had changed. Reading purposes changed. Lucia hadn't. Talk about feeling left out, or as Lucia said, "I'm stupid."

It wasn't her fault.

Considering Lucia's context, and students like her, the purpose of this chapter is to explore an affective, emotional, and perceptual response as metacognitive strategies, a means of establishing dialog with text (Probst, 1988). Here we encourage students to invest themselves as thinkers through their responses (Burke, 2010) and perceptions—a scaffold into deeper, strategic reading to ease the burden of "remembering everything and to make reading an opportunity to discover the joy of learning and being involved with a text. We examine the following strategies to support students' comprehension and use emotions to connect with the text:

- Tracking Literary Elements
- Affective Annotations
- Clarifying
- Empathy and Identification

Tracking Literary Elements

At this point, despite all her attempts at reading, I noticed that Lucia didn't understand how to *organize* the information she was reading. It makes sense why she said the book was boring. On one hand she thought she had to *remember everything*. On the other, she couldn't make sense of the characters, settings, or any conflicts. Think, for instance, when our literacy leaders say, "Any reader can struggle depending on what they read" (Beers & Probst, 2013; Marinak & Gambrell, 2016). This was it. While there are various ideas about monitoring for comprehension (Athans & Devine, 2010; Keene & Zimmerman, 2007; Routman, 2003), sometimes returning to comprehension fundamentals by keeping track of characters, settings, and conflicts makes a huge difference.

I had to show Lucia that comprehension is more than recall. Comprehension, or interacting with text, is a process that requires deliberate actions (Gill, 2008) and invites students to monitor their thinking (Frey, Fisher, et al., 2009). Smith and Wilhelm (2010) remind us, "Elements can help students understand and navigate their daily lives" (p. 7). We were going back to barebones, literary elements.

I had to show Lucia that comprehension is more than recall.

Tracking Literary Elements is for maturing readers who demonstrate difficult time making sense of what is happening or can't "find" the joy of reading their peers express, who need the strategy for basic survival within the reading experience. Tracking Literary Elements is a deliberate act to record the whos (characters), wheres (setting), and whats (conflicts) of the reading in a place where students can continually refer back to (e.g., two to three sticky notes that serve as at-a-glance references). In doing so, the reader's action relieves the stress of remembering everything.

Keep in mind, as I attempt to mirror the individuality and giftedness back to each reader, some students like Lucia will recognize the benefit of something like Tracking Literary Elements. I wouldn't "force" Lucia to use tracking. The idea is to show her how her application of tracking benefitted her ability to recall, comprehend, and engage with the text—or the joy she felt reading because she understood what was happening. Tracking Literary Elements is a launching pad of interpersonal interactions, or where the reader injects themselves into the text.

To show students how to Track Literary Elements, we co-construct a chart using a common text and a shared reading approach (Dorn & Jones, 2012; Dorn & Soffos, 2003; Fisher, Frey, et al., 2008; Frey & Fisher, 2013) within the gradual release of responsibility model (Fisher & Frey, 2008). Shared reading is an instructional approach where all readers experience the same text simultaneously. In shared reading, I can scaffold readers by reading aloud while students follow along. Within this process, I can model "think alouds" before readers experiment for themselves. I show readers that characters, settings, and conflicts should be attended to. There is a means to an end. For example, Fisher and Frey (2009) created a list of questions like, "How does the setting influence the characters." If students don't have a basic understanding of who the characters are and what the setting is, there is the likely possibility that they won't understand that characters change within different contexts.

In any event, we have to consider the following:

- Characters invite us to see ourselves or meet new friends.
- Settings invite us into new worlds or help us see that our world can be universal.
- Conflict invites us into others' struggles and helps us realize we are not alone in our struggles.

All three aspects are integral to our interest and reading enjoyment. We want to find characters who are like us, who share our struggles, harkening back to *Windows, Mirrors, and Sliding Glass Doors* (Sims, 1990). Whether the fantasy of Hogwarts or the familiarity of the town you know or are from, as my students feel about *Paper Things*

(Jacobson, 2017) or *Crashing Into Love* (Jacobson, 2022), the setting has a strong impact on how we interact and visualize text. Last, we are drawn to drama. Conflicts excite us and keep us engaged. What fun is a book with no drama? Eventually, maturing readers will realize that Tracking Literary Elements influences their perceptions about a text and their comprehension.

I introduce tracking with the use of a matrix. Using large chart paper, I make a matrix with four headings: **Chapter, Characters, Setting,** and **Conflict** (Figure 5.1). You may recall something similar in our 30 Books in 30 Days read aloud strategy. Tracking, in this case, is specific to a single text rather than comparing and contrasting a number of texts. Students use their own version of the matrix to follow along (see the digital resources). Lessons are typically sequenced over a week.

5.1 Tracking Literary Elements Matrix

Chapter	Characters	Setting	Conflicts

I prefer to start our shared read with a biography, such as *George Crum: Inventor of the Saratoga Chip* (Taylor, 2006) or *Nacho's Nachos: The Story Behind the World's Favorite Snack* (Nickels, 2020). I choose biographies like this because they have unfamiliar personalities that are connected to things we love (food) and conflicts that we recognize within ourselves and our own experiences. On day one, we begin with characters. Using the common text, I read the text aloud initially, as we write down the names of the main characters involved. I record the information on chart paper, and the students record the same information in their graphic organizers, known as a *Literary Elements Matrix* (see Figure 5.2). At the end of the reading, we review who is involved and recount their role in the story.

5.2 ***George Crum and the Saratoga Chip*** **Tracking Literary Elements Matrix**

Characters	Description	Setting	Conflict(s)
George Crum	He was a nervous and anxious person who was easily frustrated. He loved to cook and experiment with food. He wanted to be a cook in Saratoga Springs. Famous for cooking wild game and fish. Didn't tolerate bad customers. Lost his patience with customers over time. He started up his own restaurant based on the popularity of his chips.		
Kate Crum	Helped keep George's temper in check. Encouraged George and was his best friend (and sister).		
"French Fry" Woman	Ordered French fries and complained they were too thick. She fell in love with the potato experiment George created.		

During the second day, I introduce the setting. I reveal variations of settings using an inverted pyramid from "broad" to "most precise" (see Figure 5.3). We start by discussing the broad terms of a setting, which could be a country or a time period, like Middle Earth or the Dark Ages. The inverted pyramid suggests to readers that an author will "zoom in" on the setting as the narrative moves along. I also begin to gradually remove myself since I've already read the text once. On this occasion, I read a page of the text modeling how and where I found the setting. At the end of the page, I pause to jot down the settings. Students continue as I read the text, but they highlight where the settings exist in the passage. The following day, we revisit what a setting is by reviewing the inverted pyramid. During the third reading, students work together to find more explicit, less evident settings.

5.3 Settings Pyramid

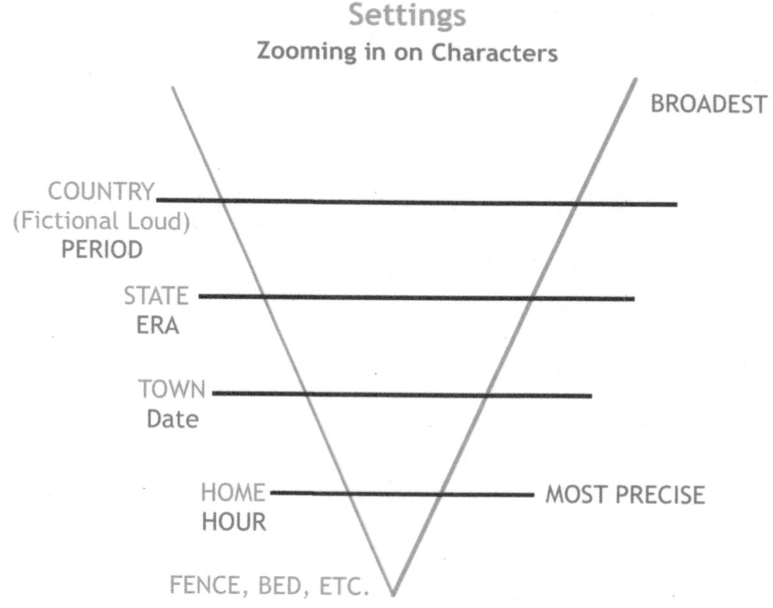

Our discussion of conflicts encompasses two more days. First, I introduce what a conflict is. Often it is easy to make generalizations about the conflict, but the idea is to find evidence in the text that defines things like internal struggles and arguments between characters. After the lesson, again, I read the first few pages to locate and highlight where the explicit conflicts are within the text. Also, like with settings, we stop after a few pages to record what information we've uncovered. From there, students read the text highlighting the evident conflicts. It's in these deliberate actions where students begin to realize that conflicts are connected with settings rather than randomized problems that a character faces.

To end the discussion of literary elements, I demonstrate how conflicts are more often than not inferred, which means students have to determine where conflicts might be.

After I've concluded, students read the books for themselves looking for the implied conflicts, or conflicts that are not explicitly stated, but they recognize a similar experience. In the end, when students have entered their conflicts into the matrix, we discuss what was discovered.

Affective Annotations

Affective reading is traditionally defined as a mix of reading attitudes, interests, and motivations (Cramer & Castle, 1994; Guthrie & Wigfield, 1997, 2000; Vaughn & Fisher, 2020; Žolgar-Jerković et al., 2018). You might find it odd or presumptuous that I redefine affective reading within a context of strategic reading.

Maybe it's become second nature to us because of the text-based world we live in, but affective responses are an everyday part of our world. Think about all the ways we can share our emotions in response to something on social media or even text messages—we can like, love, care about, laugh at, and even express shock—all using emojis.

With respect to affective reading, we should consider a few things (Bassett et al., 2020). Interest and motivation have strong links to pleasure reading and comprehension (Krashen, 2004, 2011). So, what happens when students lose interest because of negative reading experiences, increased volume of complex text, reading assignments, and testing or negative self-perception? Without support or attention to dispositions, as text complexity and demands increase, we lose readers (Biancarosa & Snow, 2006; Gallagher, 2010; Hall, 2011). As readers transition from primary grades into intermediate and middle grades, which Reoperez (2019) defines as "the stage where they will be needing advanced literacy skills to be able to cope with the challenges of content reading, which is the thrust of the tertiary level curriculum," we need to provide readers with a reading process that scaffolds "coping with difficult text."

Without support or attention to dispositions, as text complexity and demands increase, we lose readers.

Affect Theory and Its Significance for Readers

Foundational shame researcher Tomkins (1965) introduced the phenomenology known as *Affect Theory.* Tompkins asserts that our bodies respond to certain stimuli (Nathanson, 1992) causing a visible response. Beers (2003) clues us into the affect of struggling readers with her book *When Kids Can't Read.* Children blush, hang their heads, or hide behind mama. Readers slump, withdraw under hoodies, or lay their heads down. When considering affect, students reveal a physical or emotional response while they are reading. This is observed as frustration, facial discoloration, discomfort sitting in a single place, or silence. All are cues to something internal, which is likely impeding comprehension. Carrying this knowledge into the classroom, I can *see* readers respond to a text, more so than they see (or feel) for themselves.

I might have lost Lucia by the end of December had I not provided her with a new way of engaging with text. Tracking worked, for sure. But even Lucia knew there had to be more to reading than simply marking down evidence of literary elements. The problem was that Lucia had no observable affect—no physical or emotional response, as I discussed at the beginning of this chapter. She was reading enough to retell and even answer questions appropriately, but she still wasn't enjoying reading, nor was she moved by any experiences. I needed to set her up to explore a text on a deeper level but on her terms before those of anyone else.

Borrowing from Clay's (1995) *Observational Survey,* I watched Lucia's affect as she read aloud from her current book, *Letters from Cuba* (Behar, 2021). She read the following line: "You had no choice but to leave Poland to find work and take care of all of us" (p. 2).

After she finished the page, I stopped her.

I asked her, "Lucia, did you feel your face shift!"

She acknowledged a sensation.

"What did you feel?"

"I felt kinda funny. I felt sad 'cause he had to leave, but I'm just supposed to read the book, so I shouldn't feel sad."

Mr. Stygles: "Great! Yes! You should feel something! You know what I call that?"

(Continued)

(Continued)

Lucia:	"No."
Mr. Stygles:	"I call that an 'affective response.' This means, you're letting your emotions and your thoughts guide you through your reading. When you feel it, you should pause just enough to jot the codes we've been talking about in class."
Lucia:	"Really, Mr. Stygles? That's going to slow me down."
Mr. Stygles:	"I know!!! It may slow you down, but it will also help you remember more!"

After the conversation, I told her, "You know, I can see when you're having trouble with a book." She didn't like that. (This is unwanted exposure or undesired vulnerability.) More, Lucia didn't like when I asked her what was going on. We both knew she had no idea. No evidence of any interactions appeared. So she'd give me the "Lucia stare." Apparently, by staring, Lucia presumed she could ward me off as if I had asked a ridiculous question, or worse, had the nerve to intrude on a secret she didn't want known. (She already knew how to use affect in her favor!) I didn't need her to tell me she was struggling. Body language and facial expressions said it all. Since I couldn't guess what was in Lucia's head, she needed to share her thoughts with me. This would be impossible, though, if she didn't trust me enough to teach her. To help Lucia read, I had to prove to her that she could see herself in text and that she could interact with a text meaningfully based on her own perceptions.

To help Lucia read, I had to prove to her that she could see herself in text and that she could interact with a text meaningfully based on her own perceptions.

I believe this is important because watching facial expressions and body language signals a child's inner plea for help or escape. A lack of affect suggests platitude or ambivalence. Compliant readers often show little affect. They recall the gist but often struggle with close reading. Nonetheless, maturing readers lack the ability to determine how and what their peers comprehend. All they know is a difference (or assumption). Their peers "get it," and they don't.

Feeling different than their peers often produces shame by inducing negative self-awareness and reinforcing negative self-evaluations.

Using Affective Annotations With Students

Have you ever been reading a book and shouted out loud? Ever been angry for days after reading? I have. I don't know about you, but the feeling of comprehension is, to me, the heartbeat of reading. It breaks my heart to see how many readers have never experienced *emotion* in their own reading. Perhaps the most important aspect of a reading process I seek to support students with is their emotional response to text. Using Affective Annotations, readers have a chance to embark on the world of close reading through a series of symbols, or codes, that help readers "place themselves" within the text.

Affective annotations combine physical affect with well-known symbols to invite close reading (Kissner, 2006; Owocki, 2003; Serafini & Youngs, 2007; Wormeli, 2005). Lapp et al. (2012) point out that close reading is intended to help students "readily undertake the close, attentive reading that is at the heart of understanding and enjoying complex works of literature" (p. 2). With affective coding, I'm not asking students to simply mark a symbol in a text but rather to indicate an interaction or identification with the text through a visible physical response. A feeling. Readers deserve to *feel* the text as a pathway to comprehension.

So often we hear that annotating or strategic reading kills the joy of reading. Students often express frustration because it "slows their reading down" or interrupts "being sucked into the book," as one of my students once chided me. I can see their point, to an extent. That is, until the reader doesn't recall more than the gist or is otherwise indifferent to almost every book they read. Basically, if I don't see any indication of an emotional reaction to reading, I am concerned about just how engaged the reader was or how much they really comprehended within the text.

With that said, affective annotations, or codes, marked in a text can be a supportive habit for many readers, especially struggling readers. For once, readers get to experience how they are appreciated as individual readers and thinkers with a unique way to see the world. The goal is for students to feel comfortable annotating while they are independently reading. I strongly encourage all readers to experiment for a simple reason—I want to see how they think and feel while they read. I want to see who the reader is. But ultimately, the reader has the choice to incorporate strategies into their own unique, or gifted, reading process. Lucia said it best: "I mark what I am thinking on my sticky notes because I'm having my own conversation with the book." And with this, she began to discover herself as a reader.

Ultimately, the reader has the choice to incorporate strategies into their own unique, or gifted, reading process.

As with all my mini-units, I introduce every component through individual mini-lessons. Affective annotation instruction generally lasts 2 weeks. I introduce a new symbol each day. Lessons include the introduction of the symbol and the intent of the symbol—the notation of a specific physiological or emotional response. Each lesson includes a read aloud (see Chapter 3).

During the second week, we revisit the symbols during review lessons. At this time, readers have multiple opportunities to experiment with affective coding on the same text we started the week before or a short new text to further transfer learning. If, in the end, students require more instruction, I make time for a guided reading group for an additional week or two, outside of the mini-lesson model described here. At this point, I encourage students to begin marking the codes within the margins of the text. There are rules, of course. Students almost always gasp when I say they can write in my books because they've learned that writing in books is forbidden. That's fine. I respect the values they come from, which means we have alternatives.

1. If Mr. Stygles bought the book, you can write in the book. (Other kids will get to see what you've coded, which makes reading a shared experience.)
2. If the book comes from home, ask your parents. (It helps to show them how the codes help you understand and monitor your comprehension.)
3. If the book comes from the school or public library, please do not write in it! Use sticky notes instead. (We must respect the values of others.)

If students struggle to remember the annotation symbols, allow them to create a bookmark to reference while they are reading. This helps students incorporate coding into their reading process.

4. If the book belongs to the school, use sticky notes. (It's just best. These books must last for years to come. But leave (a few of) your sticky notes in the text. Maybe it may help the next reader?!)

5.4 Reading Emojis (Fiction): A Guide for Teachers

Emoji		Affective Response	Literary Purpose
Question Mark		Confusion	Rereading, clarifying, questioning, vocabulary
Star		Seriousness	Importance, recalling, summarizing, analyzing theme, making inferences
Exclamation Point		Excitement	Analyzing theme, making inferences, analyzing resolutions, examining plot twists
Heart		Happiness	Making connections, making inferences, analyzing resolutions
Smiley Face		Curiosity	Self-monitoring, making connections, analyzing literal comprehension

5.5 Reading Emojis Example (Fiction)

5.6 Reading Emojis (Nonfiction): Sample Anchor Chart

Nonfiction Emojis			Affective Response
Moral attributes (virtuous), good ethics, positive outcomes. Advocacy, connecting to personal values. I agree with the author. Interesting fact. I'm glad I learned that.			Sad, wish it was different Something unfortunate Disagreeable, not interesting
Good aspects, evokes a smile, positive qualities. Indicates or maintains interest. Makes me feel good. Attributes of a hero.			Broken hearted, offensive Shouldn't have happened Meanness
This is amazing! I can't believe it. Awesome!	!		Mind blowing, a lot to handle TMI
What the author wants to know. The most important takeaways. Things others need to know. I didn't know that! That's surprising.			I can't do this anymore, it's too much to handle This is much more than I am ready to learn May be inappropriate I wish I didn't learn about this Horrible
I am not following. Things are confusing.	?	?	I just don't get it I can't make sense of anything Too hard

Emojis from iStock.com/jangultun, bortonia, alano design

Question marks serve an array of purposes in strategic reading. Ozckus (2010), for instance, promotes the use of the question mark to indicate clarifying when using reciprocal teaching. Concerning affect, we can see from a distance when kids should scribe question marks in their text or on a sticky note. The reader's face contorts. Some cover or press both hands against their faces. When this happens, thinking is visible through affect. They are manifesting internalizations like, "I don't understand what this word (or phrase) means?" "I don't understand what is happening?" and/or "Why did the author write like this?"

Exclamation points indicate the "Ha-ha! I was right" or "Oh snap, no she didn't!" moments of surprise readers love. These are moments where students are excited. It's not unusual to hear a reader slap a table, bolt from their table to find me, or plain jump out of their seat when something good happens. Moments where exclamation marks can be ascribed are when readers turn to each other showing what they just read, be it a joke or something incredible.

Hearts indicate something interesting or lovely or a part that grabs your attention most. Students might turn flush in their face, sneak a small smile, maybe even cry. Other readers might show a sigh of relief or an exhale of contentedness. When reading biographies, students might notice something valiant about the hero or a fact they really love in other nonfiction. A heart represents the "heart of reading" because it shows the true investment of the reader on a personal level. Thus, when moments appeal to the reader on a deeply moving, emotional level, I ask students to annotate their margins with a heart. It's not hard to imagine those texts with the most hearts are ones that rank among readers' favorites.

Stars give students a symbol for noting something as important—the theme or key takeaway. The lessons learned. The determination of importance can be personal or related to reading skills. How the reader marks the text provides another indication of how information is processed and prioritized. Commonly, readers express a sense of relief or understanding when a star can be noted. A sense of relaxation settles over them. We gain a sense of how the reader perceives their text and the uniqueness of their thinking, what they consider to be important.

Smile emojis are for places in the text that are funny and heartwarming. A smile expressed while reading begets the smiley face. Humor keeps us reading. Humor can also be an indication of figurative language. When we know how the reader is handling humor, we can gain a better sense of the reader's affective engagement, which later becomes comprehension. Smiles are a little less than hearts but distinctive because good parts keep readers motivated.

5.7 Application of Affective Coding—Emojis

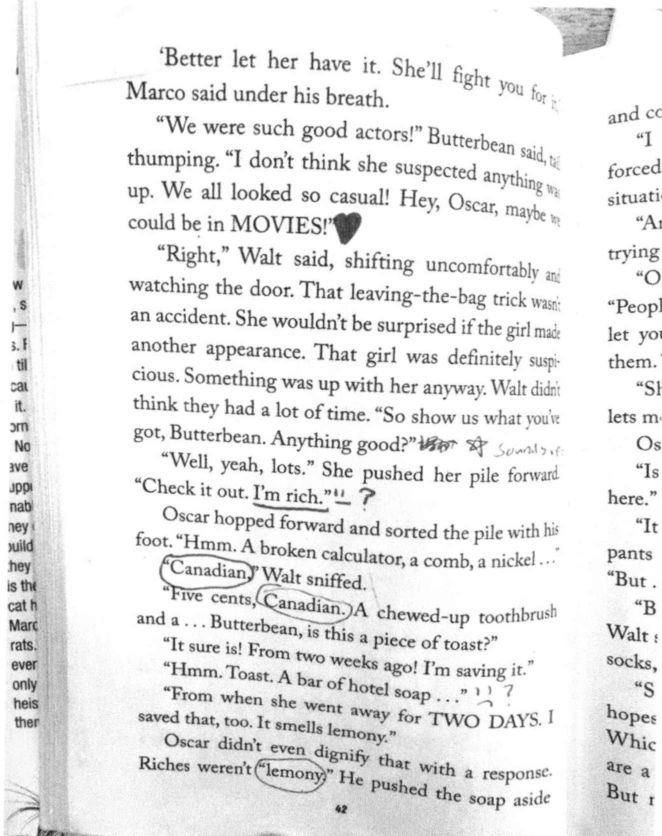

'Better let her have it. She'll fight you for it,' Marco said under his breath.

"We were such good actors!" Butterbean said, tail thumping. "I don't think she suspected anything was up. We all looked so casual! Hey, Oscar, maybe we could be in MOVIES!"

"Right," Walt said, shifting uncomfortably and watching the door. That leaving-the-bag trick wasn't an accident. She wouldn't be surprised if the girl made another appearance. That girl was definitely suspicious. Something was up with her anyway. Walt didn't think they had a lot of time. "So show us what you've got, Butterbean. Anything good?"

"Well, yeah, lots." She pushed her pile forward. "Check it out. I'm rich."

Oscar hopped forward and sorted the pile with his foot. "Hmm. A broken calculator, a comb, a nickel . . ."

"Canadian," Walt sniffed.

"Five cents, Canadian. A chewed-up toothbrush and a . . . Butterbean, is this a piece of toast?"

"It sure is! From two weeks ago! I'm saving it."

"Hmm. Toast. A bar of hotel soap . . ."

"From when she went away for TWO DAYS. I saved that, too. It smells lemony."

Oscar didn't even dignify that with a response. Riches weren't "lemony." He pushed the soap aside

42

Annotating Other Affective Responses

Negative Annotations: Annotations to denote negative feelings are invited as well. This is not something introduced right away and hopefully comes more as a result of the reader's discovery than my deliberate instruction. An example is when a student reaches a sad moment in a piece of text. For example, in Figures 5.5 and 5.7, we can see how readers added a second column. Our maturing readers are shockingly in-tune to negatives. Some are more apt to use more negative emojis, which communicates to us a message about their perceptions of the world and sense-of-self. During the mini-lesson, readers (not surprisingly my most discontent ones) will ask me what should be done if they don't feel happy but rather angry, upset, or irritated. Depending on the extent of the emotion and what best represents the reader, we have a range of symbols including tear drops, sad faces, broken hearts, or *stop* because the reader can't go on.

Unnamed Annotations: At times, students have affective responses to texts that I have not described here or haven't anticipated as a teacher. For instance, I've never come up with an annotation to represent the antithesis to a question or something that isn't important (such as already known information), or an annotation to represent information that is in contrast to current or previous understanding. Students don't adhere strictly to the codes I present in the lesson because it's important to give space to the reader to create their own system. We are best served to let readers mine these discoveries and feel the way they will on their own. The reward is that students are expressing themselves through their own codes within the text.

Even though Lucia didn't find many "good" books, she was able to find moments by marking the annotation. In such cases, I knew she was more equipped to decide on the value of a book rather than simply quitting (see Chapter 3). I taught Lucia that not every book is good, nor do you have to like the book. That doesn't mean there aren't moments that make you laugh or smile. For example, I recall once Lucia complained her book, *Walk Two Moons* (Creech, 1994), was dragging. She just couldn't get interested. Then it happened. She found out who Mike was. Lucia flipped. She carved an exclamation point into the side of the book. Slowing down to read paid off. At another point, Lucia had an epiphany of sorts when she realized she could find Words of Wisdom (Beers & Probst, 2013) on her own, not just in the lesson. She wrapped stars around the sentence "I'm sure everyone here will judge you on the merit of your character . . ." while reading an advance reader copy of *How to Completely Disappear* by Ali Standish (2020). "Mr. Stygles," she said, "I'm confused by what 'merit of your character' means, but I think this is important, so I'm asking you."

These are the interactions I love to have with students. Maybe she didn't completely understand what she was reading, but she was responsive to the signals in her body. I asked her what she thought it meant. After she gave a thoughtful clarification, I complimented her work as a thinker, as an annotator, and a risk-taker.

Within a few months, the tide shifted. Lucia read *The Bridge Home* (Venkatraman, 2019) and requested a conference. She took me page by page, note by note to show her thinking (see Figure 5.8). She was proud, not of the quantity of annotations, but that she could recount the story with less trepidation than in the past. I asked, "Lucia, what's the difference this time?"

5.8 Lucia's Text (combination of annotations and codes)

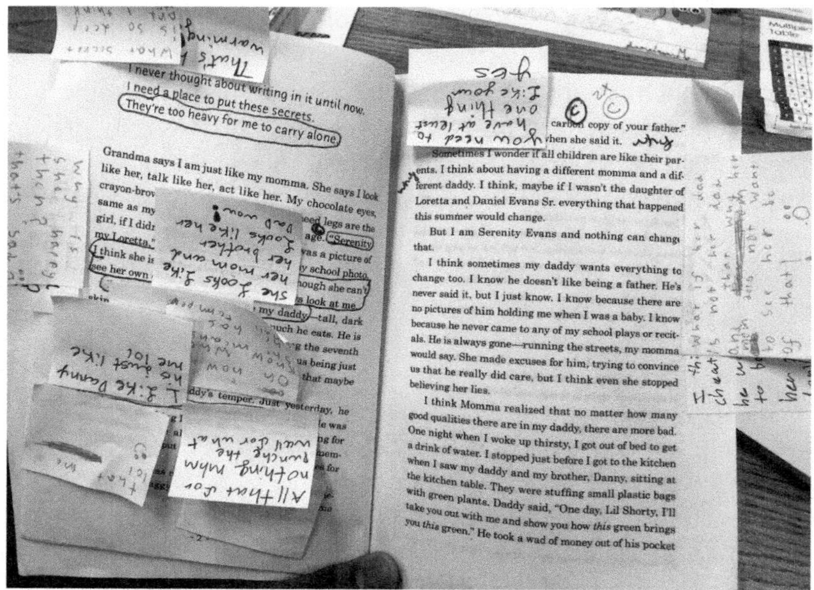

I never thought about writing in it until now.
I need a place to put these secrets.
They're too heavy for me to carry alone.

Grandma says I am just like my momma. She says I look like her, talk like her, act like her. My chocolate eyes,

carbon copy of your father."
when she said it.

Sometimes I wonder if all children are like their parents. I think about having a different momma and a different daddy. I think, maybe if I wasn't the daughter of Loretta and Daniel Evans Sr. everything that happened this summer would change.

But I am Serenity Evans and nothing can change that.

I think sometimes my daddy wants everything to change too. I know he doesn't like being a father. He's never said it, but I just know. I know because there are no pictures of him holding me when I was a baby. I know because he never came to any of my school plays or recitals. He is always gone—running the streets, my momma would say. She made excuses for him, trying to convince us that he really did care, but I think even she stopped believing her lies.

I think Momma realized that no matter how many good qualities there are in my daddy, there are more bad. One night when I woke up thirsty, I got out of bed to get a drink of water. I stopped just before I got to the kitchen when I saw my daddy and my brother, Danny, sitting at the kitchen table. They were stuffing small plastic bags with green plants. Daddy said, "One day, Lil Shorty, I'll take you out with me and show you how *this* green brings you *this* green." He took a wad of money out of his pocket

"Well, my mom made me reread it because when I read it the first time, I didn't remember anything that happened. She said I should use my strategies like you told me to. So I did. And look, I remember so much more now!"

I followed up with, "It took you more time to read, didn't it?

"Yeah, I didn't like that because I couldn't finish the book in a week."

"What matters most? Finishing the book in a week or having a quality reading experience?" I asked, seeking to merge two different reading values.

"Reading a book slowly so it makes sense! I actually liked a book this time!" Lucia concluded, leaving with a bounce in her step.

Clarifying: A Pathway to Meaning

There is more to reading than just knowing words. It's about how words are used and the meaning of those words that construct a larger meaning for us. Maturing readers seem to possess a misconception about reading. They often believe that decoding, as a meaning-making strategy (Weaver, 2009), is the same as clarifying. Most readers are aloof to the idea that clarifying is actually about determining the meaning of a word (or phrase or figurative language), often in context (Scanlon & Anderson, 2020) or morphologically (Carlisle, 2010), not just about how to pronounce the word! They've internalized word knowledge as being able to decode—to say a word accurately. Therefore, clarifying is an essential strategy where students think to themselves: (1) I can read this word, but I don't know what it means or (2) I've never seen this word before, and I need to figure it out. After all, readers are trying to identify the right word and create meaning. But there's a very murky distinction of what it means to *know* a word. Brinchmann et al. (2020) discuss the relevance of how word knowledge, as in meanings and applications, becomes prominent during the intermediate years. As a result, I've found that reading can only grow vocabulary if two things happen: (1) words are attended to, and (2) students have a vested interest in expanding their vocabularies and developing word consciousness (Scott & Nagy, 2009).

I show students that solving words helps me understand the text better and enjoy reading more.

We have to recognize that shame in reading is directly linked to literacy development (Wolf et al., 2007), language development (Nathanson, 2004), and vocabulary acquisition. To ensure that our students are ready for the rigors of academic vocabulary and incidental word learning (Beck et al., 2002; Lowell et al., 2019), we must equip them with tools, like clarifying, that will ensure perseverance and resiliency for our maturing readers.

I typically focus exclusively on clarifying for about a week using the gradual release of responsibility model (Pearson & Gallagher, 1983). In most cases, I use books, short stories, or passages from texts that are challenging to a reader but aren't so overwhelming where students are circling half the words. I've been known to use antiquated texts during a read aloud, simply to show readers that I, too, need to clarify with certain texts. (I don't believe in patronizing students, which is a shame transfer, by acting like I don't know words at their reading level. They don't appreciate the mockery either.) I've also used research studies or veterinary books, topics I'm interested in and have to study, to show them that, even in reading I enjoy, I have to "work at" words differently than I might while pleasure reading. I show them that solving words helps me understand the text better and enjoy reading more.

To teach students to clarify, I introduce an array of prompts over a sequence of a few lessons.

1. Identify a new word and look for the meaning within the text by circling it.
2. If you're unsure of a word in print, but recognize it from listening, do you remember the meaning?
3. If you can pronounce the word but don't know the meaning, can you make a guess?
4. If the word is new, can you read "around" it to see if you can figure it out from context?
5. If the word is new, what word parts do you recognize? Using those word parts, can you guess what the word means?
6. Substitute in a word you know for a word you don't know. Does it work? Could it be a synonym?
7. If the word is completely unfamiliar, use a Google Image search to help generalize a possible meaning.

Next, I back the lesson up with a read aloud to raise awareness of words within a text (Ray, 2012). Following the read aloud, we move into shared reading. Shared reading is used after lessons for all six strategies, then again to practice clarifying realizing that different strategies will need to be employed at different times for different reasons.

After practicing as a whole group through read aloud and shared reading (Bigelman & Petersen, 2016), readers interact independently (Graves et al., 2017) using the same text we've been working on, before transferring this learning to their independent reading. The reward? Word consciousness becomes a mirror of success and encourages agency.

Through this process, the students who struggle with competition or perfectionism suddenly don't feel so isolated. They look around the room to discover they aren't alone in needing to learn words and learning words is a part of the reading process. We are now reaching a point where we are collecting enough new vocabulary to read the text a second time, surely to be a more powerful experience despite the challenge of the previous endeavor.

Conferring again with Lucia, we shifted our focus to her independent reading, I asked her to circle words that were new or unfamiliar. I was scaffolding her word consciousness. In doing so, Lucia became more comfortable, acknowledging, "Hey, I don't know this." She was becoming resilient by converting what could have been an embarrassment into vulnerability. By becoming more conscious, she developed confidence and competence.

Within our reading conference, she trusted me enough that she didn't have to overcompensate or hide the truth when she didn't know for fear of losing respect, losing a desired social position, making a mistake, or worse, falling out of favor. Now I could work with her to prompt word learning in places she was stuck (Rodgers, 2016). In this case, Lucia continued reading, circling all the words she didn't know. I congratulated her for her honesty and risk-taking. She identified six words on her own. I could have pressed Lucia for more but chose to stick with what she acknowledged. Continuing in our conference, we took time to clarify and attempt to make meaning from new words.

Empathy and Identification: Seeing Yourself in a Text

Every year I have a student or two who ask me, "Why does everything in reading have to be happy?" It's a fair question if you think about it. From read alouds in the primary years to the endings of stories in middle-grade novels, aren't books overwhelmingly happy? Even conflicts don't create anxiety or fear because everything works out in the end. Of course, we know our own worlds to be very different, especially in the context of shame.

Lucia was student one who asked me this question. She'd finished reading *The Benefits of Being an Octopus* (Braden, 2017), a story of a pre-teen Vermonter who assumes a parenting role to support her mother (a virtual Alice Miller shame archetype) while trying to balance school and friends. She marched into our classroom on an overcast Wednesday morning as school started and, without even a wince, she chucked the book into the book return basket. I noticed her snarled face, which invited me to ask, "What's going on? Why are you tossing the book into the basket?"

Lucia:	"I hate it!"
Mr. Stygles:	"Why?"
Lucia:	"It's stupid!!"
Mr. Stygles:	"Ok, why?"
Lucia:	"'Cause it's not real."
Mr. Stygles:	"That's true. But isn't a lot of fiction grounded in real-life events?"
Lucia:	"Yes, and this one is, except for *the end*."
Mr. Stygles:	"What do you mean?"
Lucia:	"Look, Mr. Stygles. This book is completely fake. I know some kids have it hard and they can't control what happens in their life or what parents do. I know. That's how my life goes. In this book, she has to make decisions for her mother. Then she finds a way for her family to escape by making her family go and live with her friend and her mother in a single room apartment. That's so stupid! That's not how it actually works. That's not what happens in my life. You know how many times DHHS has come to my house? My story is never happy."

Lucia's affective response—snarled face—is a manifestation of her interactions with text—one she needed to express (At least she showed emotion! How many others just read with no emoting?). Her contempt stemmed from an empathetic connection with the main character, Zoey. Lucia noticed that she shared similarities with Zoey, with one major exception—her story would not end like Zoey's. Lucia's response was authentic. My job was to notice her.

Bishop (1990) wrote,

> Those of us who are children's literature enthusiasts tend to be somewhat idealistic, believing that some book, some poem can speak to each child and that if we have the time and resources, we can find that book and help to change that's child's life, if only for a brief time, and only for a tiny bit. On the other hand, we are realistic enough to know that literature, no matter how powerful, has its limits.

The catch is that many times we unintentionally force readers to find themselves within a book. We ask readers to be empathetic to a character or a biographical figure, without any real understanding of who the reader is for themselves. I know Bishop isn't talking about shame. Still, her statement fits the negative internalizations children see about themselves and are not allowed to identify with or articulate. A text indeed has limits. The limits represent to which extent maturing readers are allowed to identify and explore themselves or to demonstrate feelings of empathy, without forsaking their unique thoughts or feelings based on their perspectives, which are often compromised for "correct" responses to comprehension questions. The limits were that the book was fiction, and her life was reality.

Lucia's comprehension lies in her affect, the physical expression of her emotions. Sometimes all students want us to do is to value and respect their experience with a text, to be noticed, to have someone to express their feelings to, and to understand why they can feel such deep empathy with a character and/or situation or none at all. That's when reading becomes meaningful.

Brown (2010) defines empathy as, "I get it, I feel with you, I've been there" (p. 10). Empathy, therefore, as an explicit interaction with text, must be reader specific, not teacher driven. Shame-bound individuals often have a difficult time recognizing the plight of others. Yet it's common to expect students to feel or recognize empathy for a character without experiencing compassion for the reader's own bevy of circumstances.

Shame-bound individuals often have a difficult time recognizing the plight of others.

When I asked Lucia if she felt empathy toward the character's situation, she glared at me. "I don't like talking about empathy because it makes me angry." I was intrigued.

"Mr. Stygles! Do you know what it's like when you can't do your homework because you have to take care of your brother? Do you know what it's like to not have friends because you have to go to your mom's work after school? I hate when we move to different places!"

The empathy was there. So was the heartbreak. Lucia deserved every reason in the world to show her affective response to the text as her pathway in reading. Empathy cannot be contrived. It has to be experienced. We have to give our readers space to express themselves.

Empathy cannot be contrived. It has to be experienced. We have to give our readers space to express themselves.

Empathetic Connections

When I first teach about empathy, I ask students to share what they know about it. Many say things like "feel what someone else feels" or "be in their shoes." After that, I explain that we can consider empathy using a piece of text, as we think about the context of the characters and their trials in conjunction with our own experiences. On the surface, there are morally and ethically correct ways to treat people. There is also a deeper connection we can make where we can identify with someone or a character because we've lived that experience. Sharing personal examples of times I've felt empathy after reading different novels, I end by telling them that empathy is not about a right or wrong way to feel but rather how we connect with characters because we've been there. We see ourselves in the characters, which means we are not alone.

Empathetic Connections: Lesson 1 Coding With "ME"

One children's book that I like to use to discuss empathy is titled *Unicorn Thinks He's Pretty Great* (Shea, 2013). It's an easy read to introduce the idea of empathy annotations, and it invites students to think deeply about their own experiences with frenemies. The idea is not to assess students' ability to think using a lower-level text but rather to comfortably introduce readers to the strategy before application in future shared readings with grade-level texts, in guided reading groups, and ultimately, before transferring into independent reading.

Building off the concept of mirrors, windows, and sliding glass doors, "me" is a distinct annotation where students identify a portion of text that represents them, positively or negatively. Much like affective coding, I teach students to mark their text (in the margin or using a sticky note) with a circled "me," a code that indicates the reader has made potentially meaningful connections with the text (McGregor, 2007; Miller, 2002). While a student is reading, they simply jot "me" by the sentence or paragraph as a reference point. At this point, I'm not concerned with students explaining self-to-text connections in as much as I know the students are staking landmarks in their reading. The codes merely represent connections or staging points to reveal empathy.

Empathetic Connections: Lesson 2 Summarizing

The second phase of this instruction encourages students to stop after reading to summarize. Students often push back on this at first because I'm changing their expectations of independent reading. At the end of our independent reading time, I ask students to revisit their reading. They jot down in their own words how "me" was represented in the text. This summary can be as simple as writing on a sticky note or a page in their Reading Response Journal, with bullet points that outline how the reader saw themselves in the text. By providing students time to think after reading in the classroom, I am hoping they will transfer the process to their own reading environments.

Empathetic Connections: Lesson 3 Empathizing

The third and final phase of empathetic annotations (see Figure 5.9) is a dedicated reflection. After students summarize the moments of self-reflection in text, I use a portion of our instructional time to launch writing about reading (see more in Chapter 7). At this point, readers again revisit their text and complete the first two columns of the chart for each circled "me."

Finally, I ask students how they empathize. The empathy encourages readers to explain how they would empathize with the character because they've experienced something similar. They write about those thoughts in the third column of the chart. In the case of *Unicorn Thinks He's Pretty Great* (Shea, 2013), students can empathize with either character. Some believe Unicorn is treated poorly because he isn't accepted as the newbie. A majority of students empathize with Goat. Take Lucia's response, "I empathize with Goat because he [Unicorn] was toxic and wanted to be the best at everything." Although her response lacks specificity, which she and I agree to work on together over time, Lucia has a basic sense in knowing what it's like to have someone be better at everything. Ultimately, the stage is set for longer written responses and conversations about the text, which is soon to follow.

5.9 Empathetic Annotation Template

Empathetic Connections

Page	How is this like me?	Why I empathize?

5.10 Ryleigh's Empathic Connections

Empathetic Connections

Unicorn Thinks He's Pretty Great

Page	How is ______ like me?	Why I empathize?
1	once my friend moved into my school and things were alot diffrend.	I empathize because things were alot diffrent because I really had no one to play with but then I didn't because my friend moved to my school.
2	When I rode my bike to school because I had never done it before.	I empathize because once I rode my bike to school and I felt so cool because it was my first time.
3	Everyone has that friend who is a really big showoff.	I empasithed because I thought that everyone has that friend who is a showoff.
4		
5	my friend thought that she was "so" good at bakeing and I felt left out.	I empasiced because I thought of that friend who is really good at bakeing and apolontally that I'm not.
6	I always have that one talent that I do when I am at a talent show.	I empasiced because whenever I am at a talent show I always do that talent.

Final Thoughts

We have to understand how, what, and why readers think or see the world as they do. We cannot entice students to be empathic if we do not understand them first. When we understand their perceptions—making the reader first—we can then introduce our readers to new ideas or ways of thinking. We may not agree or understand how students think, but by expressing our interests in their perceptions (above our own), we can lead them to better understanding of the world.

Similarly, we have to understand our reader's capacities. The transition from a passive reading for pleasure purpose that readers are accustomed to entering the intermediate and middle grades should be handled delicately. For one, teaching a student to "stop and jot" when they have internalized passive reading since first grade is difficult. Next, students are not yet developed enough to balance the pressure of having to read for a period of time while making rapid progress through a book, all the while jotting down instances that are meaningful to them. Finally, reading (and annotating) is just as much physiological as it is cognitive. A lot goes into play before students can simply annotate or become close readers. We have to be empathetic so our readers can show their empathy.

We have to be empathetic so our readers can show their empathy.

Researchers like Paulo Freire (1970) inform us that the reader has to explore their identity and their perceptions to understand how they see the world. This, in turn, begins to create a space for readers to consider empathy as a means for *feeling* and understanding the circumstances of others. Maturing readers deserve to have frequent, positive, meaningful interactions they can call their own. The frequency of seeing one's competence in a small group encourages them to the development of identity, agency, and positive self-perception; students deserve the chance to evaluate characters through their own perceptions and celebrate the uniqueness of internal thinking, associations, and connections.

When I first met Lucia, she didn't possess an ability to enjoy reading. Her desire was squelched. She'd fallen short of her own ideals, noting she didn't read anything like her friends. Nor did she use any reading strategies. *Lucky Broken Girl* (Behar, 2017), became a plea for help and the eventual turning point. After learning affective coding and annotations, her attitude changed. Later, Lucia asked to confer about her new book, *Slider* (Hautman, 2019).

I asked her right away, "How's the book?"

I didn't hear "good" or "fine." I heard, "It's hard."

"Why are you reading a hard book if you chose it?" I followed.

"Because Mr. Stygles. I'm finally getting it. See, I've been annotating. I know so much about this book. I'm not reading it fast, but I understand it. If I didn't use my strategies, there would be no way I could pay attention to what I am reading!"

Lucia was on her way to autonomy! If we are to consider shame-resilience, we cannot deny readers. We have to let students take risks and experiment (using our guidance within the interpersonal bridge) with a unique style of strategic processing and the ability to share successes. Autonomy cannot be manipulated or confined to blocks of time, but rather through a genuine partnership within the interpersonal bridge.

Reflect and Act

Use these reflection questions to consider the information shared in the chapter and how you can apply it in your own classroom.

1. What are your beliefs about independent reading? Should students be provided opportunities to engage with text, which might alter their understanding of "pleasure reading"?
2. What value is there in students monitoring their comprehension that might be new to your understanding?
3. Going forward, what ways can you help a reader re-engage with a book before they potentially miss out on a "good" book?

6

RETHINKING INTERVENTION

When It's Time to Go "Eye-to-Eye, Knee-to-Knee"

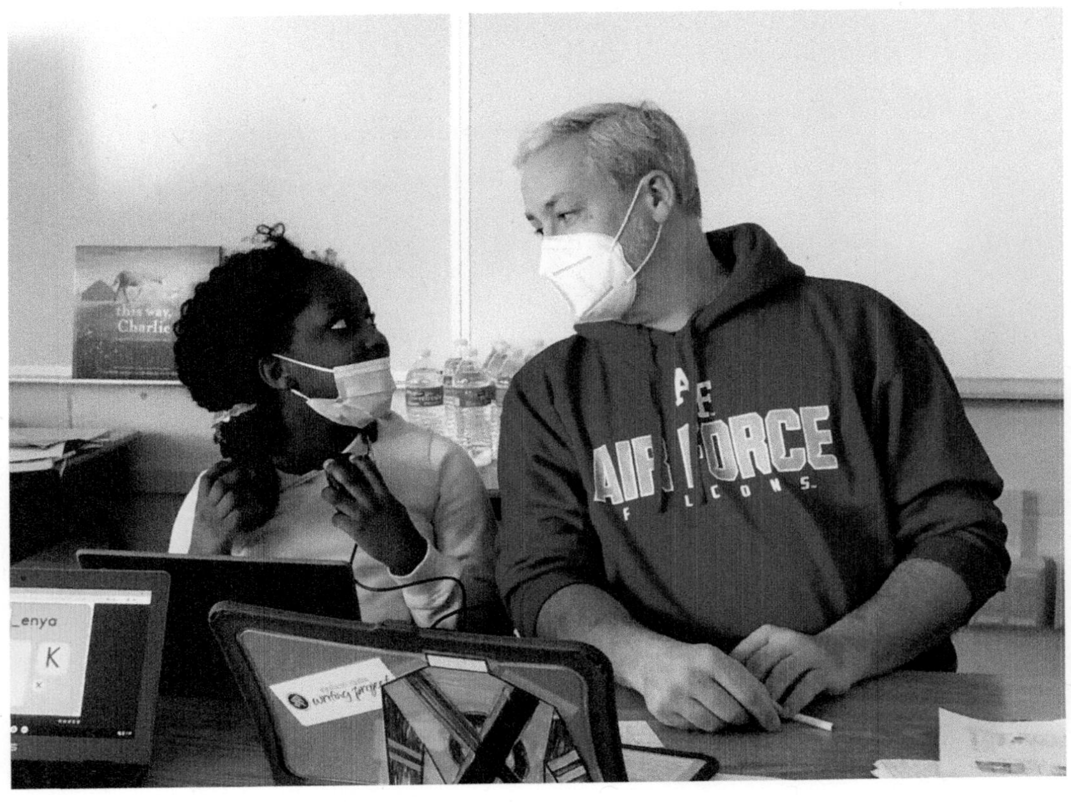

Did you ever experience a time where you felt like you're doing all the work for a reader? You've set up small groups. You've met in reading conferences. You've even walked by, tapped the kiddo on the shoulder and said, "Keep reading," "Stay on task," or "You're doing great!" No matter what, though, you sense a distance between you and your reader(s). I'll be the first to admit, in the midst of everything else we think about during a school day, it can be tough to recognize, or prioritize, the relationship between you and the readers in your classroom. If you're looking for a change, take a moment to look through the eyes of those "distant" readers. As maturing readers are beginning their journey into finding their unique identity, some students are apt to:

- Seek the same recognition as their peers
- Identify themselves as "good" readers
- Pretend to enjoy reading like you or other "favored" students

In other words, students try to be like others to gain attention. When students are unable to create their "self-concept" or are embattled with negative self-perception, they create distance as a means to avoid exposure of what they seemingly "cannot be."

Did you ever experience a time where you felt like you're doing all the work for a reader?

Our classrooms are inherently equipped with opportunities to compare, internalize, and measure self-worth—most of the time without even making it apparent! It's the only thing we, as educators, cannot control in the classroom—a student's internal thinking. Nor can we control how a student creates a valuation of themselves, or with what hypothesis. As a result, shame begins to be internalized. What students know is that since they are "different," *they are deficient*. A case scenario might include students affixed with a label (Smith et al., 2021): *at risk*, *struggling*, or even *striving* based on reading behaviors they may not be ready to articulate. From there, readers dissociate. Since they, perceptually, cannot read as well as their peers, or have been identified as a deficit, they attempt to become a reader they think will be accepted, thus disguising and avoiding whatever complications inhibit their abilities to manifest as joyful readers. Apathy ensues, which is a signal that the student is withdrawn and distant.

How can we fix this? You. Unlike other problems we face, the distance between some of our readers and us is mendable. Shame-bound students want someone to notice them, a mirror that reflects their goodness back, respects them for their current situation, and provides them the opportunity to develop new assets. In other words, when we take notice of them and explore the internal operations of the reader, we can help readers discover their true self-concept and build self-efficacy.

When there is distance, we must lean in. We must strengthen our dedication to the reader within the interpersonal bridge. The essential nature of our relationship is predicated on their feeling valued by us as a significant player in the relationship. As discussed previously (see Chapter 1), Kauffman (1993) calls this *mutuality of response*. In his words, "*mutuality of response* is indispensable to feel that one is in a real relation . . . feeling wanted for oneself" (p. 13). In other words, students don't want to be labels, identified by reading levels or test scores, or have their worth measured by the number of books they read (they aren't racehorses). They desire recognition based on their unique progress, achievements, and the broader development of identity, or sense of self, grounded in the significance of the students' whole being. We can enhance the mutuality of response through explicit, authentic interactions with students, focused on an outcome that reveals the readers unto themselves, more so than the outcomes (i.e., standards-based) someone else desires.

When there is distance, we must lean in. We must strengthen our dedication to the reader within the interpersonal bridge.

To understand others, to engage empathetically, we must examine ourselves as readers. If we teach reading, we need to be readers. We surround ourselves with readers and social media outlets that foster the image that *everyone* is reading in volume. That can be a hard mirror to look at for other reading teachers. For *we* are certainly readers, we just don't read as much. Among our other interests, attempts to maintain a work-life balance, and ever-changing demands in our classrooms, reading can get "lost in the sauce."

Our Reading Lives Play a Significant Role

I'm the first to admit that finding time to incorporate regular reading into my busy life is not always easy, albeit necessary. As links between students and the wider world of children's literature, we have the opportunity to engage in regular reading of texts appropriate for our students' age and interest for several reasons. We need to:

- stay up to date with current releases,
- maintain our integrity,
- model the complexities of a reading life, and
- demonstrate personal investment in readers.

Stay up to date with current releases. Many of us love the music from our childhood. But we also know our music is out of date. In the same vein, forgive my blasphemy, most of our students don't find *Ramona and Beezus* (Cleary, 1955), *The Best School Year Ever* (Robinson, 1994), or *Misty of Chincoteague* (Henry, 1947) appealing anymore. These are legendary books, but times have changed. By keeping abreast of what is current, we adapt to the social climate of our students and their interests. Otherwise, we implicitly ask readers to conform to what *we* know, making reading a task not an experience, which inhibits their ability to use text for self-discovery.

It's not easy to stay abreast of what's current. I receive countless emails that I study. I spend plenty of time in bookstores. I tend to scour book exhibits at conferences. I invest in what is current, to the extent that I can, because I am looking out for my readers. It's not easy, but it's worth it.

Maintain our integrity. If we relax or take current literature for granted, we run a risk of creating a divide between readers and ourselves. When we don't know what our students are reading, distance ensues. We cannot authentically understand how our readers interact and identify with text or how they relate because we lack the context. On occasion, it's important to outsource the reading of a new text to students. We save ourselves time and empower readers. However, when we aren't reading, how can our readers learn to take reading seriously and see how meaningful and impactful it is? We risk our integrity as reading teachers if we are not reading. Readers ask themselves, "If my teacher isn't reading, why am I?" In other words, if we're asking students to read but we're not, then that's where "Do as I say, not as I do" has a critical impact on our reading community.

After working an 11-hour day, I can't say that reading before bed is my favorite thing to do. Remember, I handicap horses. I have plenty of interests that consume my time. This is where I connect with my readers best—the "oh man, I have to read. . . ." It's real, and I own it. As I write this, there is a pile of books I want to read. Finding the time against the fatigue of my day is hard. But I have to walk into my classroom tomorrow ready to share how I made time. My students' belief in me as a reader and one who can relate with them about the books is important to me. If my integrity, even as a struggling reader, is damaged, I could turn my students off from the only pillar of reading they might have. Their reading depends on it.

> **As I write this, there is a pile of books I want to read. Finding the time against the fatigue of my day is hard. But I have to walk into my classroom tomorrow ready to share how I made time.**

Model the complexities of a reading life. More and more students do not have models of reading at home. Be it two parents working, a single parent with two jobs, the student bearing the responsibility of other siblings or significant household oversight, or maybe they just come from an environment that isn't necessarily conducive to support reading, such realities leave students void of reading experiences.

Maturing readers deserve reading models to relate and empathize with. Reading is hard. Making time to read is hard, especially when varied interests and pressing distractions permeate our consciousness. Yes, we have busy lives. Our students live busy lives, which they don't control. Our blessing is that we can help maturing readers strike a balance by inquiring and guiding them with ideas about how to integrate reading into their lives and serve as models of perseverance. Otherwise, students might choose to abandon reading. Who can blame them?

From my own experience as a distracted, somewhat reluctant reader, when I show my reading struggles and challenges, as well as how I overcome these difficulties, it makes a difference with my students. They don't quite believe me at first, but through my own Reading Passport and emotional responses to text, readers begin to recognize they aren't alone. They begin to see that it's almost human to have shortcomings and face hurdles with reading interest, stamina, or attention. Most important, what it shows my students is that I empathize with their day-to-day reading experiences. It may just be my best characteristic as a reading teacher.

Demonstrate personal investment in readers. We have to read because of our personal investment in readers. Students deserve someone who takes a vested interest in what they are reading. Our readers know when we haven't read a book. For one, they can sense when we are asking generic, surface-level questions. Our own affect reveals our lack of knowledge around a text. When students become accustomed to answering questions that lack substance or can be answered without reading a text, reading becomes purposeless and boring. Students deserve a teacher who knows a text well enough to drill down to harness a richer, deeper perspective of the content. If I don't have a solid understanding of the text, conferring becomes an interrogation—and a collection of answers—not a conversation. All this proves to a reader is that we are not interested in them, thus eroding the interpersonal bridge. Students stop reading. And why not? If reading is meant to be a task, then students will treat it as a task, not an experience.

If I don't have a solid understanding of the text, conferring becomes an interrogation—and a collection of answers—not a conversation.

It's fair to say that if we don't take a vested interest in what our students are reading, we cannot expect maturing readers to take a vested interest in themselves. If we only see the student superficially, we cannot discover their authenticity, which is internal. Now the question is, besides reading what they're reading, how do we dive deep to find out what's inside our readers?

Purposeful Reading Interventions and Support

In this chapter you will learn about Michael. Michael is a 12-year-old boy from a single-parent household. He qualifies for free-and-reduced lunch. His trauma history is extensive, and he struggles with rage. When I met him, he couldn't have cared less about reading. He joked about how he tricked his fourth-grade teacher, always misrepresenting what he read. He was a regular for intervention "pull-outs." Michael casually spoke of his boredom with re-reading "easy" texts and the fact that, no matter what he did, his reading level never improved. It would be the book *One for the Murphys* (Mullaly-Hunt, 2013) and the reading process we used that finally invited Michael to see himself as a reader. How did this happen? Well, I had to *look* at Michael. I not only had to look at the data, but I also had to look beyond the data.

As we delve into the idea of purposeful reading interventions and support, let me ask again, is your relationship with your readers strong enough to push into discomfort? Do you have time to stay in the discomfort with your readers? Can you make the time to show your dedication to your readers and be "knee-to-knee" to help them overcome challenges? In this chapter, we consider:

- Assessments That Provide a Voice to Readers
- Self-Perception and Social Contexts
- Conferring and the Interpersonal Bridge

Assessments That Provide a Voice to Readers

As we begin to examine assessment, let's take a look at a discussion I had with Michael.

Mr. Stygles:	"Hey, do you want to talk about your book?"
Michael:	"No."
Mr. Stygles:	"Really? What's going on?"
Michael:	"I don't want to talk about the book. First, you're gonna make me read it out loud then tell me all the errors I made or that I didn't read fast enough."
Mr. Stygles:	"Hold on, am I assessing you or asking you to talk about your book?"
Michael:	"I don't know. You know I'm bad at reading. Why should I talk to you about it?"
Mr. Stygles:	"Well, I'm interested in what you think about your book. What it's like to be you, as a reader. I want to see how you think."
Michael:	"What? That's dumb. Why would you care what I think when I'm a bad reader?"
Mr. Stygles:	"You tell me."
Michael:	"What do you mean?"
Mr. Stygles:	"I mean, why do you think I want to listen to *you*, a 'bad' reader?"
Michael:	"I don't know. I never really thought about it. All people say is I'll get better soon, and I don't. Why would they want to talk to me about books when they keep saying I can't read?"
Mr. Stygles:	"So let me go back to my question, can I talk to you about what you're reading, to see what's going on in your world?"
Michael:	"I mean, you can try. But why would you care about what I read?"
Mr. Stygles:	"Because, Michael, the only way you're going to believe in yourself as a reader is if we look at how you think about reading. I want to know you as a reader. Is that ok?"
Michael:	"I guess."

Michael is representative of so many readers I've worked with. Conferring is a self-perception death march. Michael thinks I've made up my mind about him. But Michael is saying something, albeit defensively. I want to give him a shot, but to do so, I need to know what's creating this defensiveness, this shame manifestation that inhibits the interpersonal bridge.

Reader Self-Perception Scale Revisited: Diving Deep Into the Reader's Internal Thinking

Not all assessments are created equal. Many are damaging. Many are given to collect data, which has little influence (Barshay, 2022). Assessments that provide readers a voice are the greatest asset. The Reader Self-Perception Scale (*RSPS*; Henk & Melnick, 1995), see page 172, is an interim assessment described in Chapter 3 that helps students define their narrative with ideas they are coming to understand. To best build the interpersonal bridge, I need to "hear" Michael's voice. The *RSPS* was probably the first time Michael could define himself, or a first opportunity at vulnerability. It wasn't that Michael was a struggling reader; it was that he carried negative self-perceptions, or shame, that inhibited any reading interest and that he could he explain.

Michael's RSPS (see Figure 6.1) revealed several important attributes about his self-perception:

- "Low" self-perception related to Social Feedback, Observational Comparison, Physiological States, and Progress.
- More than half of his responses related to Progress were Undecided (3), Disagree (2), or Strongly Disagree (1).
- All subcategories for Observational Comparison and Physiological States were undecided.

Taking a deeper look that the RSPS, here's what I found. On the positive side, Michael didn't seem overly concerned about himself in regard to others. His Observational Comparison was low but on the higher side of low. This didn't surprise me since he mentioned that his identity as a bad reader came from feedback received during instruction. His regular group of friends regularly abstained from reading, leaving him little to compare with. I felt Michael had an opportunity to grow because we would focus only on him, not how he rates against peers.

6.1 Michael's Reader Self-Perception Scores

In this assessment, student responses are reported in the form of a number for easy calculations.

5 = strongly agree

4 = agree

3 = undecided

2 = disagree

1 = strongly disagree

Question	Fall	Self-Perception
Social Feedback	27	Low
2. I can tell my teacher likes to listen to me read.	3	
3. My teacher thinks that my reading is fine.	3	
7. My classmates like to listen to me read.	3	
9. My classmates think I read pretty well.	3	
12. People in my family think I am a good reader.	3	
17. My teacher thinks I am a good reader.	3	
30. Other kids think I am a good reader.	3	
31. People in my family think I read really well.	3	
33. People in my family like to listen to me read.	3	
Observational Comparison	18	Low
4. I read faster than other kids	3	
6. When I read, I can figure out words better than other kids.	3	
11. I seem to know words more often than other kids when I read.	3	
14. I understand what I read as well as other kids do.	3	
20. I read better than other kids in my class.	3	
22. I read more than other kids.	3	
Physiological States	23	Low
5. I like to read aloud.	2	
8. I feel good inside when I read.	3	
16. Reading makes me feel happy inside.	3	
21. I feel calm when I read.	3	

Physiological States	23	Low
25. I feel comfortable when I read.	3	
26. I think reading is relaxing.	3	
29. Reading makes me feel good.	3	
32. I enjoy reading.	3	
Progress	**29**	**Very Low**
10. When I read, I don't have to try as hard as I used to.	3	
13. I am getting better at reading.	3	
15. When I read, I need less help than I used to.	5	
18. Reading is easier for me than it used to be.	3	
19. I read faster than I could before.	3	
23. I understand what I read better than I could before.	3	
24. I can figure out words better than I could before.	3	
27. I read better than I could before.	3	
28. When I read, I recognize more words than I used to.	3	

Michael also rated himself as low with respect to Social Feedback. I had taken notice of Michael's lack of participation in whole-class and small-group settings. He didn't reveal much in the way of vulnerability around other readers. His RSPS suggested he hadn't received much in the way of positive feedback from teachers, parents, or peers. So despite his low score, it could have been worse. Reflecting back to Michael what he could do as a reader would be our priority.

With this information, I could orchestrate interactions, or interventions, that would help Michael improve his self-perception and develop self-efficacy. Furthermore, I could help Michael discover what he could be as a reader.

Self-Perception and Social Contexts

One of my favorite genres to read is reading research. But I've also grown quite wary when people quote "research." I'm not saying the effect size of research isn't valid, or that research shouldn't influence our practice. I just don't like when research backfires on me because I didn't do enough *research*. Such was the case when I attempted partner reading intervention.

I'd paired Michael with an "expert" peer, as research suggested. Michael's negative self-perceptions suggested otherwise. While working with his classmate, Michael snapped.

Michael:	"I'm not sharing. The girls say all the answers anyway. I'm stupid! You just made me read with someone because I can't read, which means I'm stupid! See, she's smart. I'm dumb."
Cassandra:	"Well, I already read a lot and I'm a good reader, so I already know a lot."
Mr. Stygles:	"Cassandra, can you hold on for one second. You didn't do anything wrong. Do you mind if I talk to Michael for a few minutes? "Michael, I completely understand what you're saying. In fact, I know how you feel. Once I had to read with a girl in my class. I felt so small. Is that where you're at?"
Michael:	"Mr. Stygles, do you know how hard it is? Those girls are always called on in class. Ever since first grade, nobody cares what anyone else thinks. The girls are always perfect. They are always the teacher's favorites. I hate reading because of it."
Mr. Stygles:	"I can see your point. I recall a situation like that when I was in sixth grade with a girl named Jessica. I sat next to her. She was nice and all, but she was perfect. I always felt dumb next to her. Like you, I had to sit by her because she was smart and my teacher thought I was smart, too. He thought we'd be a good pair. Is that what it's like for you?"
Michael:	"Not really. They just know everything. I never ever get to talk. I'm stupid. 'Cause of school. The girls know everything. I know nothing. That's why I had to redo first grade. I can't read like everyone else in the class. The girls read everything right, 'look at me I can read *Moby Dick*.' 'I'm at the highest reading level.' 'Call on me I know the answer.' It's stupid. Every year I am put in the same class as them. They are the teacher's pets. I'm just dumb."
Mr. Stygles:	"You must feel stressed out?"
Michael:	"All the time. It's the same thing every day. Not one teacher likes me."

By age 9, boys develop strong attitudes about reading (Lever-Chain, 2008). Maturing readers will compare themselves to other readers when there isn't enough feedback to influence or prop up their self-concept. In this case, Michael had all he could take of being reminded that he was a low, struggling reader, who apparently needed help learning how to read. The comparison to peers was evident. Readers measure themselves against others because they don't know how to measure themselves successfully (see Chapter 2). But it's the last sentence that struck me most: "Not one teacher likes me." It was in this moment—social context—that I recognized the shame burdening Michael. Thankfully, we developed a strong connection, but I looked at Michael in a different light. I failed to account for the fact that students carry memories of rejection, abandonment, and failure, which aren't easy to overcome (Gausel et al., 2012). I needed to start giving him feedback to improve his self-perception, which started with smarter choices of instructional practice.

But it was the last sentence that struck me most: "Not one teacher likes me." It was in that moment that I recognized the shame burdening Michael.

The Various Roles and Impacts of Social Feedback

Let's attend to social feedback for a moment. A reader is apt to face several forms of unspoken feedback. Internally, students struggle with labels, distractions, excessive monitoring, and self-imposed comparisons to "better" readers, which can be condemning. It's not beyond reason to confer, for example, with students on their perceptions and how they compare themselves. After all, we know, developmentally (Erikson, 1968), students are prone to focus on these facets as early as third grade. Well-intended leveled-reading practices, for example, can potentially inhibit readers because they are confined to a designation, fostering shame through a form of social feedback. Therefore, if we don't discuss the qualifiers of social feedback, our readers are at risk of creating nasty internalizations, such as faulty (I'm dumb) or unworthy (I'm horrible), thus disassociating further from reading, which comes in the form of "I hate reading."

That aside, (leveled) reading instruction is based primarily on cognition. Reading comprehension and reading processes are largely grounded in cognition (Schwanenflugel & Knapp, 2016). Like cognition, *affect* is a concept explored in psychology. It just doesn't garner the same attention. Why? There's little reliability in measurement, unlike cognition (e.g., standardized testing). Why am I talking about this? We have to understand that affect and shame have direct influences on the reading process and comprehension. How? Social context and social capital.

Social capital is an emotional and/or affective influence. Social capital is how we see ourselves and the value in which peers place on us. These perceptions have an incredible influence on our ability to engage in peer collaboration. Our maturing readers are not immune to this because they are children. We should be more attuned to it because their ever-forming perceptions become foundational experiences to relationships in the future.

Social capital is how we see ourselves and the value in which peers place on us.

With that said, peer collaboration, a favored instructional vehicle aimed at inspiring readers (Frey et al., 2009; Prescott-Griffen, 2005), can have a significant impact on the readers' beliefs about reading and self-perception. Psychology and shame research is rich in the discussion of social roles, anxiety, rejection, and so on that occurs within small groups (Gilbert, 2000; Shahar et al., 2015). When we group readers together, based on levels, for example, or we insist a student shares out in the name of participation, there is a potential of negatively influencing self-perception when social capital isn't accounted for.

Just after the winter break, I asked students to share out what they had read and their opinions of those books. Alex was a voracious reader. He also had incredible insight into his reading. I wanted him to celebrate that with his peers, and maybe his peers could celebrate him? Little did I know, I set him up for failure when his turn came. He didn't want to be noticed in front of a larger audience.

Mr. Stygles:	"Alex, can you tell us what you read over the break?"
Alex:	"I don't want to."
Mr. Stygles:	"OK. Can I come back to you?"
	This time, no response.

	After I called on each student sitting in the circle in our gathering area, I asked again.
Mr. Stygles:	"Alex? Are you ready to share what you read?"
	Silence. With that, I ended the morning discussion as we moved into the mini-lessons. During independent practice, I made a point to catch up with Alex.
Mr. Stygles:	"Alex, you read so much over the break. How come you didn't want to say anything?"
Alex:	"You know I don't like to talk out loud in front of the class."
Mr. Stygles:	"I know. But what stopped you?"
Alex:	"The other kids don't like me. They make fun of me, Mr. Stygles. I don't like being smart in front of them. They ignore me."
Mr. Stygles:	"Oooh. I'm sorry. I didn't realize that."
Alex:	"I know."

For some of us with low social capital, we're teased for what we do well. Our accomplishments are held against us. Alex tragically, though brilliant, was a withdrawn student for good reason. He wasn't admired for his talent. In turn, he had low social capital. It took a little while for me to restore the interpersonal bridge. I can assure you, any books he read from that point on were shared with me and no one else. We may desire for students to work collaboratively, but if executive function is focused on perception amongst peers, even our best efforts can be nullified. The last thing any maturing reader desires is public failure in the eyes of their peers.

We may desire for students to work collaboratively, but if executive function is focused on perception amongst peers, even our best efforts can be nullified.

"I'm Not the Only One?" Using Deficits to Celebrate and Grow

Conversely, social interactions can be quite supportive when social capital is not an influence. Michael was socially active, but when it came to reading, he was withdrawn. Withdrawal can be a problem because the isolations grant students indefinite time to reinforce negative internalizations. How then, can students benefit from our efficient teaching and improve the circumstances so students can be enriched as readers through social learning? It may sound silly, but it starts with simply helping students recognize they aren't alone or "they aren't the only ones."

I was in a conference with Michael who was having a hard time clarifying new vocabulary. Michael turned to me and asked, "Am I the only one who can't read aloud well?" I knew the answer to that question, so I replied, "Absolutely not. Most of us struggle with that. Even me at my age!" My comment fulfilled his curiosity in that moment but enticed mine. I wondered why he came up with such an internalization. After school, I took time to review his mid-winter RSPS administered after the winter break.

6.2 Michael's Mid-Winter Social Feedback Ratings

Other readers think I'm a good reader.	Disagree (2)
My classmates like to listen to the way I read.	Strongly Disagree (1)
My teachers think I'm a good reader.	Undecided (3)
My teachers think that I try my best when I read.	Undecided (3)
People in my family like to listen to me read.	Strongly Disagree (1)
My classmates think I read pretty well.	Disagree (2)
I can tell my teachers like to listen to me read.	Undecided (3)
My teachers think I do a good job of interpreting what I read.	Undecided (3)
My teachers think my reading is fine.	Undecided (3)

Once again, Michael was communicating his narrative in a way that was crystal clear to anyone but him. Actually, he was implicitly seeking help. The RSPS confirmed this. Now, moving away from the data, I called Michael to "look at the child next to me." He brought over his current book, *A Handful of Stars* (Lord, 2015). Like a stadium announcer, Michael reminded me, or more lamented, that he didn't want to read aloud again, despite asking if he could read well. (What an irony, though a reality of internalized shame.) I sought to learn more about Michael's burden.

Mr. Styles:	"Michael, why is it you don't like reading out loud?"
Michael:	"When I read, I make too many mistakes. I'm not perfect. I get words wrong, then everyone knows I'm bad."
Mr. Styles:	"You make a few mistakes? That makes you bad?"
Michael:	"When I was in second grade, my teacher took books from me and gave me easier ones until I read them right. I hated it. I was always nervous. Now I just hate reading aloud. When I read out loud, I watch you mark the paper. I can feel the mistakes I'm making, and I know I'm not reading fast enough."
Mr. Styles:	"How do you know others aren't in the same situation?"
Michael:	"Because. I listen to the way you talk to them. They're all better than me."
Mr. Styles:	"Michael, can I invite Evan over to read aloud to you?"
Michael:	"I guess."
Mr. Styles:	"Evan, do you think you read aloud very well?"
Evan:	"No! I make mistakes all the time. When I come to words I don't know I try to figure them out."
Mr. Styles:	"Evan, can you read aloud for Michael? I think he might be interested in listening."
Michael:	"Hey, you made the same mistakes in the same places I did!"
Evan:	"Yeah. These words are new."
Mr. Styles:	"Yes, they are, those are the multi-morphemic words we're starting to learn about. Michael, it's ok to make mistakes. We all do it. It's doesn't make us bad. It means we get to learn. It's how we work *through* those mistakes that make a difference.

(Continued)

(Continued)

Tell you what boys, what if we do this. Let's listen to each other read. The only thing I ask is that you don't correct your friend while they are reading. Instead, give advice after reading by saying, 'I noticed . . . Here is a way you can fix that.' Or you can tell us how you came across a troublesome word or a new word you had to clarify. Tell us how you solved it. After that, jot down your new learnings on sticky notes so we can preserve this moment. What do you think?"

Before I knew it, the boys were off reading and laughing together. A few weeks later, Michael said he didn't mind reading aloud anymore. I asked him why. Whimsically he replied, "Mr. Stygles, I'm not a good reader, but I'm not going to be better if I don't try, even if that means making mistakes."

When I design small groups, be it pairs or groups of four or five, I must recognize that these small groups might be the only opportunity for maturing readers to be close to someone who cares about them and their reading, to provide feedback in a social context. The goal is to create a sense of security, which improves self-perception, which is to say, "I'm a good reader!"

Literature Maps: A Confluence of Close Reading, Shared Perspectives, and Small Groups

I remember reading Nancie Atwell early in my career. In her book *The Reading Zone* (2007), she noted:

> Metacognition was interfering with the reading zone. The sticky notes intruded on the zone, disrupted the flow of a great story, ate up precious time that could have been devoted to living inside another great story and wasted their time as a reader. (p. 54)

Atwell closely observed how her readers acted to improve their experience as independent readers.

Similarly, Fountas and Pinnell (2012) wrote, "Small-group teaching is needed for the careful observation and specific teaching of individuals that it allows, as well as for the efficiency in teaching and the social learning that benefits each student" (p. 275).

With that said, can you imagine the intense pain other readers feel when they are unable to experience this "living in a story" as their peers do? We've already seen Michael's explosion—the feeling of despair when peers rave about reading while you desperately disguise your struggles? Compounding the issue, Michael, for example, was cavalier with his reading. He portrayed an image that he understood his reading, but rarely could speak of characters or setting, let alone specific details that ignited deeper thinking about text.

Can you imagine the intense pain other readers feel when they are unable to experience this "living in a story" as their peers do?

The reality is, readers think, feel, and respond differently, which means, they require differentiated instruction (Tomlinson & Imbeau, 2010). I notice my readers differently than Atwell did hers, but close reading (Boyles, 2014; Fisher et al., 2016; Frey et al., 2015) has changed the lives of many readers who needed a means to navigate reading comprehension. Close reading instruction can be a means to work with a small group to help students realize and actualize their potential. Through close reading, I'd observed Michael respond favorably in a supportive social context. Now he needed a strategy to interact with the text meaningfully, while obtaining positive feedback from peers (influenced by his winter Social Feedback ratings; see Figure 6.2). For that purpose, I introduced Michael to literature mapping.

Sobel (1998) contextualized mapping in this way: "Not only do we have to put a picture together, but we have to find what's beyond their yard, beyond the end of the road." Our students grow and learn, we gain clarity, and barriers fall when we take time to listen and understand the reader's thinking. Therefore, literature mapping serves as multimodal or semiotic representation of comprehension

(Aukerman, 2013; Barone & Barone, 2017). Put another way, it is a means for readers to convert textual evidence into a visual form so that they physically see the results of their close reading to express their unique articulations, thereby creating competence. Literature mapping is not about right or wrong answers but about using textual evidence to support a vision that is unique to the reader, in turn improving self-perception. Furthermore, the map becomes an external hard drive of sorts that preserves students' contextualizations (Fisher et al., 2009).

> **Literature mapping is not about right or wrong answers but about using textual evidence to support a vision that is unique to the reader.**

Who Would Benefit From Literature Mapping?

To determine who will best benefit from literature mapping, I consider those students who:

- might otherwise be inhibited by vocabulary or language constraints;
- are reluctant to engage with peers and demonstrate their perception or understanding of a text because of anxiety or perceived social capital and/or negative self-perceptions;
- have a clear struggle locating specific details, or who like to recall as much as possible;
- are less eager to share in front of a small group; and
- need immediate feedback.

Literature mapping is an opportunity to "reframe the narrative" of close reading and self-concept. When I told Michael and his group about the intervention, he remarked, "Why are we making maps? Isn't that something the kids in Ms. Belvoir's class do?" (Ms. Belvoir teaches the Gifted and Talented class.)

After I determine who will benefit from the intervention, I gather students and explain that "we're going to learn how to make sense of our reading when we get lost, confused, or overwhelmed." I define that we will be reading a book they may not necessarily like and that we might have to slow our reading down to help us make better sense of what's going on when we read.

To begin the intervention, students read aloud within the group as peers follow along and highlight text evidence connected to setting. After a student reads, we take time to share out what evidence is highlighted. At other times, students read independently locating information before regrouping and discussing our findings. Our next step is to outline our maps.

For example, Michael's group read *The Dollar Kids* (Jacobson, 2019). The author spent quite a bit of time describing the town that Lowen Grover and his family had just moved to. Collaboratively, students designated the specific locations or landmarks and the transitional phrases that approximate their locations within the text. Next, students sketched text evidence onto 12″ x 18″ blank white paper using a pencil (house, school, playground, etc.). By identifying key places, such as Mom's bakery, students developed anchors to the text, or locations where they could pinpoint specific events, characters' actions, important conflicts, and turning points, which would become the foundation for our forthcoming group discussions.

6.3 Michael's Literature Map for *The Dollar Kids*

As we read further, we added details that provided greater clarity about the setting, which becomes an anchor to students' strategic reading. Once we've moved past the portion of a book where our setting remains constant, students added color to their maps using colored pencils during a designated writing about reading block, first thing in the morning.

Working to mitigate shame, the emotional or affective purpose of this small-group design is to help readers develop a sense of security or sense of self amongst others by demonstrating competence, which improves social feedback and observational comparison. In other words, I know students are comparing themselves. Rather than risk students comparing themselves silently, thereby internalizing shame, students can compare what is done in the form of sharing what details have been included. Moreover, they hear affirmation from others, and immediate feedback from me, which helps them develop a sense of pride, or improved self-perception. I wanted to empower Michael, to reverse his negative self-perceptions. I wanted him to value himself rather than saying, "I can't do this because it's something that the 'smart' kids do." It's opportunities like this where we help maturing readers alter their self-perceptions. He viewed his own work through several mirrors: the positive feedback of his peers and affirmation of his comprehension when he (1) contained the same features and details as his peers and (2) added features he felt were relevant that his friends didn't include. Moreover, Michael realized he could comprehend text reasonably well and had no reason to see himself as inferior.

Conferring and the Interpersonal Bridge

Have you ever noticed that we expect kids to make cognitive leaps simply because we taught something? Like transfer is automatic? It's not like Michael suddenly found the joy of reading because of close reading or realizing that he wasn't alone. In fact, Michael still hadn't "bought in" per se. For instance, Michael complained (a shame-based avoidance tactic) every time we considered writing a new reading goal together. After a few conversations, it became clear that Michael had no real purpose to read, not to mention his previously discussed negative perception and manifestations. At one point he mentioned that he rarely felt a sense of accomplishment reading. He just *had* to read. Whatever that meant. Acknowledging his recent success with literature mapping, Michael was at a crossroads: He knew he was a better reader, but did he want to pursue reading? Now we had the chance to build his sense of accomplishment as an independent reader, which would come through the interpersonal bridge via investment and accountability around his reading life. There was no more "keeping him at a distance."

Reading teachers continuously dedicate themselves to building reading communities and adopting core values posited by honored literacy leaders. These values often include:

- Turning students on to reading (Kindig, 2012; Kittle, 2013)
- Volume and wide reading (Miller, 2010; Wilde, 2013)
- Scaffolding readers through text (Beers, 2003; Lesesne, 2010)

What I have found though, is that readers don't automatically embrace these values just because we embody them in our personal identity or promote them as part of a rigorous learning environment. These beliefs are contingent on the willingness of the student. This is why we must be willing participants—patient, forgiving, empathetic, compassionate, and impartial about our own desires inside the interpersonal bridge or reading conference. We can't force willingness. We can't demand vulnerably.

**We can't force willingness.
We can't demand vulnerably.**

More so, inspiring students to go beyond what they've already accomplished can be somewhat dubious. First, pushing them further increases the potential for shame, especially if I, for instance, am not satisfied with their progress, or they fail. Conversely, allowing students to become complacent increases the risk of shame in the future. Students tend to develop affinities and stay in their comfort zones (don't we all!). And sometimes, it feels ok to accept that. While there is research to support the value of reading within one's comfort zone, research also

> indicate(s) that weaker readers, using texts at two, three, and four grade levels above their instructional levels with the assistance of lead readers [other, better reading, students], outscored both proficient and less proficient students in the control group across multiple measures of reading achievement." (Shanahan, 2017, para. 10)

What did this mean for Michael? I had to keep challenging him. First, he had to start reading independently. Second, I wouldn't patronize him with easy books. Together, we would find what he felt comfortable with and encompassed some level of challenge.

To make this happen for students like Michael, we had to build the interpersonal bridge through conferring. Though conferring is easy to forsake because of time constraints, there is nothing more essential than the dedicated conference (Serravallo & Goldberg, 2007; Yates & Nosek, 2018).

Effective conferring requires a strong and honest relationship between teacher and student. Kaufman (1993), clinical psychologist and shame researcher, states the following about working one-on-one with a client. As you read his words, substitute the word *teacher* for *therapist* and *student* for *client*:

> **Effective conferring requires a strong and honest relationship between teacher and student.**

> Each must come to know the other as a real, very human person. And the relationship must be honest. In these ways the therapist will increasingly gain the client's confidence and the client will permit the therapist increasingly to enter his or her experiential world inside. The power to gain entry resides solely within the client. (p. 134)

With this in mind, sometimes we have to sit knee-to-knee, eye-to-eye to move maturing readers beyond their comfort (reading) zones. Together, Michael and I would experience the vulnerability of his reading struggles and the discomfort he needed to continue his progress as a reader and adopt reading into his "whole self." Conferring is about consistently showing up to talk with readers about their progress. Otherwise, the values posited above will mean nothing to our readers.

I try to meet with each student at least once a week, in one capacity or another (see Chapter 2) for 15 minutes about independent reading, if not more. One style of conferring I often use with students is a Reading Reflection conference. The point of this conference is to celebrate new achievements the reader has experienced or to dive deeper into the hurdles the reader is facing to stay engaged. Within this conference, I ask a variety of questions including

Reading Interest

- How did you maintain or find interest in your book?
- In what ways do you think you should make adjustments (before quitting a book)?

Physiological Reading

- Were you able to find a comfortable space to read?
- What did you feel like as you read?

Reading Satisfaction

- Did you face any distractions? If so, how did you deal with them?
- What would you like to try differently to make reading more successful?
- Were you happy with your reading situation?

Self-Monitoring

- Were you able to maintain a steady reading rate?
- Were you able to manage your time to complete the book in a timely fashion?

By engaging in such conversations, I explore the reader. I inquire into the narrative of their experience and journey. Together, we reinforce the role someone like Michael has had in managing his own reading. For instance, Michael and I talked about "weird" things like the physiological state, or the physical comfort of reading. *Good readers* feel calm and joy when reading. We talked about the trauma that impacts his progress. *Good readers* aren't distracted by trauma or on guard for the next interruption. *Good readers* aren't ridiculed or harassed because they made the choice to read instead of doing something else, because it's a priority or their personal interest. Michael and I shared our experiences with these at length.

Conferring is about having a strong sense of how various struggles and opportunities for each student are unfolding and evolving over time (Szymusiak et al., 2008). To ever associate the feeling of reading with a love for, or even basic appreciation of, books maturing readers need to explore their act of reading, turn the mirror inward, and locate the opportunities within themselves for finding interest and motivation.

I want to show my readers that I value them. That our relationship is an investment in who they are because they are that important!

A Student-Centered Approach to Success

Measures of success are not the same for all students. Success changes as students mature along their reading journey. Readers are unique. For some students, success might be determined by the genres and content they explore outside their comfort zones. For others success might be measured in how they surpass their own read goals, like time or pages read. Ultimately, students need to know their capabilities, establish reasonable and honest expectations for themselves, and determine how to challenge themselves beyond their status quo. The gift of the interpersonal bridge is to co-construct and reflect with students as they develop goals that promote self-concept, efficacy, and agency as readers.

> The gift of the interpersonal bridge is to co-construct and reflect with students as they develop goals that promote self-concept, efficacy, and agency as readers.

Boundary Setting: Personalized Accountability as a Defense Against Shame

When it came to reading, book selection was not Michael's forte, nor did he understand any *boundaries*, or parameters, that would help him find success. I use the term *boundary* to talk about the capabilities a reader possesses to ensure successful reading. Boundaries is a term that helps readers identify what conditions of reading they can control. I adapted the definition from Brené Brown (2010). In her seminal text *The Gifts of Imperfection*, she writes, "If we really want to practice compassion, we start by setting boundaries and holding people accountable for their behavior" (p. 17). Before I go further, I recognize that "boundaries" in Brown's sense is establishing limitations with those around to protect yourself and escalated emotions. In the sense that I use the term, I'm modeling, co-creating, and inviting students to set the parameters in which they can read successfully. "Read for 45 minutes" as a homework assignment is not a boundary or a parameter. It's a command—one that can easily be ignored or manipulated. By establishing boundaries, students develop a sense of how the act of reading can work for them. Essentially, I am asking students to say, "Here's what I know I can do to take care of myself as a reader." In return, I hold students accountable to these boundaries as a means of compassion, an interest and dedication to their reading development. My role is to accept what readers establish for themselves, ensure they fulfill the expectations set for themselves, and eventually challenge them (within reason) to expand their abilities. You may say to yourself, "Isn't this goal setting?" Sure, goal setting may be a reasonable term. I would advise that the difference between *boundaries* and *goal setting* is the self-awareness a student possesses about their reading and their self-efficacy—the belief they can read successfully within the parameters established for themselves.

During the class's weekly trip to the library, Michael did something I've seen a hundred times before. He rushed up to me, revealing his two new books. In one hand, he had *Harry Potter* and in the other was *Dogman*. I flashed a smile and asked for his rationale while recognizing that he was signaling to me that he didn't understand how to manage a reading life with appropriate boundaries. I've found that students often select combinations of books like this, not because they are reading, but because they are putting up an image of being a reader. Indeed, he gleefully responded, "I've read them before."

Things didn't connect. I knew Michael faced numerous hurdles with his reading and he's "read" *Harry Potter*? I'm not one to tell a student they cannot read a book. That would defeat the point of learning how to establish successful boundaries. I wanted to learn about Michael's motive, and I wanted him to realize his abilities and limitations without me saying so. In this way I wouldn't shame Michael, but I would allow him to develop a sense of his own capabilities.

Boundaries are attributes that help students compose their identity as reader. They allow students to find a baseline of what they can do as readers and later reflect on how much they have grown as readers. Students like Michael don't necessarily have this sense because they have a set of go-to books that they lean on. Students need to learn how to balance the dynamics (mentioned above) that constitute this "pleasure" called *reading*. Successful readers know their abilities and limitations. That's part of what makes reading enjoyable.

The key is that we teach readers how to negotiate a plan for reading for themselves, which occurs through trust and respect of the interpersonal bridge. Simultaneously, we must not impose a rigid set of expectations that automatically discourages our readers. Instead, we have to discuss, or negotiate, what the reader believes they are capable of accomplishing within a reasonable set of boundaries, which includes

> **We must not impose a rigid set of expectations that automatically discourages our readers.**

- An understanding of who they are as readers
  - What books do I like?
  - What books should I try to explore?
  - Is this book too easy, or what is a reasonable challenge?
- The capacity to set realistic expectations for themselves and hold themselves accountable
  - Can I read this book in a week?
  - How many pages can I complete in a day?
  - If I choose *Harry Potter*, how long will it reasonably take to complete?
  - What strategies might I need to employ to feel successful with this book?

In other words, when students don't feel they can achieve something like the 40-book challenge, what is it we can help readers do to see what books they can read and how they can make this happen reasonably?

Setting Goals: Creating a Definition of Success

Within the reading conference, Michael and I had to determine what he could reasonably accomplish. I wanted Michael to complete a chapter book inside a week. Michael was content with his famously ambivalent approach, "I'll read if I can." This meant we had to start small and work big: What book are you reading and what's the plan to complete it? As the teacher, it's my job to lead the way.

"Which book will you start with first, *Dogman* or *Harry Potter?*" I asked.

Michael answered, "I think I'll read *Harry Potter* first. I haven't read this since last year."

"All right." I replied. "Will it take one or two weeks to finish the book?"

Michael returned, "What do you mean?"

I followed up with, "I'll tell you what. Why don't you read a page for me and let's see what you might be able to accomplish?"

As it turns out, based on his oral reading rate, *Harry Potter* could have taken him 900 minutes to read. Even if he was reading at the expected 45 minutes a night, it would have taken Michael 3 weeks to complete the book—and that's if he read nightly for 3 consecutive weeks. Based on his reading past, this was a lofty goal. With that, he decided on *Dogman*, which we both knew would only take him the evening, if that.

This ended our conference, but we'd only just begun. We'd meet again the next day because he'd need another book. Second, we needed to start finding what books would be meaningful reads that he could reasonably tackle within 4–8 days. The goal wasn't so that he would complete his nightly reading. The goal was to find what would keep Michael interested in reading. That, too, was an evergreen discussion we would continue within the interpersonal bridge.

We show our compassion by holding loved ones accountable to themselves.

The biggest takeaway is that I left Michael's dignity intact. I knew he hadn't read *Harry Potter* before. His reading fluency suggested as much. His book selection was what I consider to be on the "continuum of extremes," which is easy on one side to very difficult on the other, or what I kindly consider the "keeping up appearances" end of the continuum. Even though Michael knew he couldn't balance *Harry Potter*, he was certainly willing to risk his reading experience to play the part.

Throughout this negotiation, it is important that readers recognize we are working together. If the student does not meet the expectation, such as missing a night of reading, that's fine. Let's consider what inhibited reading and adjust the expectations accordingly. The point is, I am holding the student accountable as a means of scaffolding their ability to do so. It's also because I am showing compassion. Again, Brown (2010) points out, we show our compassion by holding loved ones accountable to themselves. Michael didn't need to be released back into reading on his own devices. He needed someone he could always come back to, a mirror to reflect back possibilities.

Quitting Books

Quitting books is a contentious topic at literacy conferences. Everyone has their opinions and rationales. I don't allow kids to quit books; it's more that I want to know why they choose to quit as a means to help readers define the boundaries in which they can read successfully. I've found that some students develop a habit of quitting books, which is tough to reverse. Simultaneously, students call these books "boring," or they "just aren't interested." Again, I'll be a bit of a curmudgeon, but I am curious about what exactly makes a book boring or not interesting. More often it's not the content or text complexity that deters the student, it's their ability to engage meaningfully with the text. In other words, it's the reader's lack of a reading process.

More often it's not the content or text complexity that deters the student, it's their ability to engage meaningfully with the text.

Long story short, when Michael discovered his reading process, it was a very unlikely book that became his favorite book of all time (indicated on his Favorites Bookshelf; see Chapter 7). Michael's breakthrough book, or book that changed his self-perception as a reader, was far removed from his former reading interest about football. The book was titled *One for the Murphys* (Mullaly-Hunt, 2013). Michael read the book four times over the 2 years I was able to teach him. It was the very book that he recognized his boundaries as reader and worked within those capabilities. If we had not worked together to develop those boundaries, persevere through a challenge by simply quitting the book, who knows when Michael would have found himself as a reader.

Ultimately, when I see readers changing books every day, something is up. My point is, before a reader chooses to quit a book, I need to intervene, for the sake of the reader. Together, we need to consider what the impetus for quitting is. Do we:

1. *need to reconsider the boundaries that were established for successful reading?* At times, students quit books because they aren't reading at all. I've had readers share with me that they quit the book to make it look like they are "interested" in reading books. This is completely real and forgivable. I'm sure a few of us have been down this road before. The readers I work with are really just lost and looking for a bit of connection and mentorship.
2. *consider the reading process that students are using to make meaning?* In my experience, students reach a critical juncture in their reading lives between grades four and six. Books are no longer always *easy*. Nor do they *get good* before page 100. But a number of readers believe that reading is either word calling or strictly for pleasure. When nothing makes sense, it's not necessarily because of behaviors that can be represented on a running record, it's because readers need to approach a book more strategically. I teach my students—and many testify later—that strategic reading helps them find their joy in reading.
3. *understand that some books just don't appeal to readers?* Every year, my class has a reading assignment devoted to our state book award list. Unfailingly, I have a few readers who use poor boundaries to select a book. A month later, they are stuck in quagmire. In their minds, they have to complete the book because they've heard me say, "Try to not quit a book." Expectedly, students use an array of excuses like "I didn't have time to read" or "My mom made me read something different." These are likely true statements. Why? Because the book is just not appealing, and it never got better. I'd prefer to catch this trend after a week rather than wait a month and lose 2 to 4 weeks of reading experiences, but when I see reader slogging through books, using excuses to compensate, it's just not worth it. We've discussed boundaries and strategic reading. We've talked about what could make the book enjoyable. If it's just not working, it's time to be done.

If none of those considerations work, then by all means quit the book. Reading need not be torture. Move on to something different. Nonetheless, I would rather exhaust my resources, sitting side-by-side a reader, helping them find interest in a book rather than leaving them shortchanged of diverse, in-depth reading experiences that they will likely need to draw from later in life rather than abandoning them to their own devices. When these experiences are void—say high school or college, or beyond—then the student will likely experience shame in a very different way. I know. I was that reader. Nowhere did I feel that pain more than when I became a "reading teacher."

Conversely, there are good reasons why a student needs to abandon a book. Sophie comes to mind. One morning she slapped her book down on my table with a sticky note without speaking a word. The look in eyes declared her intent. "Mr. Stygles, I'm not reading this anymore" (see Figure 6.4). Still, I asked why. Sophie steadfastly said, "I'm almost halfway through this book and I can't take it anymore. It makes me cry every time I read. I don't want to keep crying."

"Okay" was all I said in return. There was no need to insist or demand that she kept reading. Emotions told the story of her engagement. She was planning for her emotional well-being at the time. I'm completely down with that. She displayed appropriate boundaries and demonstrated a reading process. She was in control of her reading.

6.4 Sophie's Book Feedback

Perception Reveals Identity

Comprehension, if not already a challenging concept to measure, can be very difficult with the uniqueness of every reader. Comprehension has largely been measured by correct answers to questions, which clearly tell a reader whether they are right or wrong. This again is cognition. However, it is obviously important to know whether or not the student is accessing the basics of the book. Now, personally, can you think of a time you read a book, talked about it with others, and well, just didn't see it the same way others did? Or even love it, like others did, but wonder, "Did we read the same thing?" Our maturing readers aren't quite at this stage, but they do wonder whether they are allowed to comprehend a text in a way that is solely based on their understanding.

Reading comprehension is also about perspective—how one sees the world. As mentioned in the previous chapter, reading is about connecting; it's about affect and emotion. It's in this realm of comprehension where students *see* themselves in text, connect with characters and more, and find value in the book. This is where we find the windows, mirrors, and sliding glass doors. Without it, whatever is the point of reading?

Our intermediate, middle, and high school readers are ready to interpret a text through their own lens (Appleman, 2006). But how often do we stifle their experience because we must chase after test scores and reading levels? Further, whether because of insecurity, social capital, or compliance, rarely do we hear what our readers really want to say. In turn, they keep their uniqueness, their giftedness, bottled up; a treasure they keep only for themselves, protected from any potential threat. The result is loneliness. When readers have no one to share their reading experience and all the emotions that come with it, why should they continue reading? This is especially apropos for our readers who are seeking to gain confidence and social capital. Fountas and Pinnell (2016) also suggest that we have a responsibility as much to our students' academic needs as their social-emotional needs, which can be highly at risk in small groups, leaving students exposed and vulnerable. If we truly believe in equity, we will respond to our call by cherishing the perceptions and vulnerability our students are willing to share.

Our maturing readers who struggle with poor self-perception or no perceived social capital are silent, if not unintentionally repressed. Moreover, some might begin to question themselves or engage in negative self-talk that influences their narrative. Questions these readers may ask themselves, with no intention of ever being heard include

- Why is everyone else always right and not me?
- Why do I not see the world like everyone else does?
- What am I reading? Do I even read right?

It's in these thoughts, which become internalizations, that readers begin to evaluate themselves and compare themselves to peers (Observational Comparison). It doesn't have to be this way. We just have to explore what's happening inside our readers and help them feel valued for it.

By year's end, Michael showed a complete change in persona and attitude about reading. Based on his Reader Self-Perception Scale, Michael indicated many positive changes within his perceptions of his reading, including Social Feedback. But the intriguing part was in the realm of his perceived progress. He didn't improve, according to his responses, but this isn't unjustifiable. Afterall, the more you learn, the less you know. Michael became a "better" reader. He knew himself better and measured his progress more accurately. Michael developed "healthy shame" (Brown, 2010), a clear sense and understanding of himself that he could grow from. For example, Michael still "strongly disagreed" that "When I read, I don't have to try as hard as I used to." But instead of deficit thinking, as in an "I can't do this," because his self-perception changed, he could say, "Yeah this is hard, but I keep trying," showing a growth mindset (Dweck, 2015). Moreover, he became a resilient reader who no longer latched on to "I hate reading." Improvements like this are rooted in work around social feedback, including teacher feedback and interaction with peers. Thus, Michael ended the year on a high note. He opened himself to reading because he was noticed by way of his reading process, engagement, thoughts, and perceptions toward reading. Michael simply needed an avenue to overcome the belief that he was a bad reader.

Final Thoughts

Closely working with students is easy to take for granted. It's easy to confer with a reader just by stopping at their desk and checking in. It's easy to find solace in the fact that students continuously read books. But at day's end, our readers deserve our true dedication.

Our mindful dedication to readers matters. I must teach readers to believe in themselves. Each student must believe that I can help them discover who they are as readers (teacher credibility). To promote shame resiliency or improve self-perception, I must invest time in helping the reader reconstruct negative internalizations that inhibit their progress and pathways to knowledge.

To promote shame resiliency or improve self-perception, I must invest time in helping the reader reconstruct negative internalizations that inhibit their progress and pathways to knowledge.

Reading interest and engagement is not the result of a lesson but rather willing participation in a relationship that defines success and invites appropriate adaptions to shortcomings or misunderstandings. It's about seeing oneself in a mirror and as worthy in the eyes of a respected other—You—the one who can propel a reader into authentic reading. Yes, there is something ironic about the fact that reading is a solitary activity learned in a social context. In Michael's case, he'd learned to read but rarely had the opportunity to practice those habits to make them beneficial. He was sent off to be an independent reader (meaning isolated) without yet developing a sense of himself through any social context. Michael deserved to take an interest in reading not because he was required to but because he built up the belief that he, and others, saw him as a reader.

Too often, we are asked to forsake relationships with students because we have assessment demands and curriculum requirements that must be met—out of fear of repercussions to us. Relationships are tender. Overlooking our relationships with students, or maintaining superficial connections, will cause us problems in the end. Our investment in our readers can alter a child's trajectory in the form of intervention we are ready to sit *knee-to-knee, eye-to-eye* (Cole, 2003).

Reflect and Act

Use these reflection questions to consider the information shared in the chapter and how you can apply it in your own classroom.

1. Think about your current understanding of Tier I interventions. How do the strategies presented in this chapter mesh with or differ from your understanding?
2. When a reader says a book is boring or that they want to quit a book, how do you handle the situation? What does the reader say about their book that leads to their conclusion?
3. How can you monitor students' changing attitudes about reading, and how can you respond with compassion and interest?

7

FINDING THE READER THROUGH WRITING ABOUT READING

Over the years, I've seen a distinct trait among resilient readers: They're willing to write about their reading. Throughout their reading pasts, these readers have seen themselves as determined by someone else. But writing about reading changes that. Readers' responses through writing are evidence of comprehension that mirrors back competence and confidence.

Katie Wood Ray once told me, "Writing is a legacy." Writing about reading gives students a chance to document landmarks in their thinking and perceptions, undergoing a metamorphosis into unique, gifted readers before our eyes, a declaration of who the reader is and how they perceive reading on their terms. In turn, writing about reading has a significant impact on self-concept and self-efficacy.

Writing about reading gives students a chance to document landmarks in their thinking and perceptions.

Of course, maturing readers don't magically demonstrate brilliant comprehension simply because they write about their reading. Like everything else to this point, there is a process—a process that helps with self-actualization and improves their self-efficacy.

William, age 10, is representative of many students who embraced the possibilities connected with writing about reading in their journey to become resilient readers. It wasn't easy, though. As a fifth grader, William's benchmark assessments and state test results suggested he was a capable third-grade reader. He lacked reading stamina and "didn't remember" much about his book during discussions. Along those lines, he wasn't the most invigorated writer.

One asset I had was William's fourth-grade Reader's Notebook, passed along from his previous teacher. I was curious to what extent William did comprehend text or documented his thoughts about reading. I thumbed a few pages before noting a trend. One late September morning, I invited him to a reading conference so that we could discuss what I noticed.

Mr. Stygles:	"William, something tells me you don't exactly enjoy writing in your Reader's Notebook."
William:	"Why?"
Mr. Stygles:	"Well, either you're a fantastic writer or you borrowed your writing."
William:	"How can you tell?"

Mr. Stygles:	"I'll be straight up. Last night, I read your Reader's Notebook from last year. I couldn't help but notice that there was a lot of narrative writing. I found that interesting since you had written on top of most of the pages, "Summary." You weren't by chance copying from the book, were you?"
William:	"Maybe."
Mr. Stygles:	"That's kinda funny. Let me guess, you didn't want to read, and you didn't want to get in trouble, did you?"
William:	"Yeah! We had to write a summary about what we read every night. I hate writing."
Mr. Stygles:	"I hear that! I might have been known to do the same thing a time or to when I was your age. In fact, I recall getting a C+ on a book report that was mostly copied. And I know, you won't be the last kiddo to try that on me. What I really want to know is why you did it? Are you willing to tell me about it?"
William:	"I hate that I try to read before bed then I have to write a summary before I go to bed. Most of the time I fall asleep then I forget to write in the morning. If we don't have everything done, I have to stay in for recess and recess is the only time during school I get to do something fun."
Mr. Stygles:	"Thanks for the honesty. But here's the thing: When I read responses about reading, I look for the reader, you, in the response."
William:	"What does that mean?"
Mr. Stygles:	"It means, I'm looking for what you think. I am interested in what you want to talk about after reading. But I know none of that can be done if you are NOT reading."
William:	"Does that mean I have to spend more time writing responses?"
Mr. Stygles:	"I don't think I need to answer that question. The question might be, 'Are you ready and willing to be honest about what you experience as a reader?'"
William:	"Experience?"
Mr. Stygles:	"Yeah. In the Reading Response Journal, I don't want you to write about reading because it's an assignment. I want you to discover yourself and then show what you think about your reading. It's your place to tell the world how you see things; the way only you can see."

(Continued)

(Continued)

William:	"Wow. That seems like a lot."
Mr. Stygles:	"It is. And it's going to take some time for us to figure it all out. I'll be honest, you're going to be writing a lot. Is it something you can do?"
William:	"I don't know. I'll try?"
Mr. Stygles:	"That's all I can ask."

Writing about reading is a way to look into the reader's soul. Shame festers with the absence of voice. William didn't have an outlet for articulation or self-expression, which begs the question, what's the point of reading? He adapted to complete assignments, not to reveal his perception. The catch is, any time we ask our readers to reveal themselves, it's our responsibility to attend to them and their vulnerabilities. Without that connection, the *mutuality of response* is tarnished. Mentoring and inquiry are absent, leaving no sense of value in the reader. In reality, writing about reading is a part of our world (book reviews in the *New Yorker*, blogs, tweets, etc.). Why not foster the contributions our students can make to our world? Who was William writing for? How was he creating or documenting *his* legacy?

My guess is that William had no intention of writing about reading when he entered my class. As demonstrated in the conversation, William's idea of reading was more about getting assignments done, not revealing his own thoughts and perceptions. The time-honored reader's notebook (Buckner, 2009), or in my class, the Reading Response Journal, is a means to explore the vulnerability behind a reader's perceptions, not purely as an accountability tool. In the world of shame, one thing was predominately clear: William felt that his thoughts had no value. If he could get away with copying, who would value what he really wanted to say? Nor did William understand how to articulate his thinking about reading. So, masterfully, he manipulated (a shame-based behavior) the assignment to ease his burden.

Shame festers with the absence of voice.

Naturally, William melted when he realized I'd caught on. He was shocked because I'd exposed him, without his approval. But he wasn't hurt. I didn't condemn him; rather, I kept his integrity intact by connecting with him. William didn't have a means to make sense of a text. He compensated to avoid the inadequacy he knew to be real. William may have felt shame through the exposure discussed in our conversation, for which I am sorry. But sometimes we have to learn the truth and lean into the discomfort. In truth, *it wasn't his fault*. Thus, the critical shift I needed to make with William was to make writing about reading about William.

> **Any time we ask our readers to reveal themselves, it's our responsibility to attend to them and their vulnerabilities.**

In this chapter, I share a multifaceted approach to writing about reading. These strategies become distinct legacies of the reader's development, integral to their self-perception as readers.

- Reading Response Journals and Perception-Based Responses
- Perception Exit Slips
- VOWELS Checklist
- Top Ten Bookshelf

Reading Response Journals and Perception-Based Responses

Comprehension instruction (Beck & McKeown, 2006; Collins-Block & Pressley, 2002; Daniels, 2011; McKeown et al., 2009; Pearson, 1985; Rafael et al., 2006) has been largely based on cognition. Students are typically expected to produce an answer that can either be found "right there" or inferred. These responses are not affective or tied to the individual's physical or emotional response, which is distinctive and individual, or what Muhammed (2020) defines as "genius." Rosenblatt (2005) reflects, "I couldn't ignore the fact that each [reader] brought different personal experience and sometimes quite different assumptions about people and society to the reading" (p. xxi).

Beers and Probst (2013) add:

> We'd like to see them independently, confidently, and competently noticing those points in the story that they think might yield the most insight into a text, the author's intention, and the characters' motives. We want them to notice those moments that trigger their memories and thoughts about their own lives, about other texts they have encountered, and about events in the world. (p. 4)

If we do not adhere to this advice, we run a tremendous risk of asking readers to dissociate from their own experience and to devalue their interactions with a text to show understanding that is already predetermined (likely by an adult). The consequences are that the reader's experience is forsaken, and the reader believes they should all comprehend a text the same way for what might be judged as accurate. This potentially asks that maturing readers think like adults. In such a case, we must refer back to Miller (1995), who reminds us that shame manifests when we ask students to forsake themselves to live out the expectations of our authority figures. Therefore, expression of the reader's unique experience with a text cannot be forsaken, whether it be to work within the four corners of the text or to obtain a test score to determine the reader's identity. Writing about reading is an experience that becomes a landmark within the reader's development—an indication of their comprehension abilities (Collins et al., 2017; Eason et al., 2012).

In my experience, students often arrive in my classroom with little knowledge of writing about reading. Their background generally includes answering questions on worksheets or in discussions, rarely including text references or evidence, a practice that becomes more widely expected during the year. Therefore, we reach a point, whether through read aloud (Beck & McKeown, 2001; Robb, 2013) or small groups (Fisher & Frey, 2010), where I want students to explore their comprehension and thinking through writing (Silver et al., 2012). Additionally, my job is to scaffold written responses such that maturing readers meaningfully comprehend text, meaning I can verify their understanding and inquire about their perceptions. To do so, I developed perception-based writing prompts that would be meaningful to readers and informative for my own practice. Perception-based responses allow a reader to consider themselves, their experiences, and their interpretations, in conjunction with and through interactions with text. This style of writing about reading incorporates elements of close reading, serving as a preliminary step to text-dependent questions or writing about reading that expects a reader to assume the role of an expert (Daniels, 2002), for example, *Questioning the Author* (Beck & McKeown, 2006; McKeown et al., 1993).

The Reading Response Journals we use are a reader's unique space where they tackle prompts or questions about text that integrate various text evidence, background knowledge, logic, and experience to create the maturing reader's ***perception***. The journal is a daily collection of personal thoughts about reading, reflections, documentation of the reader's development, and a record of their unique interactions with texts that set them apart from others—their own perspectives (Wilhelm, 2008). The difference for William (and all readers) lies in that his journal and entries wouldn't be about accountability but rather evidence of his involvement, interaction, and experience with his reading.

Making writing about reading meaningful to readers (Hicks, 2015) takes front-loading (Cummins & Quiroa, 2012), deliberate implementation, reinforced routine, and practice. The prompts scaffold text-dependent questions (Cherry-Paul & Johansen, 2014) by seeking to show how a student recognizes literary devices, and by revealing their interactions with text and their ability to engage in close reading and critical literacy (McLaughlin & DeVoogd, 2004; Vasquez, 2010). They also provide a unique expression of the reader's affect. The prompts, by venturing through the reader's perspective first, reduce the burden of shame by providing students an opportunity to express their own unique voice rather than risking the exposure of differences or misinterpretations. In this way they are unlike traditional questions, which often leave readers vulnerable.

Here are some sample prompts, tied to universal themes we study throughout the year:

My Reading Life

- What was it like for you to read last night?
- How did you make time to read yesterday (or not)?
- Is this book an easy, "just-right," or challenging book for you? Why?
- Why did you choose the book you're currently reading?
- What challenges do you face with reading? What would you like help with?
- As you are reading, is your book getting better or worse?

My Opinions About Books

- What is the best part of the book so far?
- What is the worst part of the book so far?
- What is your opinion of the book so far?
- Is the book a worthwhile read?
- Would you recommend the book to anyone? Why or why not?

Characters

- Do you agree with the choices the main character makes?
- Are you happy with a certain character?
- Do you find any inspiration in a character?
- If you could change something about a character, what would it be?
- What are the qualities that make the character likable?
- What is your opinion about how characters are treated by others?

Conflict

- What are some of the conflicts in your book?
- What are your thoughts about a conflict?
- What is the backstory behind a certain conflict?
- How does a character respond to a conflict?
- Are the conflicts keeping you interested in the story?

Connections

- How does the setting match what you know about your world?
- What places have you been to in your life that the characters have also been to?

- Do you see yourself in the main characters or other characters? How come?
- How are the conflicts similar to challenges in your life?

Strategic Thinking

- What do you think will happen in a particular setting or to characters?
- How will certain conflicts be resolved?
- What are the three main points another reader should take away from what you've read?
- What new words did you clarify in your reading? How did you figure them out? What do you like about those words?
- What questions did you write for other readers?
- What is the backstory for these questions?

If I Were the Author

- Would you have ended the book the same way?
- Would you have resolved a certain conflict differently than the author?
- At the end of your reading, write what might happen next.
- If you're not happy with a section of your book, take some time to rewrite it the way you think it should have gone.

Settings

- What is new to you about the setting?
- What have you learned about places because of the author's details about a setting?
- Could the story be written in different places?
- What makes the setting a good place for the story?

Perception-Based Response in Action

To begin, I introduce to readers response structures that are similar to examples already in existence (Cole, 2009; Wang et al., 2016). Readers who are new to written responses require a foundation on which to write. In that vein, I ask students to restate the question. Their initial response includes a statement of their perception since the prompts I've provided are open-ended and based on their thinking. Next, students include text references or evidence. Without a reference or evidence, readers have nothing to base their perception on. This is not asking for recall or what the student remembers; it is about what impacted them. Additionally, references or evidence stated by the reader are what they believe to be essential, which clues me in to their understanding of the text or ability to comprehend. Readers conclude responses with explanations or validations for the evidence chosen.

Tip: Over time, you can invite readers to deviate creatively in their perception-based responses, as long as text evidence supports their perception.

One book I use to initiate perception-based responses is multiple-award-winning *One Crazy Summer* (Williams-Garcia, 2010). Bringing William back around, as a group of us were working together, I asked the following prompt, "What is your opinion about how kids are treated by others?"

William wrote:

> *I think the kids whore [were] treated poorly because their mom wocked [walked] fast and when she did. Look back that whore told keep up. It was almost like the mom pot a mute butten on the kids. Because she would cut off the oldest every time she treed [tried] to talk. (Paragraph 1)*

If you notice, William provided an answer in this opening statement. This tells me he gets the gist or at least is capable of literal comprehension. I am confident he is following the text. He also includes a text reference. I define a text reference as when a student recalls a sample of text but doesn't provide exact textual evidence in the form of a quote. His response lacks a perception, or concluding thought, which identifies what he needs to learn next.

Adding Depth to Perception-Based Responses

To extend the heart of a response, I invite readers to unpack additional thinking (Walsh & Sattes, 2017), namely connections to text and background knowledge, or schema (Pearson, 1982). The heart of a reader's perception is the depth to which they identify text evidence (Hasty & Schrodt, 2015; Lehman & Roberts, 2014) and to what extent they can explain their thinking. Perception-based responses are intended to provide space so a reader can communicate—which includes developing and expanding on any annotations—the raw, authentic thoughts and perceptions the reader captured in the heart of the moment. Using a different prompt, I ask students how readers saw themselves in the text, building on the concept of windows and mirrors. I sought to nudge William by identifying as many possible connections he made with Delphine (the main character in *One Crazy Summer*) as possible. William offered the following connection:

To extend the heart of a response, I invite readers to unpack additional thinking.

We both act responsible one.

We both have sibling that like to fit [fight], but when one edes hurts one of them it's not ok. I have moved a lot more.

We both have summer camps to go to.

Delphen and I have a pritty similar but the detls [details] are different like I have moved sevrl times in my life. Dalphen's mom left when she was little. I didn't know ho my dad was intill about eight years old. Daplhen is a mini mom to vanenta and Fren. I have got 2 stichi's both in my grandmother Palas cusidey.

Dalphen mom was arrested when her and her soster whar [sister was] visiting. My dad has an x wife and it isn't my mom. Dalphen siblings all come from the same 2 people. Both granmas and moms don't like each other.

Despite his spelling and grammatical errors, William's response offered me insight into his perceptions. Regardless of abilities, I owe it to students to focus on their thoughts and perceptions first. Presentation alone was enough to invite William to withdraw and quit. But he revealed distinguishable traits of comprehension. Ironically, he left out the text evidence, but it's clear he was referring to the text. Not bad for someone who skated through his previous grade by copying text, not to mention the vulnerability he showed because of his spelling challenges. Once I dug into William's perceptions, I learned he possessed a virtual superpower. He could process questions and identify essential text references to support his thinking!

Exit Slips

There's a reality in all our classrooms. We love certain books, and we enjoy expressing our affinity. But on occasion (or more often than not if students really feel secure), some of our readers just don't feel the same way about a book as we do. I used to get upset when students disagreed with me. I couldn't understand why. I had to look in my own mirror and realize that the reading experience in the classroom was not about me. I had to start looking through their lens. I needed to ask students what they thought about what I read or what they read. Was it beneficial to them? Did they have thoughts they wanted to express without my influence? Each of these drives at perceptions readers possess within themselves, perceptions that are not often sought out or given space.

I've found that an efficient way to overcome this is to enter their world and to honor the perception of the reader through the use of exit slips (Marzano, 2007). Exit slips help me understand how a student viewed a book and allow their peers to honor and factor in the voice of another student reader—rather than my adult self—when making book selections.

Book Review Exit Slips are a popular means for students to share their perceptions of books with their peers. It's a tool to project the voice and opinion of even our most reserved readers. While I prefer to use this strategy when advance reader copies of a book are available in my classroom or to promote wide reading of books on our annual state book list, the reality is, such a tool is especially useful when students are willing to read books that would otherwise go unopened. Additionally Book Review Exit Slips are exceptionally helpful for slow readers or for those students who simply withhold their brilliant perspectives because they believe they cannot compete or keep up with their peers in discussions.

Book Review Exit Slips are a popular means for students to share their perceptions of books with their peers.

The exits slips are simple for students to complete and are not overly time demanding, which allows readers to begin their next book quickly. The exit slips are usually written on a small index card and include the following:

- One-sentence summary
- One-sentence opinion
- Target audience
- Star rating (1-5 scale)

To establish the habit of writing Book Review Exit Slips, the entire class locates their most recent book finished. I begin by sharing the book I most recently finished. Placing an index card underneath a document camera, I write out my response as a model. We continue this practice once a week for the next 3 to 4 weeks. As readers complete their independent reading books, they begin completing the exit tickets on their own. I typically collect them for a quick read-through before affixing them to books. (This only applies to books I've purchased.) Often, I confer with the readers before I attach the cards to help students project their voice most accurately and competently. Following a conference, I attach the card to the book's back cover to hide the comments or summary provided by the publisher. This places the emphasis on the readers in our classroom. In turn, students are more likely to read a new or different book because of reviews from their peers (see Figure 7.1). If we run out of space, tickets are posted on a bulletin board in the classroom library for students to reference. The Book Review Exit Slips also create a space for withdrawn readers to help them add their voice and become involved within the reading community in a less apprehensive manner. Additionally, the exit slip can be a post-reading companion to the Reading Visa presented in Chapter 3.

The Book Review Exit Slips also create a space for withdrawn readers to help them add their voice and become involved within the reading community.

7.1 and 7.2 Sample Book Review Exit Slips

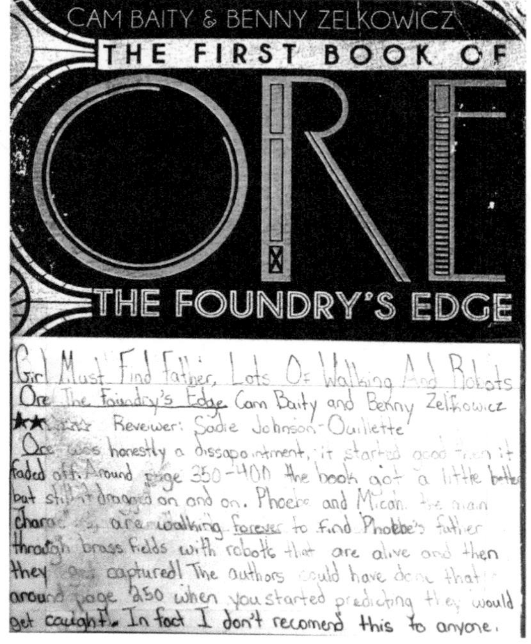

Girl Must Find Father, Lots Of Walking And Robots

Ore The Foundry's Edge Cam Baity and Benny Zelkowicz

★★☆☆☆ Reveiwer: Sadie Johnson-Ouillette

Ore was honestly a dissapointment, it started good then it faded off. Around page 350-400 the book got a little better but still it dragged on and on. Phoebe and Micah the main characters are walking forever to find Phoebe's father through brass fields with robots that are alive and then they get captured! The authors could have done that around page 250 when you started predicting they would get caught. In fact I don't recomend this to anyone.

Book tittle: Elvies and the underdogs ★★★★★+

Ather: Jenny Lee

Name: kaitlyn Pelletier

Three kids go washington. D.C. to save a dog.

I chose a 5t rateing because it's the best book I have ever readed. I like how the three friends don't quit intill thay now how stay together. I rack amand this book to kids that like a chaling book. It is fun. It tells you to have fath in your friend. But that is not all....

VOWELS Checklist

Writing about reading isn't just about comprehension. It's also about the act of reading or reading process. When we consider the internalized shame of a reader, the best way to keep a reader feeling safe is to be mindful of their inner thoughts including challenges, celebrations, and confusions around the reading process. I do this by providing readers a space to write metacognitively about their reading process so they can consider where they've been and where they're going, making their journey visible (Hattie, 2012). If the reader's development is the centerpiece of our instruction, reading becomes something they are part of rather than something done to them.

If the reader's development is the centerpiece of our instruction, reading becomes something they are part of rather than something done to them.

In Brown's (2010) *The Gifts of Imperfection*, she uses vowels (A-E-I-O-U) as a means of self-reflection (p. 74), called a "vowel check." Brown's premise, which she adopted from a friend, is meant to evaluate where one is at and consider ideas to move forward. This same premise can help students consider their reading development. If a person can gain a strong sense of their inner voice, and that inner voice can be nurtured, defeating negative self-talk, readers can begin to develop resilience or gain confidence. Students like William can become less dependent on what I think, or how I score them as the definition of their value. The VOWELS checklist works to empower readers' ownership and reflection on their affect (their motivation and engagement with reading) to reduce apathy and develop the integrity of their reading identities.

Depending on your classroom, the VOWELS checklist can be done weekly, biweekly, or monthly. I prefer that students review their affect (engagement and motivation) at the conclusion of a week. In turn, we can create goals for the coming days. Normally, students have about 15 minutes to complete the document. Should time allow, I confer with students to help them embellish their reflection or to mine for information that will guide future reading conferences. We typically start documenting our legacies through VOWELS checklists late in the fall once we've created the reading community and initiated strategic instruction (see Chapter 4).

Tip: The VOWELS checklist can be used in a hard-copy format or digitally via a shared document, should you be inclined to make digital portfolios.

7.3 Managing My Reading Life: The VOWELS Checklist (Beginner Version)

Vowel	Reflection
Acknowledgment How did I deal with my excitement, anxiety, distractions, and/or concerns that might disrupt my reading?	
Exercise How did I give myself an appropriate amount of time to practice my reading this week?	
I What did *I* do for myself as a reader this week that makes me enjoy reading or helps me become a "better" reader?	
Others How did I help others in my class or family to become better readers?	
Unexpressed What am I irritated or upset about that prevents me from reading? What should I talk to my teacher about?	
Yay! What is my major celebration for reading this week?	

Here are descriptions for each vowel in the checklist.

Acknowledgment: This prompt asks readers how they dealt with excitement, anxiety, distractions, and/or perseverating concerns. Readers deserve to address the factors that are swirling around in their heads before they attempt to read. When we acknowledge these, we can better prepare ourselves for a joyful reading experience.

Exercise: Every reader needs to honestly look at when and how much was read during the week. I'm not looking for fake reading logs that include 30 minutes no matter what, the same time, every night. I want the reader to think about their actions and how they are made. It's time to exercise their reading habit.

I: If we want to move away from compliance and dependency (Beers, 2003), *I* needs to have a role. Not "Mr. Stygles, what do I do next?" but "Here's what I did for myself." Did *I* choose a better book? Did *I* intentionally use a strategy to make sense of what I read? *I* is the most important aspect of believing in oneself.

Others: Not to say *I* is bad, but charity is great, too. Maturing readers are developmentally narcissistic. Yet to build capacity, communication, and collaboration, readers should be mindful to consider how they help others. Did they offer a book suggestion, strategy, advice? Help clarify a word? Read aloud to a tired friend? We can help each other read rather than take away by talking to neighbors during class.

Unexpressed: Shame loves silence. We can be buried in our ruminations, the thoughts we leave unexpressed. Kids don't want to say that reading aloud stinks. Or strategies stink. Or that they are irritated they cannot read because home, school, or the classroom is too loud. Shame resilience is predicated on feeling safe. This document can be a space where the reader can unload for a minute. It's my responsibility to maintain the trust within the interpersonal bridge when I read what is recorded.

Shame resilience is predicated on feeling safe. This document can be a space where the reader can unload for a minute.

Yay! Everyone deserves a celebration! Students deserve to feel pride from within. What is it they accomplished without external feedback? There is a time for external feedback. At this point, I want to start building toward intrinsic motivation.

The VOWELS checklist reflections are not as easy as distributing and asking students to complete them. Rather, reflections are apt to reveal *things* about reading that the reader would much rather keep private, like not reading, for example. Moreover, some readers are forced into a dual layer of shame when they lack the language to complete thoughts efficiently and effectively. William had always had a history of reluctance, which would better be reframed as apprehension. He didn't warm up to the VOWELS checklist, and why should he? William had to trust that the revelations he made wouldn't indict him and that they would be meaningful to me. So after I modeled and set readers on their way, I walked around the room to check their initial thoughts. William glared at an empty page.

"How are things coming along?" I asked him.

"I'm thinking." He returned. Three minutes later I checked in again. Page still blank.

"William," I said, leaning into the interpersonal bridge, "Let's work together over at the roundtable. I'll listen to what you might be avoiding writing. I would like to see where you're at. Maybe we can come up with some ideas and get you into a good position." Off we went.

Dylyn, one of William's close friends, had similar attitudes. He was delightful to talk with, though reluctant when it came to reading. He didn't have as much apprehension about completing the checklist, though we had some mechanics to work on. Dylyn's responses to the VOWELS Checklist (Figure 7.4) reveal how self-perception and reading purpose merge.

7.4 Dylyn's VOWELS Checklist (Advanced Version)

Vowel	Action	Specific Examples
Acknowledgment: How did I deal with my excitement, anxiety, distractions, and/or concerns that might disrupt my reading?	I just ignored her and said, "Go play in your room."	My sister kept coming into my room while I was reading and wanting to play.
Exercise: How did I give myself an appropriate amount of time to practice my reading this week?	I sat on my bed and kept on reading.	I read every day.

Vowel	Action	Specific Examples
I: What did *I* do for myself as a reader this week that makes me enjoy reading or helps me become a "better" reader?	I shut my door and sat in the corner.	I read 3 books in 2 days!!
Others: How did I help others in my class, or family, become better readers?	?	? I didn't help anyone.
Unexpressed: What am I irritated or upset about that prevents me from reading? What should I talk to Mr. Stygles about?	??	My sister always comes into my room and doesn't leave! And she takes my books!
Yay! What is my major celebration for reading this week?	*Kew Kid*, *Camp*, and *Black Death*.	I read 3 books in 2 days.

As you can likely tell, even with these short responses, there is a lot to glean from Dylyn's VOWELS checklist. For starters, he tended to mix up his actions with specific examples. For instance, his "action" for "exercise" should have been "I read every day." The specific example, then, would have been what he listed as an "action." We can also see that Dylyn has made strides to improve his reading life and his reading environment because he:

- acknowledged that he had distractions, namely his sister. Students with younger siblings certainly face such distractions, which can negatively impact their reading experiences.
- exercised his reading by making time every day. Notice he doesn't specify the time, but his location. This could become a goal, not for time and pages, but to reveal how productive his time could be.

- took care of himself ("What did I do for 'I?'") by defining a space of his own to read. He notes "Yay" as well, pointing out that physiological self-care produces benefits.
- didn't express frustration (lacking language, perhaps?); although, he expressed that his sister, well, acts like a little sister. Though frustrated, my suggestion to Dylyn would be to read to his sister.
- celebrated the completion of two graphic novels and a nonfiction trade book. In context, this is a marked improvement over recent reading. Dylyn deviated into unfamiliar books, including nonfiction, for self-selected reading. Until that point, he'd only reread the popular run of graphic novels.

He left "Others" with question marks. Helping other readers is often a newfound concept, at least in my experience. Depending on the time of year, this can be okay. By year's end, I would like to see students defining "helping others" as helping with unknown words, book suggestions, and reading together by choosing books to read together or starting book clubs, all actions that improve self-perception. I would often pair Dylyn and William together as thinking buddies just to show William he wasn't alone, even if he often felt that way. *Thinking buddies* are peer partnerships I establish with students early in the school year. The intent is for every student to have a reliable companion to share their reading and writing with when I am not available.

Reflections such as the VOWELS checklist make the interpersonal bridge essential. I'm diving deep into their vulnerabilities, which I must honor with the utmost respect. The question is "Who is in charge of their reading life?" The VOWELS checklist creates an agentive answer!

My Favorites Bookshelf

Writing about reading is an opportunity to turn what is commonly seen as a vice into a strength. William had a loud, outspoken, and judgmental nature that had not yet been used for reading. He was often outspoken and disruptive, but extremely sensitive, too. William was a near-perfect example of how individuals buried in shame cope: loud and attention-seeking, aimed to protect and shelter the deeply rooted negative internalizations. Once I caught on to this trait, I redirected William. Sometimes students need to have their "vices" converted to talents.

Milestone projects like the Favorites Bookshelf give readers like William a chance to be the critic about books they have read up to this point in their reading lives. For once, all the judgments and options they had around books they had to read can finally be aired out!

Milestone projects like the Favorites Bookshelf give readers like William a chance to be the critic about books they have read up to this point in their reading lives.

A Favorites Bookshelf comes at the end of the year when it's time to reflect on how we've grown. In this project, somewhat analogous to the reading autobiography, readers reflect on their previous preferences and what they have learned from the reading by selecting their top 10 read books from kindergarten to now. This can include read aloud, assigned, and independently read books as long as readers provide the title, the year read, and the experience.

To begin, readers brainstorm a list of their favorite books. Hopefully, the lists go beyond 10 titles. Next, they take the tougher step of reorganizing the list into their top 10—descending or ascending order, depending on the reader's choice. Most everyone reads their list closely to choose their absolute favorites and ultimate favorite first. To differentiate the project, based mainly on writing stamina and scheduling, some students write their top five books. Others go for a more expansive top 10. Then, readers write to explain why they chose each book. Figure 7.5 shows an overview.

For the first session of our Bookshelf unit, I give students about 20 minutes to brainstorm a list of what could very well be their favorite books of all time. William started well, thinking back to read alouds from primary grades and books read to him by his parents. He conjured up a few titles that he enjoyed from this year as well. He'd listed almost 15 books before asking me if he could revisit the Reading Passport (see Chapter 3) I'd collected throughout the year. By the time he was done, he'd reeled off 25 books—too many!! A pleasant surprise.

William ran up to me showing off his list. I asked him, "How will you parse this list down?" He had no clue, so we sat down together. I asked him, "What books can you absolutely not live without, and which one's made you feel yourself become a reader?" William took a highlighter

7.5 Favorites Bookshelf Assignment Overview

Favorites Bookshelf

The directions are as follows:

Introduction: Here you will explain what this assignment is about and reflect on reading before entering your next phase of school.

- What is the assignment?
- What are you hoping to tell your reader?

Book Headers: Your writing will be grouped into 10 sections, one for each book. Each section, though, is not its own paragraph.

Book Discussion: Since you will have different ideas about each book, each idea is its own paragraph. Here are some ideas for what you can write about for your selected books:

- How did the book appeal to you, regarding topic or emotions?
- How did the author's writing style appeal to you?
- What made a book special, more so than others?
- What moment in the book resonated with you most? Why?
- Would you recommend this book to readers? Why?
- Why is this your favorite book?
- What made this book better than others?
- How did you experience the book?
- Who was your favorite character?
- Did you "find yourself" in the story?
- Did you relate or connect to the character?
- What parts of the plot did you connect to?
- What conflicts did you recognize in your own life?
- What conflicts kept you interested in the story?
- What writing styles did the writer use that kept the book interesting?
- What kept you hooked? Or interested in reading?

Conclusion: Here, you will write about your experiences overall in elementary school.

- Did you like reading?
- What were the best parts about reading?
- What were some of your best experiences reading?
- Or you can write about the negative stuff.
- Finally, what is a lesson you learned about reading, good or bad, or that you would suggest to another student in the future?

to indicate which books meant the most. We stopped there, celebrating success.

On the second day of a 2-week unit, students easily begin writing about their favorite books. I model each lesson. From book selection to writing about the book, I share with my students an example of my writing from my own bookshelf (see Figure 7.6).

7.6 Model Paragraph for Top 10 Bookshelf

#1 Book of All Time - *Rump* by Liesl Shurtliff (2013)

Rump is my favorite book of all time. I forgot the reason I read the book, but I instantly fell in love with Rump, the main character. Rump is short for Rumpelstiltskin. It's funny for obvious reasons. Rump falls in love with a girl who couldn't care less for him. That's the main reason I like Rump so much. He goes on a journey to discover himself, but he's really out to rescue the girl, Opal, with whom he is in love. Opal's husband, the king, treats her like dirt. You'd think Opal would be thrilled for a boy like Rump, especially after Rump rescues her. But she isn't.

When I read this book, it felt like the story of my life!! Rump and I are soul brothers. He's insecure like I am, and he fell in love with a girl who didn't love him. I should have expected the ending. Rump finds himself a "better" life, but I don't buy it.

I loved reading this book to my class because I cracked jokes and made silly comments while I was reading. I was always making predictions and asking questions because I felt like I was talking to myself. No other book made me smile inside like this one!

Generally, I have students write about their favorite book first because that is the one that will likely represent the best run of memories, experiences, and learning. William started experimenting on his own using the prompts I'd offered. Over the next few days, William had some challenges because he was writing retells for every book. And they were long! Even though his final product was mainly retelling (see Figures 7.7 and 7.8), they are significant reductions. To help him, because it is very easy for writers to get lost in larger projects, I asked William the prompts, then recorded the notes for him. One question I asked him was "Why is this book on your bookshelf?" I recorded the notes and gave him feedback before he returned to writing.

You can see the result in what he wrote for his top two books:

1. *My Big Fat Zombie Goldfish* (5th)

   I choose this book because it's a very good book. It is filled with an adventure and science. It is full of adventures and morons. If you want to find out what that means then read the book and if you have an older brother call him a moron. This book is on my bookshelf because of the battery.

2. *My Big Fat Zombie Goldfish #2* (5th)

   Same thing here but the sea equal full of eel bay and the adventures of the morons. They need to find a way to signal there dads cause they are stuck in the water looking for their son. When they are actually back at the light house. This is on my bookshelf because of the mistress upstairs in the light house.

In the first response, he eliminated his retell to include a reason he chose *My Big Fat Zombie Goldfish* (O'Hara, 2013), with a modest, though not explicit rationale. He concludes with the reason the book is on his bookshelf, leaving us hanging on this idea of a "battery." When he turned the project in, I asked him why. His reply: "I wanted to leave a cliffhanger so you would read it." William's second response assumes we've learned a lot from his first book with his opening sentence, before leaving us with another cliffhanger about the "mistress."

At first blush, the final project is nothing overwhelming. It's full of grammatical errors and awkward writing. However, he's come a long way from his perception-based responses earlier in the chapter. There is a dramatic shift in his writing. Even in his tone of voice, it's quite apparent that William is more responsive to writing and expressing his perceptions about reading.

7.7 and 7.8 William's Favorites Bookshelf

my book shelf

1) My Big Fat Zombie Goldfish (5th)

I choose this book because it is a very good book. It is filled with an adventure and science. It is full of adventures and morons. If you want to find out what that means then read the book and if you have a older brother call them a moron. This book is on my book shelf because of the battery.

2) My Big Fat Zombie Goldfish #2 (5th)

Same thing here but the sea equal full of eel bay and the adventures of the morons. They need to find a way to signal there dads cause they are stuck in the water looking for there son. When they are really back at the light house. This is on my bookshelf because of the mistress upstairs of the light house.

3)Star Bounders Rebellion (5th)

This is a outer space adventure it is were a boy named Zachary has to save the outer verse from bison and more creators. You may be thinking why did bison go into the outer verse well they are not bison that are here on earth they are a outer space creature that try's to stop them from saving and to find out more read star bounders rebellion. This book is on my bookshelf because of the outer space motor cycles and how they get to earth.

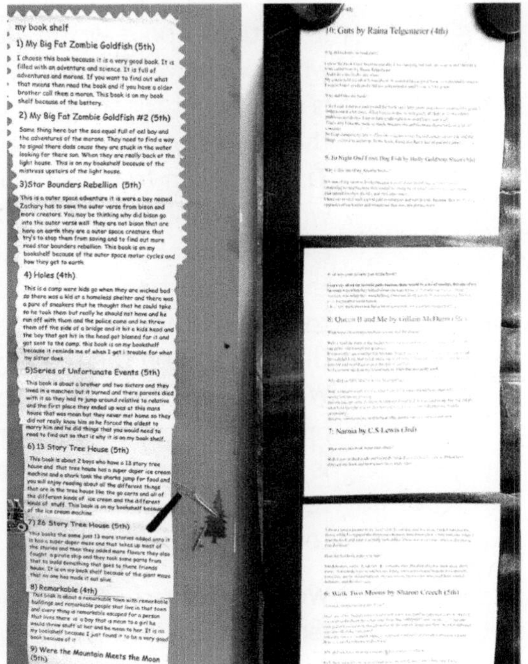

my book shelf

1) My Big Fat Zombie Goldfish (5th)

I choose this book because it is a very good book. It is filled with an adventure and science. It is full of adventures and morons. If you want to find out what that means then read the book and if you have a older brother call them a moron. This book is on my book shelf because of the battery.

2) My Big Fat Zombie Goldfish #2 (5th)

Same thing here but the sea equal full of eel bay and the adventures of the morons. They need to find a way to signal there dads cause they are stuck in the water looking for there son. When they are really back at the light house. This is on my bookshelf because of the mistress upstairs of the light house.

3)Star Bounders Rebellion (5th)

This is a outer space adventure it is were a boy named Zachary has to save the outer verse from bison and more creators. You may be thinking why did bison go into the outer verse well they are not bison that are here on earth they are a outer space creature that try's to stop them from saving and to find out more read star bounders rebellion. This book is on my bookshelf because of the outer space motor cycles and how they get to earth.

4) Holes (4th)

This is a camp were kids go when they are wicked bad so there was a kid at a homeless shelter and there was a pare of sneakers that he thought that he could take so he took them but really he should not have and he run off with them and the police came and he threw them off the side of a bridge and it hit a kids head and the boy that got hit in the head got blamed for it and got sent to the camp. this book is on my bookshelf because it reminds me of when I get i trouble for what my sister does.

5)Series of Unfortunate Events (5th)

This book is about a brother and two sisters and they lived in a manchen but it burned and there parents died with it so they had to jump around relative to relative and the first place they ended up was at this mans house that was mean but they never met home so they did not really know him so he forced the oldest to marry him and he did things that you would need to read to find out so that is why it is on my book shelf.

6) 13 Story Tree House (5th)

This book is about 2 boys who have a 13 story tree house and that tree house has a super doper ice cream machine and a shark tank the sharks jump for food and you will enjoy reading about all the different things that are in the tree house like the go carts and all of the different kinds of ice cream and the different kinds of stuff. This book is on my bookshelf because of the ice cream machine

7) 26 Story Tree House (5th)

This books the same just 13 more stories added onto it it has a super doper maze and that takes up most of the stories and then they added more flavors they also fought a pirate ship and they took some parts from that to build something that goes to there friends house. It is on my book shelf because of the giant maze that no one has made it out alive.

8) Remarkable (4th)

This book is about a remarkable town with remarkable buildings and remarkable people that live in that town and every thing is remarkable escaped for a person that lives there it a boy that is mean to a girl he would throw stuff at her and be mean to her. It is on my bookshelf because I just found it to be a very good book because of it

9) Were the Mountain Meets the Moon (5th)

When William emailed me his 10-page, single-spaced, document, I thought I was in for a long painful read. Instead, I had the delight of reading the most expressive document William ever wrote. He later said to me, "Wow. I read a lot, and I hate reading! These books weren't easy." William was proud of himself. I was proud of him, too, and he knew it.

> **The experience of reflecting on his reading for himself changed William's perception of himself as a reader forever.**

Writing about reading gave William a reason to define himself. Gone were the days of copying pages from books to mask his decision to avoid reading. The experience of reflecting on his reading for himself changed William's perception of himself as a reader forever. When he graduated from high school, I learned that William's Favorites Bookshelf was the longest paper he'd ever written. Rarely do we have a chance to encapsulate our experience in a manner that mirrors back a positive image of ourselves. William had that. It remained with him until he graduated.

Final Thoughts

If we think about writing about reading as the inner voice of the child whom we have to give space for expression, then writing about reading is paramount for students to define their perceptions and individuality, thereby establishing a legacy. The problem is, we don't always do it. Time is taken from us regularly. Yet we cannot ignore the potential of writing about reading. We must strike a balance between reading and expressions about reading. I've made the mistake of silencing readers through questions that had one right answer or not giving them space to express their thoughts at all. As time slips away, we may increase the pressure on the reader about what they should know and perform. Writing about reading is lost. When we do this, the reader bears the brunt. Their opportunity to share their perspectives and to be accepted is replaced by the teacher's voice, and this creates shame. Then our readers give up. If there is no way to share a voice, there is no reason to read. This is shame.

Writing about reading is successful because it is used as the vehicle to express individuality, uniqueness, and best of all, giftedness. I want to hear the voice of readers. I want readers to capture their reading experiences and cherish that as a legacy. William didn't get to have this experience until fifth grade. William made himself apparent in my classroom, where previously he had covered up his pain. To self-actualize and improve his self-concept, he needed someone who would not judge his faults. More important, he needed a safe place to reveal his inner voice.

> **Writing about reading is successful because it is used as the vehicle to express individuality, uniqueness, and best of all, giftedness.**

William had come a long way in 1 year. Based on the Favorites Bookshelf, eight of his 10 favorite books came from our year together. William's grand total of books may not have beaten my 40-book challenge, but for a student who started the year copying text, he'd certainly become a *reader*! Moreover, he dared greatly, if you will, to write about *his* reading.

William shifted from insecurity about discussing books to articulating through writing—the most important skill related to comprehension in later years where everything seems to be a response to text (namely in college). As for now, it's time for readers to shine! Let them write!

Reflect and Act

Use these reflection questions to consider the information shared in the chapter and how you can apply it in your own classroom.

1. How does writing about reading currently occur in your classroom, and how is it integrated into your literacy instruction? What opportunities might you have to make writing about reading look different?
2. How might the writing about reading strategies presented in this chapter influence the role of student voice and agency in your classroom?
3. Choose one writing about reading strategy. How do you think it will make the most immediate impact in your classroom and will benefit readers?

AFTERWORD

When I started writing this book nearly a decade ago, I had an idea borne from my own recovery. To be honest, I wanted to write a book that detailed every connection between shame and reading. Somewhere on an external hard drive rests a stream of consciousness about what shame is, and several stories that confirm shame exists in classrooms and why.

Instead, what has resulted from my journey, professional and personal self-reflection, and time spent writing, is a book about relationships. Kate Atkinson, literacy coach at Lyseth Elementary School, took time to read a chapter just before I wrapped up my final revisions. She noted how much care I put into my student readers. How I set high expectations and join them on the journey toward those expectations. As I wrote and the book evolved, the integrity of content I shared was revealed through my relationships with students, both good and bad. So as you walk away from reading this book, you might be thinking how wonderful it must be in my classroom.

It didn't used to be that way.

When I first started teaching, I prided myself on being a fun teacher whom kids liked. I took my students for granted, caring more about what they could do for me—how they could make me look good. I focused on accolades that other teachers ending up winning. In light of my personal interest in professional development, I struggled dearly against beliefs that programs were more effective than teachers. I'd bought into the mindset that test scores—increasing those scores and closing the achievement gap—were more important than anything else. While I was fantastic at gaining those desired test scores and increasing the number of students who scored in the meeting or exceeding ranges, my professionalism became an epic nightmare.

I didn't realize it at first, but I had a pronounced impact on my classroom. Students loved being in my classroom. Until they didn't. John Lennon and Paul McCartney once expressed, "The love you make is equal to the love you break." My students worked hard to impress me. They didn't want to fail or let me down. Little did I know, my students wanted me to value them. No matter how hard they worked, I was never satisfied. When readers experienced a transgression, something like not reading at home, I was quick to point out their failures. What my students learned as a result of my behaviors was that they couldn't be good enough. Students began to realize I was willing to make them feel incapable as a means to meet my expectations.

The easiest way for my students to adapt was to withdraw. The blank expressions on their faces and the apathy toward their assignments were the only ways they could reasonably fight back. So indeed, what my students were willing to give in affection, they were more than willing to take away through academics based on how I treated them. I'd failed at what mattered most, noticing students for who they were, how they thought, and their unique accomplishments. The smiles students showed at the start of the school year vanished. Empty faces filled the desks; apathy reigned. I wasn't about to win awards, and the cost of burdening children for the sake of data was torturing me. In a sense, I gave up.

The blank expressions on their faces and the apathy toward their assignments were the only ways they could reasonably fight back.

When I stopped competing for test scores, reading levels, and reading 40 books a year, I was able to give my heart to readers again. But even still, it took a long time to reach the point where I could communicate the information in this book in a way that would be beneficial to you, the reader. When you reach a point in your life when you don't feel valued or like you matter, there is one thing you can do: make others feel like they matter. You can acknowledge and admire the unique wonders of those who rely on you most, your students. I diverted my attention from test scores and accomplishments by focusing on my students, who just wanted to be noticed and loved. When I was able to divest myself of everything thing else that boggled my mind as an educator and place my attention solely on the experiences of my readers, the joy of teaching returned. My classroom environment shifted. My students began to walk tall, even those who traditionally struggled.

So yes, this book could only be told through relationships. Harkening back to the start of this book, it takes a relationship to feel shame, and it takes a relationship to emerge from shame. In other words, a relationship based on authority that has barriers between the teacher and students is bound to create shame. A relationship based on empathy, understanding, and connection resurrects a person from the depths of shame.

It takes a relationship to feel shame, and it takes a relationship to emerge from shame.

At day's end, there is only one silver bullet. That's you. Resiliency doesn't happen because we tell our kids to be resilient. Resiliency is not a term we can use to justify the intensity of our expectations or amount of burden we place on our students. Resiliency happens when our readers recognize that we're willing to work with them every step of the way. That we will sit with them, eye-to-eye, knee-to-knee, and support them on their reading journey.

Our maturing readers no longer need to say, "I hate reading." When you are willing to be involved with a person during their challenges and grow with a person to see them blossom, there is nothing to hate. Just love.

Resiliency happens when our readers recognize that we're willing to work with them every step of the way.

REFERENCES

Abodeeb-Gentile, T., & Zawilinski, L. (2013). Reader identity and the common core: Agency and identity in leveled reading. *The Language and Literacy Spectrum, 23*, 34-45.

Afflerbach, P. (2016). Reading assessment: Looking ahead. *The Reading Teacher, 69*(4), 413-419.

Allen, P. (2009). *Conferring: The keystone of the reader's workshop*. Stenhouse.

Allington, R. L., & McGill-Franzen, A. (2013). *Summer reading loss: Closing the rich/poor reading achievement gap*. International Literacy Association.

Anderson, C. (2000). *How's it going? A practical guide to conferring with student writers*. Heinemann.

Ang, R. P., & Khoo, A. (2004). The relationship between psychopathology and shame in secondary school students. *Pastoral Care in Education, 22*(1), 25-33.

Applegate, A. J., & Applegate, M. D. (2010). A study of thoughtful literacy and the motivation to read. *The Reading Teacher, 64*(4), 226-234.

Applegate, M. D., Applegate, A. J., & Modla, V. B. (2009). "She's my best reader; she just can't comprehend": Studying the relationship between fluency and comprehension. *The Reading Teacher, 62*(6), 512-521.

Appleman, D. (2006). *Reading for themselves: How to transform adolescents into lifelong readers through out-of-class book clubs*. Heinemann.

Athans, S. K., & Devine, D. A. (2010). *Quality comprehension: A strategic model of reading instruction using read-along guides, Grades 3-6*. International Reading Association.

Atwell, N. (2007). *The reading zone: How to help kids become skilled, passionate, habitual, critical readers*. Scholastic.

Atwell, N. (2015). *In the middle: A lifetime of learning about reading, writing, and adolescents* (3rd ed.). Heinemann.

Aukerman, M. (2007). When reading it wrong is getting it right: Shared evaluation pedagogy among "struggling" fifth grade readers. *Research in the Teaching of English, 42*(1), 56-103.

Aukerman, M. (2013). Rereading comprehension pedagogies: Toward a dialogic teaching ethic that honors student sense making. *Dialogic Pedagogy, 1*, A1-A30.

Barnes, J. (2020). Promoting student agency in writing. *The Reading Teacher, 73*(6), 789-795.

Barnhouse, D., & Vinton, V. (2012). *What readers really do. Teaching the process of meaning making*. Heinemann.

Barone, D., & Barone, R. (2015). Students' understandings of what is important in the teaching of reading. *Voices From the Middle, 23*(1), 10-18.

Barone, D., & Barone, R. (2017). Rethinking reader response with fifth graders' semiotic interpretations. *The Reading Teacher, 71*(1), 23-31. https://doi.org/10.1002/trtr.1563

Barone, D., & Barone, R. (2018). The persuasive art of responding. *Journal of Practitioner Research, 3*(2), Article 1. https://doi.org/10.5038/2379-9951.3.2.1085

Barshay, J. (2022). Researchers blast data analysis for teachers to help students: Data pinpoints problems but not solutions for teachers. Hechinger Report.

Basset, H. H., Denham, S. A., Mohtasham, M., & Austin, N. (2020). Psychometric properties of the book readings for an affective classroom education (BRACE) coding system. *Reading Psychology, 41*(4), 322-346.

Baumeister, R. F., & Leary, M. R. (1995). The need to belong: Desire for interpersonal attachments as a fundamental human motivation. *Psychological Bulletin, 117*(3), 497-529.

Beck, I. L., & McKeown, M. G. (2001). Text talk: Capturing the benefits of read-aloud experiences for young children. *The Reading Teacher, 55*(1), 10-20.

Beck, I. L., & McKeown, M. G. (2006). *Improving comprehension with questioning the author: A fresh and expanded view of a powerful approach.* Scholastic.

Beck, I. L., & McKeown, M. G. (2008). *Creating robust vocabularies: Frequently asked questions and extended examples.* Guilford Press.

Beck, I., McKeown, M. G., & Kucan, L. (2002). *Bringing words to life: Robust vocabulary development.* Guilford Press.

Beers, K. (1998). Choosing not to read: understanding why some middle schoolers just say no. In K. Beers & B. Samuels (Eds.), *Into focus: Understanding and creating middle school readers* (pp. 1-27). Christopher Gordon.

Beers, K. (2003). *When kids can't read: A guide for teachers K-12*. Heinemann.

Beers, K., & Probst, R. E. (2013). *Notice and note: Strategies for close reading.* Heinemann.

Beers, K., & Probst, R. E. (2017). *Disrupting thinking:* Why *how we read matters.* Scholastic.

Beers, K., & Probst, R. E. (2020). *Forged by reading: The power of a literate life.* Scholastic.

Biancarosa, G., & Snow, C. E. (2006). *Reading next: A vision for action and research in middle and high school literacy: A report from the Carnegie Corporation of New York* (2nd ed.). Alliance for Excellent Education.

Bigelman, L. G., & Peterson, D. S. (2016). *No more reading instruction without differentiation*. Heinemann.

Bishop, R. S. (1990, Summer). Mirrors, windows, & sliding glass doors. *Perspectives, 6*(3), ix-xi.

Blachowicz, C., & Ogle, D. (2001). *Reading comprehension: Strategies for independent learners*. Guilford Press.

Block-Lewis, H. (1990). Shame, repression, field dependence, and psychopathology. In J. L. Singer (Ed.), *Repression and disassociation: Implications for personality theory, psychopathology, and health* (pp. 233-258). University of Chicago Press.

Boyles, N. (2014). *Closer reading, grades 3-6: Better prep, smarter lessons, deeper comprehension*. Corwin Literacy.

Brassell, D. (2006). *Readers for life: The ultimate reading fitness guide, K-8.* Heinemann.

Brinchmann, E. I., Hjetland, H. N., & Lyster, S. H. (2020). Lexical quality matters: Effects of word knowledge instruction on the language and literacy skills of third and fourth-grade poor readers. *Reading Research Quarterly, 51*(2), 165-180. https://doi.org/10.1002/rrq128

Brown, B. (2007). *I thought it was just me (but it isn't): Making the journey from "What will people think?" to "Am I enough."* Gotham Books.

Brown, B. (2010). *The gifts of imperfection: Let go of who you think you're supposed to be and embrace who you are*. Hazeldon.

Brown, B. (2015). *Daring greatly: How the courage to be vulnerable transforms the way we live, love, parent, and lead.* Avery.

Brown, B. (2017). *Rising strong: How the ability to reset transfers the way we live, love, parent, and lead.* Random House.

Brown, B., Hernandez, V. R., & Villarreal, Y. (2011). Connections: A 12 session psychoeducational shame resilience curriculum. In R. L. Dearing & J. P. Tangney (Eds.), *Shame in the therapy hour.* American Psychological Association.

Buckner, A. (2009). *Notebook connections: Strategies for the reader's notebook.* Stenhouse.

Burke, J. (2012). *The English teacher's companion* (4th ed.). Heinemann.

Burke, J. (2010). *What's the big idea? Question-driven units to motivate reading, writing, and thinking.* Heinemann.

Cambria, J., & Guthrie, J. T. (2010). Motivating and engaging students in learning. *New England Reading Journal, 46*(1), 16-30.

Carlisle, J. (2010). Effects of instruction in morphological awareness on literacy achievement: An integrative review. *Reading Research Quarterly, 45*(4), 464-487. https://doi.org/10/1598RRQ.45.4.5

Cervetti, G. N., & Heibert, E. H. (2015). The sixth pillar of reading instruction: Knowledge development. *The Reading Teacher, 68*(7), 548-551.

Chambers, A. (1996). *The reading environment: How adults help children enjoy books.* Stenhouse.

Cherry-Paul, S., & Johansen, D. (2017). *Teaching interpretation using text-based evidence to construct meaning.* Heinemann.

Claesson, K., & Sohlberg, S. (2002). Internalized shame and early interactions characterized by indifference, abandonment, and rejection: Replicated findings. *Clinical Psychology and Psychotherapy, 9*, 277-284.

Clay, M. M. (2005). *Literacy lessons: Designs for individuals, Part II.* Heinemann.

Cole, A. D. (2003). *Knee to knee, eye to eye: Circling in on comprehension.* Heinemann.

Cole, A. D. (2009). *Better answers: Written performance that looks good and sounds smart* (2nd ed.). Stenhouse.

Collins, J. L., Lee, J., Fox, J. D., & Madigan, T. P. (2017). Bringing together reading and writing: An experimental study of writing intensive reading comprehension in low-performing urban elementary schools. *Reading Research Quarterly, 52*(3), 311-332. https://doi.org/10.1002/rrq.175

Collins-Block, C., & Pressley, M. (2002). *Comprehension instruction: Research-based practices.* Guilford Press.

Cornelius-White, J. (2007). Learner-centered teacher-student relationships are effective: A meta-analysis. *Review of Educational Research, 77*(1), 113-143.

Cramer, E. H., & Castle, M. (1994). *Fostering the love of reading: The affective domain in reading education.* International Reading Association.

Cummins, S., & Quiroa. R. E. (2012). Teaching for writing expository responses to narrative texts. *The Reading Teacher, 65*(6), 381-386. https://doi.org/10.1002/trtr.01057

Daniels, E., & Pirayoff, R. (2015). Relationships matter: Fostering motivation through interactions. *Voices from the Middle, 23*(1), 19-23.

Daniels, H. (2002). *Literature circles: Voice and choice in book clubs and reading groups.* Stenhouse.

Daniels, H. (Ed.). (2011). *Comprehension going forward: Where we are/what's next.* Heinemann.

Davis, A., & Forbes, L. (2016). Doing the impossible: Motivating middle school students. *Voices from the Middle, 23*(4), 14-18, 548-551.

Dearing, R., & Tangney, J. P. (2011). *Shame in the therapy hour.* American Psychological Association.

DeYoung, P. A. (2015). *Understanding and treating chronic shame: A relational/ neurobiological approach.* Routledge.

Dorn, L., & Jones, T. (2012). *Apprenticeship in literacy: Transitions across reading and writing, K-4* (2nd ed.). Stenhouse.

Dorn, L., & Soffos, S. (2003). *Teaching for deep comprehension: A reading workshop approach.* Stenhouse.

Dweck, C. (2015). Carol Dweck revisits the growth mindset. *Education Week, 35*(5), 20-24.

Eason, S. H., Goldberg, L. F., Young, K. M., Geist, M. C., & Cutting, L. E. (2012). Reader-text interactions: How differential text and question types influence cognitive skills needed for reading comprehension. *Journal of Educational Psychology, 104*(3), 515-528.

Ellery, V. (2008). *Creating strategic readers: Techniques for developing competency phonemic awareness, phonics, fluency, and comprehension* (2nd ed.). International Reading Association.

Erikson, E. H. (1968). *Identity: Youth and crisis.* W. W. Norton.

Fisher, D., & Frey, N. (2008). *Better Learning through structured teaching: A framework for the gradual release of responsibility.* Association of Supervision and Curriculum Development.

Fisher, D., & Frey, N. (2009). Purpose: The foundation for high-quality teaching. *Principal Leadership, 14*(5), 58-61.

Fisher, D., & Frey, N. (2010). *Guided instruction: How to develop confident and successful learners.* Association of Supervision and Curriculum Development.

Fisher, D., Frey, N., Anderson, H., & Thayre, M. (2015). *Text-dependent questions: Pathways to close and critical reading.* Corwin Literacy.

Fisher, D., Frey, N., & Hattie, J. (2016). *Visible learning for literacy: Implementing the practices that work.* Corwin.

Fisher, D., Frey, N., & Lapp, D. (2008). Shared readings: Modeling comprehension, vocabulary, text structures, and text features for older readers. *The Reading Teacher, 61*(7), 548-556.

Fisher, D., Frey, N., & Lapp, D. (2009). *In a reading state of mind: Brain research, teacher modeling, and comprehension instruction.* International Reading Association.

Fisher, D., Frey, N., & Lapp, D. (2016). *Text complexity: Stretching readers with text and tasks* (2nd ed.). Corwin Literacy.

Fisher, D., Frey, N., & Law, N. (2020). *Comprehension: The skill, will, and thrill of reading.* Corwin Literacy.

Fisher, D., Frey, N., & Smith, D. (2020). *The teacher credibility and collective efficacy playbook, Grades K-12.* Corwin Literacy.

Fountas, I. C., & Pinnell, G. S. (2012). Guided reading: The romance and the reality. *The Reading Teacher, 66*(4), 268-284.

Freire, P. (1970). *Pedagogy of the oppressed.* Continuum. https://archive.org/details/pedagogyofoppres0000frei

Frey, N., & Fisher, D. (2013). *Rigorous reading: 5 access points for comprehending complex text.* Corwin Literacy.

Frey, N., Fisher, D., & Berkin, A. (2009). *Good habits, great readers: Building the literacy community.* Allyn & Bacon.

Frey, N., Fisher, D., & Everlove, S. (2009). *Productive group work: How to engage students, build teamwork, and promote understanding.* Association of Supervision and Curriculum Development.

Frey, N., Hattie, J., & Fisher, D. (2018). *Developing assessment-capable visible learners, grades, K-12: Maximizing skill, will, and thrill.* Corwin.

Gallagher, K. (2010). *Readicide: How schools are killing reading and what you can do about it.* Stenhouse.

Gausel, N., Leach, C. W., Vignoles, V. L., & Brown, R. (2012). Defend or repair? Explaining responses to in-group moral failure by disentangling feelings of shame, rejection, and inferiority. *Journal of Personality and Social Psychology, 102*(5), 941-960.

Gilbert, P. (2000). The relationship of shame, social anxiety, and depression: The role of the evaluation of social rank. *Clinical Psychology & Psychotherapy, 7*(3), 174-189.

Gilbert, P. (2003). Evolution, social roles, and the differences in shame and guilt. *Social Research, 70*(4), 1205-1230.

Gilbert, P. (2004). Evolution, attractiveness, and the emergence of shame and guilt in a self-aware mind: A reflection on Tracy and Robins. *Psychological Inquiry, 15*(2), 132-135.

Gilbert, P., & Andrews, B. (1998). *Shame: Interpersonal behavior, psychopathology, and culture.* Oxford University Press.

Gill, S. R. (2008). The comprehension matrix: A tool for designing comprehension instruction. *The Reading Teacher, 62*(2), 106-113.

Goldberg, G. (2016). *Mindsets and moves: Strategies that help readers take charge.* Corwin Literacy.

Gordon, B. (2018). *No more fake reading: Merging the classics with independent reading to create joyful, lifelong readers.* Corwin.

Graves, D. (2004). *Testing is not teaching.* Heinemann.

Graves, M. F., Schneider, S., & Ringstaff, C. (2017). Empowering students with word learning strategies: Teach a child to fish. *The Reading Teacher, 71*(5), 533-543. https://doi.org/10.1002/trtr1644

Guthrie, J. T., & Wigfield, A. (1997). *Reading engagement: Motivating readers through integrated instruction.* International Reading Association.

Hall, R. A. (2011). Affective assessment: The missing piece of the educational reform puzzle. *Delta Kappa Gamma Bulletin, 77*(2), 7-10.

Hattie, J. (2012). *Visible learning for teachers. Maximizing impact on learning.* Routledge.

Harvey, S., & Goudvais, A. (2000). *Strategies that work: Teaching comprehension for understanding and engagement.* Stenhouse.

Harvey, S., & Goudvais, A. (2007). *Strategies that work: Teaching comprehension for understanding and engagement* (2nd ed.). Stenhouse.

Hasty, M. M., & Schrodt, K. E. (2015). Using writing to support close reading: Engagement and evidence from the text. *Voices from the Middle, 22*(4), 20-24.

Hattan, C., & Lupo, S. M. (2020). Rethinking the role of knowledge in the literacy classroom. *Reading Research Quarterly, 55*(S1), S283-S298.

Henk, W. A., Marinak, B. A., & Melnick, S. A. (2012). Measuring the reader self-perceptions of adolescents: Introducing the RSPS2. *Journal of Adolescent & Adult Literacy, 56*(4), 311-320.

Henk, W. A., Marinak, B. A., & Melnick, S. A. (2013). Measuring the reader self-perceptions of adolescents: Introducing the RSPS 2. *Journal of Adolescent & Adult Literacy, 56*(4), 311-320.

Henk W. A., & Melnick, S. A. (1995). The reader self-perception scale (RSPS): A new tool for measuring how children feel about themselves as readers. *The Reading Teacher, 48*, 470-482.

Hicks, T. (2015). Beyond the book response: Digital writing and reflection for deeper engagement. *Voices from the Middle, 22*(4), 31-35.

Hoffman, J. V. (2017). What if "just right" is just wrong: The unintended consequences of leveling readers. *The Reading Teacher, 71*(3), 265-273.

Hudson, A. K., & Williams, J. A. (2015). Reading every single day: A journey to authentic reading. *The Reading Teacher, 68*(7), 530-538.

Jackson, R. (2018). *Never work harder than your students*. Association of Supervision and Curriculum Development.

Jacobs, J. E., & Paris, S. G. (1987). Children's metacognition about reading: Issues in definition, measurement, and instruction. *Educational Psychologist, 22*, 255-278.

Jaeger, E. L. (2015). Literacy and vulnerability: Shame or growth for readers who struggle. *Talking Points, 26*(2), 17-25.

Jang, B. G., Conradi, K., McKenna, M. C., & Jones, J. S. (2015). Motivation: Approaching an elusive concept through the factors that shape it. *The Reading Teacher, 69*(2), 239-247.

Johnson, N. J., Koss, M. D., & Martinez, M. (2017). Through the sliding glass door: #Empowerthestudent. *The Reading Teacher, 71*(5), 569-577.

Johnson, P. (2006). *One child at a time: Making the most of your time with struggling readers, K-6*. Stenhouse.

Johnston, P. H. (2004). *Choice words: How language affects children's learning*. Stenhouse.

Jones, S. (2020). Measuring reading motivation: A cautionary tale. *The Reading Teacher, 74*(1), 79-90.

Jordan, M. C. (2015). Extra! Extra! Read all about it. Teacher scaffolds interactive read-alouds of a dynamic text. *Elementary School Journal, 115*(3), 358-383.

Kaufman, G. (1993). *Shame: The power of caring*. Schenkman Books.

Keene, E. O., & Zimmerman, S. (2007). *Mosaic of thought: The power of comprehension strategy instruction* (2nd ed.). Heinemann.

Kelley, M. J., & Clausen-Grace, N. (2009). Facilitating engagement by differentiating independent reading. *The Reading Teacher, 63*(4), 313-318.

Kindig, J. S. (2012). *Choosing to read: Connecting middle-schoolers to books*. Heinemann.

Kissner, E. (2006). *Summarizing, paraphrasing, and retelling: Skills for better reading, writing and test taking*. Heinemann.

Kittle, P. (2013). *Book love: Developing depth, stamina, and passion in adolescent readers*. Heinemann.

Krashen, S. (2004). *The power of reading: Insights from research*. Heinemann.

Krashen, S. (2011). Protecting students against the effects of poverty: Libraries. *New England Reading Association Journal, 46*(2), 17-21.

Laminack, L. L., & Wadsworth, R. M. (2006). *Learning under the influence of literature and language*. Heinemann.

Lapp, D., Moss, B., Johnson, K., & Grath, M. (2012). *Rigorous real word teaching and learning—Teaching students to closely read texts: How and when*. International Literacy Association.

Layne, S. L. (2015). *In defense of read-aloud: Sustaining best practice*. Stenhouse.

Learned, J. L. (2016). Becoming "eligible to matter": How teachers' interpretations of struggling readers can disrupt deficit positioning. *Journal of Adolescent & Adult Literacy, 59*(6), 665-674.

Lehman, C., & Roberts, K. (2014). *Falling in love with close reading: Lessons for analyzing texts—and life*. Heinemann.

Lesesne, T. (2010). *Reading ladders: Leading students from where they are to where we'd like them to be*. Heinemann.

Lever-Chain, J. (2008). Turning boys off? Listening to what five-year-olds say about reading. *Literacy, 42*(2), 83-91.

Lowell, R., Pender, K. W., & Binder, K. S. (2019). Impact of informative context's meaning consistency during incidental vocabulary acquisition. *Reading Research Quarterly, 55*(4), 679-697.

Lupo, S. M., Strong, J. Z., Lewis, W., Walpole, S., & McKenna, M. C. (2018). Building background knowledge through reading: Rethinking text sets. *Journal of Adolescent & Adult Literacy, 61*(4), 433-444.

Malloy, J. A., Marinak, B. A., & Gambrell, L. B. (2010). *Essential readings on motivation.* International Literacy Association.

Marcell, B., DeCleene, J., & Juettner, M. R. (2010). Caution! Hard hat area! Comprehension under construction: Cementing a foundation of comprehension strategy usage that carries over to independent practice. *The Reading Teacher, 63*(8), 687-691.

Marinak, B. A., & Gambrell, L. B. (2016). *No more reading for junk: Best practices for motivating readers.* Heinemann.

Marzano, R. J. (2007). *The art and science of teaching: A comprehensive framework for effective instruction.* Association of Supervision and Curriculum Development.

McClure, E. L., & Fullerton, S. K. (2017). Instructional interactions: Supporting student's reading development through interactive read-alouds of informational text. *The Reading Teacher, 71*(1), 51-59.

McGregor, T. (2007). *Comprehension connections: Bridges to strategic reading.* Heinemann.

McKenna, M. C., Conradi, K., Lawrence, C., Jang, B. G., & Meyer, J. P. (2012). Reading attitudes of middle school students: Results of a U.S. survey. *Reading and Research Quarterly, 47*(3), 283-306.

McKeown, M. G., Beck, I. L., & Blake, R. G. K. (2009). Rethinking reading comprehension instruction: A comparison of instruction for strategies and content approaches. *Reading Research Quarterly, 44*(3), 218-253.

McKeown, M. G., Beck, I. L., & Worthy, M. J. (1993). Grappling with text ideas: Questioning the author. *The Reading Teacher, 46*(7), 560-566.

McLaughlin, M., & DeVoogd, G. (2004). Critical literacy as comprehension: Expanding reader response. *Journal of Adolescent and Adult Literacy, 48*(1), 52-61.

McLaughlin, M., & Overturf, B. J. (2010). *The Common Core: Teaching K-5 students to meet the reading standards.* International Reading Association.

Middleton-Moz, J. (1990). *Shame and guilt: Masters of disguise.* Health Communications.

Miller, A. (1995). *Pictures of childhood.* Meridian. (Original work published *Bilder einer Kindheit,* 1985).

Miller, A. (1997). *Drama of the gifted child: The true search for self* (3rd ed.). Basic Books. (Original work published *Drama des begabten Kindes,* 1979).

Miller, D. (2002). *Reading with meaning: Teaching comprehension in the primary grades.* Stenhouse.

Miller, D. (2010). *The book whisperer.* Jossey-Bass.

Miller, D., & Kelley, S. (2014). *Reading in the wild.* Jossey-Bass.

Monroe, A. (2009). Shame solutions: How shame impacts school-aged children and what teachers can do to help. *Educational Forum, 73,* 58-66.

Mordrcin, M. (2016). *Treating shame in clinical practice: Somatic strategies and self-compassion.* PESI.

Morrison, V., & Wlodarcyzk, L. (2009). Revisiting read-aloud: Instructional strategies that encourage students' interactions with text. *The Reading Teacher, 63*(2), 110-118.

Moss, B., & Young, T. A. (2010). *Creating lifelong readers through independent*

reading. International Reading Association.
Mueller, P. N. (2001). *Lifers*. Heinemann.
Muhammed, G. (2020). *Cultivating genius: An equity framework for culturally and historically responsive teaching*. Scholastic.
Muris, P. (2015). Guilt, shame, and psychopathology in children and adolescents. *Child Psychiatry & Human Development, 46*(2), 177-179.
Muris, P., & Meesters, C. (2013). Small or big in the eyes of the other: On the developmental psychopathology of self-conscious emotions as shame, guilt, and pride. *Clinical Child Family Psychology Review, 17*, 19-40.
Muris, P., Meesters, C., Cima, M., Verhagen, M., Brochard, N., Sanders, A., Kempener, C., Beurskens, J., & Meesters, V. (2014). Bound to feel bad about oneself: Relations between attachment and the self-conscious emotions of guilt and shame in children and adolescents. *Journal of Child and Family Studies, 23*(7), 1278-1288.
Nathanson, D. (1992). *Shame and pride: Affect, sex, and the birth of self*. W. W. Norton.
Nathanson, D. (2004). The role of emotion in learning to read—How shame exacerbates reading difficulties. http://www.childrenofthecode.org/interviews/nathason.htm
Ness, M. (2017). *Think big in think alouds, Grades K-5: A three-step planning process that develops strategic readers*. Corwin Literacy.
Newkirk, T. (2017). *Embarrassment: And the emotional underlife of learning*. Heinemann.
Ortlieb, E., & Schatz, S. (2020). Student's self-efficacy in reading: Connecting theory to practice. *Reading Psychology, 41*(7), 735-751. https://doi.org/10.1080/02702711.2020.1783146
Owocki, G. (2003). *Comprehension: Strategic instruction for K-3 students*. Heinemann.
Ozckus, L. (2010). *Reciprocal teaching at work, K-12: Powerful strategies for improving reading comprehension* (2nd ed.). International Reading Association.
Palinscar, A. S., & Brown, A. L. (1986). Interactive teaching to promote independent learning from text. *The Reading Teacher, 39*(8), 771-777. http://www.jstor.org/stable/20199221
Parsons, L. T. (2009). Readers researching their reading: Creating a community of inquiry. *Language Arts, 86*(4), 257-267.
Payne, R. (1998). *A framework for understanding poverty* (4th ed.). Aha Process.
Pearson, P. D. (1982). A primer for schema theory. *Volta Review, 84*(5), 25-33.
Pearson, P. D. (1985). Changing the face of reading comprehension instruction. *The Reading Teacher, 38*(8), 724-738.
Pearson, P. D., & Gallagher, M. C. (1983). The instruction of reading comprehension. *Contemporary Educational Psychology, 8*(3), 327-344.
Piff, P. K., Martinez, A. G., & Keltner, D. (2012). Me against we: In-group transgression, collective shame, and in-group hostility. *Cognition and Emotion, 26*(4), 634-649.
Potter-Efron, R. (2002). *Shame, guilt, and alcoholism: Treatment issues in clinical practice* (2nd ed.). Haworth Press.
Prescott-Griffen, M. L. (2005). *Reader to reader: Building independence through partnerships*. Heinemann.
Probst, R. E. (1988). Dialogue with a text. *English Journal, 77*(1), 32-38.
Raphael, T. E., Highfield, K., & Au, K. H. (2006). *QAR now: A powerful framework that develops comprehension and higher-level thinking in all students*. Scholastic.
Ray, K. (2012). Wonderous words. *The Reading Teacher, 66*(1), 9-14. https://doi.org/10.1002/TRTR.01106
Redford, K. (2020). For reading comprehension, knowledge is power. *Educational Leadership, 77*(5), 52-56.

Reoperez, M. G. D. C. (2019). Mediators of reading motivation among Filipino collegiate students. *International Journal of Education and Literacy Studies, 7*(1), 18-24. doi:10.7575/aiac.ijels.v.7n.1p.18

Reynolds, M. (2004). *I won't read and you can't make me: Reaching reluctant teen readers*. Heinemann.

Rizvi, S. L., Brown, M. Z., Bohus, M., & Linehan, M. L. (2011). The role of shame in the development and treatment of borderline personality disorder. In R. L. Dearing & J. P. Tangney (Eds.), *Shame in the therapy hour*. American Psychological Association.

Robb, L. (2013). *Unlocking complex text. A systematic framework for building adolescents' comprehension*. Scholastic.

Rodgers, E. (2016). Scaffolding word solving while reading: New research insights. *The Reading Teacher, 70*(5), 525-532. https://doi.org/10.1002/trtr1548

Roorda, D. L., Koomen, H. M. Y., Split, J. L., & Oort, F. J. (2011). The influence of affective teacher-student relationships on students' school engagement and achievement: A meta-analytic approach. *Review of Educational Research, 81*(4), 493-539. https://doi.org/10.3102/0034654311421793

Rosenblatt, L. (1995). *Literature as exploration* (5th ed.). Modern Language Association.

Rosenblatt, L. (2005). *Making meaning with texts: Selected essays*. Heinemann.

Routman, R. (2003). *Reading essentials: The specifics you need to teach reading well*. Heinemann.

Sanden, S. (2012). Independent reading: Perspectives and practices of highly effective teachers. *The Reading Teacher, 66*(3), 222-231.

Scanlon, D. M., & Anderson, K. L. (2020). Using context as an assist in word solving: The contributions of 25 years of research on the interactive strategies approach. *Reading Research Quarterly, 55*(S1), S19-S34.

Schwanenflugel, P. J., & Knapp, N. F. (2016). *The psychology of reading: Theory and applications*. Guilford.

Scott, J. A., & Nagy, W. E. (2009). Developing word consciousness. In M. F. Graves (Ed.), *Essential reading on vocabulary instruction* (pp. 102-113). International Reading Association.

Serafini, F. (2004). *Lessons in comprehension: Explicit instruction in the reading workshop*. Heinemann.

Serafini, F., & Youngs, S. (2007). *More (advanced) lessons in comprehension. Exploring student's understanding of all types of text*. Heinemann.

Serravallo, J., & Goldberg, G. (2007). *Conferring with readers: Supporting each student's growth and independent*. Heinemann.

Shahar, B., Bar-Kalifa, E., & Hen-Weissberg, A. (2015). Shame during social interactions predicts subsequent generalized anxiety symptoms: A daily-diary study. *Journal of Social and Clinical Psychology, 34*(10), 827-837.

Shanahan, T. (2017, May 14). New evidence on teaching reading at frustration levels. *Shanahan on Literacy*. http://www.shanahanonliteracy.com

Sibberson, F., & Szymusiak, K. (2003). *Still learning to read: Teaching students in grades 3-6*. Stenhouse.

Silver, H. F., Dewing, R. T., & Perini, M. J. (2012). *The Core Six: Essential strategies for achieving excellence with the common core*. Association of Supervision and Curriculum Development.

Sims, R. B. (1990). Windows, mirrors, and sliding glass doors. *Perspectives, 6*(3), ix-xi.

Smith, D., Fisher, D., & Frey, N. (2021). *Removing labels, grades K-12: 40 techniques to disrupt negative expectations about students and schools*. Corwin.

Smith, M. W., & Wilhelm, J. D. (2010). *Fresh takes on teaching literary elements: How to teach what really matters about character, setting, point of view, and theme*

(2nd ed.). Scholastic; National Council of Teachers of English.

Sobel, D. (1998). *Mapmaking with children: Sense of place education for the elementary years*. Heinemann.

Stahl, K. S., & McKenna, M. C. (2010). *Assessment for reading instruction* (2nd ed.). Guilford Press.

Stiggins, R., & Popham, W. J. (2010). *Assessing students' affect related to assessment for learning: An introduction for teachers*. Council of Chief State School Officers.

Stygles, J. M. (2014). Losing control to gain readers. *Literacy Today Blog*. International Literacy Association. https://www.literacyworldwide.org/blog/literacy-now/2014/03/06/losing-control-to-gain-readers

Stygles, J. M. (2017a). *Reading passports*. Choice Literacy. http://www.choiceliteracy.com/article/reading-passports/

Stygles, J. M. (2017b). *30 books in 30 days*. Choice Literacy. http://www.choiceliteracy.com/article/30-books-in-30-days/

Szymusiak, K., Sibberson, F., & Kock, L. (2008). *Beyond leveled books: Supporting early and transitional readers in grades K-5*. Stenhouse.

Tangney, J., & Dearing, R. (2002). *Shame and guilt*. Guilford Press.

Tangney, J. P., & Fisher, K. W. (1995). *Self-conscious emotions*. Guilford Press.

Tangney, J. P., Miller, R. S., Flicker, L, Barlow, D. H. (1996). Are shame, guilt, and embarrassment distinct emotions? *Journal of Personality and Social Psychology, 70*(6), 1256-1269.

Tatum, A. (2009). *Reading for their life: (Re)building the textual lineages of African American adolescent males*. Heinemann.

Thomaes, S., Stegge, H., & Olthof, T. (2007). Externalizing shame responses in children: The role of fragile-positive self-esteem. *British Journal of Developmental Psychology, 25*, 559-577.

Tomkins, S. S., & Izard, C. E. (1965). *Affect, cognition, and personality: Empirical studies*. Springer.

Tomlinson, C. A., & Imbeau, M. B. (2010). *Leading and managing a differentiated classroom*. Association of Supervision and Curriculum Development.

Tovani, C. (2000). *I read it, but I don't get it: Comprehension strategies for adolescent readers*. Stenhouse.

Tracy, J., & Robbins, R. (2004). Putting the self into self-conscious emotions: A theoretical model. *Psychological Inquiry, 15*(2), 103-125.

Valencia, S. W. (2011). Using assessment to improve teaching and learning. In S. J. Samuels & A. E. Farstrup (Eds.), *What research has to say about reading instruction* (4th ed.). International Reading Association.

Vasquez, V. (2010). *Getting beyond "I like the book": Creating space for critical literacy in K-6 classrooms*. International Reading Association.

Vaughn, M., & Fisher, D. (2020). Affective dimensions of student literacy learning: Issue 1. *Reading Psychology, 41*(6), 513-514, https://doi.org/10.1080/02702711.2020.1783140

Vaughn, M., Jang, B. G., Sotirovska, V., & Cooper-Novack, G. (2020). Student agency in literacy: A systemic review of the literature. *Reading Psychology, 41*(7), 712-734. https://doi.org/10.1080/02702711.2020.1783142

Vlach, S., & Burcie, J. (2010). Narratives of the struggling reader. *The Reading Teacher, 63*(6), 522-525.

Walsh, J. A., & Sattes, B. D. (2017). *Quality questioning: Research-based practice to engage every learner* (2nd ed.). Corwin and McREL International.

Wang, E., Matsumura, L. C., & Correnti, R. (2016). Making a CASE: Improving use of text evidence in students' writing. *The*

Reading Teacher, 70(4), 479-484. https://doi.org/10.1002/trtr.1524

Weaver, C. (2009). *The reading process: Brief edition of reading process and practice* (3rd ed.). Heinemann.

Welford, M., & Langmead, K. (2015). Compassion-based initiatives in educational settings. *Educational and Child Psychology, 32*(1), 71-80.

Wigfield, A., & Guthrie, J. T. (2000). Engagement and motivation in reading. In M. L. Kamil, P. B. Mosenthal, P. D. Pearson, & R. Barr (Eds.), *Handbook of reading research* (Vol. 3, pp. 403-422). Lawrence Erlbaum Associates.

Wilde, S. (2013). *Quantity and quality: Increasing the volume and complexity of students' reading*. Heinemann.

Wilhelm, J. D. (2008). *"You gotta be the book": Teaching engaged and reflective reading with adolescents* (2nd ed.). Teachers College Press.

Wilhelm, J. D., & Smith, M. W. (2014). *Reading unbound: Why kids need to read what they want and why we should let them*. Scholastic.

Wolf, M. S., Williams, M. V., Parker, R. M., Nowlan, A. W., & Baker, D. W. (2007). Patient's shame and attitudes toward discussing results of literacy screening. *Journal of Health Communication, 12*, 721-732.

Wormeli, R. (2005). *Summarization in any subject: 50 techniques to improve student learning*. ASCD.

Yates, K., & Nosek, C. (2018). *To know and nurture a reader: Conferring with confidence and joy*. Stenhouse.

Zimmerman, S. (2011). Bring back the joy to reading. In H. Daniels (Ed.), *Comprehension going forward: Where we are / what's next* (pp. 34-45). Heinemann.

Žolgar-Jerković, I., Jenko, N., & Lipec-Stopar, N. (2018). Factors and reading achievement in different groups of readers. *International Journal of Special Education, 33*(18), 201-210.

CHILDREN'S LITERATURE CITED

Behar, R. (2021). *Letters from Cuba.* Nancy Paulsen Books.

Behar, R. (2017). *Lucky broken girl.* Nancy Paulsen Books.

Braden, A. (2018). *Benefits of being an octopus.* Sky Pony.

Cherry-Paul, S., Reynolds, J., & Kendi, I. X. (2021). *Stamped (for kids): Racism, antiracism, and you.* Little, Brown Young Readers.

Cleary, B. (1955). *Ramona and Beezus.* HarperCollins.

Craft, J. (2019). *New kid.* HarperCollins.

Creech, S. (2003). *Granny Torrelli makes soup.* HarperCollins.

Creech, S. (1994). *Walk two moons.* HarperCollins.

Gantos, J. (1998). *Joey Pigza swallowed the key.* Square Fish.

Gipe, G. (1985). *Back to the future.* Berkley Books.

Hautman, P. (2019). *Slider.* Candlewick.

Henry, M. (1947). *Misty of Chincoteague.* Yearling Classic.

Hiranandani, V. (2019). *The night diary.* Penguin.

Jacobson, J. R. (2017). *Paper things.* Candlewick.

Jacobson, J. R. (2019). *The dollar kids.* Candlewick.

Jacobson, J. R. (2022). *Crashing into love.* Candlewick.

Lambert, M. E. (2017). Family game night and other catastrophes. Scholastic.

Lord, C. (2015). *Handful of stars.* Scholastic.

Maldonado, T. (2018). *Tight.* Nancy Paulsen Books.

McDunn, G. (2019). *Queen bee and me.* Bloomsbury Children Books.

Miles, E. (2007). *The puppy place: Shadow.* Scholastic.

Mullaly-Hunt, L. (2013). *One for the Murphys.* Nancy Paulsen Books.

Mullaly-Hunt, L. (2015). *Fish in a tree.* Nancy Paulsen Books.

Munoz-Ryan, P. (2002). *Esperanza rising.* Scholastic.

Nickels, S. (2020). *Nacho's nachos: The story behind the world's favorite snack.* Lee & Low Books.

O'Hara, M. (2013). *My big fat zombie goldfish.* Feiwel and Friends.

Paulsen, G. (1987). *Hatchet.* Antheneum Books for Young Readers.

Peck, R. (2004). *A long way from Chicago.* Puffin Books.

Pilkey, D. (2016). *Dogman.* Graphix.

Robinson, B. (1994). *The (worst) best school year ever.* Scholastic.

Seuss, D. (1995). *Cat in the hat.* Random House.

Shea, B. (2013). *Unicorn thinks he's pretty great.* Scholastic.

Shurtliff, L. (2013). *Rump: The true story of Rumpelstiltskin.* Alfred A. Knopf Books for Young Readers.

Standish, A. (2020). *How to completely disappear.* Harper Collins.

Taylor, G. (2006). *George Crum: Inventor of the Saratoga chip*. Lee & Low Books.

Telegmeier, R. (2010). *Smile*. Scholastic.

Ursu, A. (2011). *Breadcrumbs*. Harper Collins.

Uss, C. (2018). *Adventures of a girl called Bicycle*. FSG/Margaret Ferguson Books.

Venkatraman, P. (2019). *The bridge home*. Penguin.

Williams-Garcia, R. (2010). *One crazy summer*. Scholastic.

INDEX

At Corwin Literacy we have put together a collection of just-in-time, classroom-tested, practical resources from trusted experts that allow you to quickly find the information you need when you need it.

DOUGLAS FISHER, NANCY FREY, NICOLE LAW

Using a structured, three-pronged approach—skill, will, and thrill—students experience reading as a purposeful act with this new comprehensive model of reading instruction.

PAM KOUTRAKOS

Packed with ready-to-go lessons and tools, this user-friendly resource provides ways to weave together different aspects of literacy using one mentor text.

REBECCA G. HARPER

Customizable strategies turn students' informal writing into a springboard for daily writing practice in every content area—with a focus on academic vocabulary, summarizing, and using textual evidence.

MELANIE MEEHAN, CHRISTINA NOSEK, MATTHEW JOHNSON, DAVE STUART JR., MATTHEW R. KAY

This series offers actionable answers to your most pressing questions about teaching reading, writing, and ELA.

CLN21B50

CORWIN